*A* **SOC**
**SEX** *a*

# ONE WEEK LOAN

# SOCIOLOGY *and* SOCIAL CHANGE

**Series Editor:** *Alan* **Warde, Lancaster University**

**Published titles**

*Gail* **Hawkes** — *A* **Sociology** *of* **Sex** *and* **Sexuality**

*Colin* **Hay** — **Re-stating Social** *and* **Political Change**

*Andy* **Furlong** *and Fred* **Cartmel** — **Young People** *and* **Social Change**

*Máirtín* **Mac an Ghaill** — **Contemporary Racisms** *and* **Ethnicities: Social** *and* **Cultural Transformations**

# A **SOCIOLOGY** *of* **SEX** *and* **SEXUALITY**

*Gail* **Hawkes**

**Open University Press**
Maidenhead · Philadelphia

Open University Press
McGraw-Hill House
Shoppenhangers Road
Maidenhead
Berkshire
England
SL6 2QL

email: enquiries@openup.co.uk
world wide web: www.openup.co.uk

and
325 Chestnut Street
Philadelphia, PA 19106, USA

First published 1996
Reprinted 1999, 2002

A catalogue record of this book is available from the British Library

ISBN 0 335 19316 1 (pb)     0 335 19317 X (hb)

*Library of Congress Cataloging-in-Publication Data*
Hawkes, Gail, 1945–
    A sociology of sex and sexuality / Gail Hawkes.
        p.   cm. — (Sociology and social change)
    Includes bibliographical references and index.
    ISBN 0–335–19317–X. — ISBN 0–335–19316–1 (pbk.)
    1. Sex customs. 2. Sex (Psychology)—Social aspects. 3. Sexual ethics. I. Title. 11. Series.
HQ12.H39 1996
306.7 — dc20                                                     95–26513
                                                                      CIP

Typeset by Graphicraft Typesetters Ltd, Hong Kong
Printed in Great Britain by Marston Lindsay Ross International Ltd, Oxford

*For Essie and Gibson Hawkes,
my mother and father.*

# Contents

# Series editor's preface

In response to perceived major transformations, social theorists have offered forceful, appealing, but competing accounts of the predicament of contemporary Western societies. Key themes emerging have been frequently condensed into terms like 'post-modernism', 'post-modernity', 'risk society', 'disorganized capitalism' and 'the information society'. These have important and widespread ramifications for the analysis of all areas of social life and personal well-being. The speculative and general theses proposed by social theorists must be subjected to evaluation in the light of the best available evidence if they are to serve as guides to understanding and modifying social arrangements. One purpose of sociology, among other social sciences, is to marshall the information necessary to estimate the extent and direction of social change. This series is designed to make such information, and debates about social change, accessible.

The focus of the series is the critical appraisal of general, substantive theories through examination of their applicability to different institutional areas of contemporary societies. Each book introduces key current debates and surveys, existing sociological argument and research about institutional complexes in advanced societies. The integrating theme of the series is the evaluation of the extent of social change, particularly in the last twenty years. Each author offers explicit and extended evaluation of the pace and direction of social change in their chosen area.

In this book, Gail Hawkes sets about examining the ways in which the experience and appreciation of sexuality might have changed over time. A more intriguing topic is difficult to imagine. Both continuities and transformations can be identified and their interpretation offer great opportunity for exploring social change. Dealing with writings about sex from since Classical Antiquity, she applies the insights of recent social theorists to analysing texts and discourse from different historical periods. The story of the changing regulation of sexuality necessarily involves much interpretation that is inherently controversial, for it is a sphere of struggles for power and control between moral arbiters, different groups of experts, social movements, men and women, states and citizens. A substantial proportion of the book deals with change in the twentieth century, but it is only in the context of the longer time span that the particularity of contemporary behaviour can be appreciated. This book is a fascinating vindication of the power of a theoretically informed historical sociology to throw light on the dilemmas of current experience.

Alan Warde

# Acknowledgements

Fond thanks to David Morgan, David Howell and Ian McIntosh for being there with advice, encouragement and friendship. Grateful thanks to Tim May, Bernard Leach and my Faculty at The Manchester Metropolitan University for giving me the opportunity to complete this project. Thanks also to Nick Evans, formerly of Open University Press, for his support during some difficult times, and my students on 'The Sex Course' for their insights and enthusiasm. Enduring thanks to Joseph and Sarah Smaje, who lived with the domestic chaos and unpredictable maternal moods during its production.

# Introduction

Sex and sexuality are familiar, not to say commonplace, words in late twentieth-century Western vocabulary. An ever expanding range of commodities is sold by invoking sexual imagery, while sexual desirability is increasingly presented as a leisure commodity to be acquired and utilized, whether in relation to self or others. We live, in short, in a sexualized world. Such a statement is itself a truism, received with little dissent during any social gathering. It might be imagined that woven into the social fabric in this way, sex has finally found respectability and has shed its former problematic status. Yet the commercial effectiveness of selling with sex, whether it be cars, ice-cream, holidays or magazines, suggests otherwise. A commonplace in one sense, the mere use of the word is sufficient to arouse attention if not fascination. On a scale of significance in our lives, it would be fair to say that sex occupies a position parallel to death. Both are associated with life – its beginning and end. Death is an inevitability – a question of when, not whether, and therefore perhaps easier to ignore. Sex, on the other hand (and 'sex' not 'sexuality' is the word we use spontaneously), is an ever present factor in our lives whether we choose actively to associate with it or not. Sex and death are the source of deep and powerful emotions, both positive and negative, which are the source, perhaps, of our claim to humanity. Death continues to be associated with the profoundly private, while sex, in close association with the 'modernizing process', has come to occupy equal significance in both public and private spheres. Yet, as recent catalogues of sexual fantasies suggest, what constitutes at an individual level expressions and explorations of the possibilities of sexual desire, may not necessarily coincide with the dominant parameters of 'sexuality' in the world outside the bedroom (Friday 1976, 1980). In respect of the latter, we can, without too much difficulty, recognize a set of feelings and ideas associated with sex which are in themselves instructive and illustrative: pleasure and fear, freedom and restriction, control and abandon, health and disease. These are primarily illustrative in that each pair contains a contradiction. From a lay perspective, these contradictions present few problems. We 'understand' that what appears to be self-questioning sets of ideas are actually recognitions of the variety of ways in which sex and sexuality appear in the compartments of our day-to-day lives as well as over time. So, for example, there is little difficulty in conjuring up a mental picture of a sexually repressed 'past'; nor of being able to explain how sex can be both good and bad for one's health. Such a superficial consensus suggests the presence of shared assumptions – about what 'sex' is, about who is involved and what 'turns us on'. Any doubts about the presence of such assumptions can be dispelled by the ubiquitous sexual imagery in advertising, to offer one supporting illustration. Yet the familiarity of these ideas, and the ease with which the complexities are negotiated, invites further critical attention. Looking, as Bauman (1990) suggests, 'at the familiar in unfamiliar ways', would allow us to question the process by which heterosexuality has become a 'given' and what in itself it constitutes. Any such deconstruction of assumptions and commonplaces necessitates reference to what has gone before, for 'there is no true understanding without a certain range of comparison; provided, of course, that the comparison is based on differing and, at the same time, related realities' (Bloch 1967: 42).

Gay and lesbian scholarship has, in the past three decades, critically and importantly challenged the primacy of heterosexuality and the negative constructions of erotic alternatives to the orthodoxy. Yet from within the mainstream there has been little to match this. Sociological analyses have explored the social significance of sex and sexuality in relation to health issues, the politics of reproduction and gender relations. While these have been illuminating in respect of the consequences of certain aspects of sexual behaviour, and even of the ideas, judgements and norms which surround them, they have not necessarily addressed the sources of these deep-seated and easily recognizable notions. For the most part, sexual desires, the erotic, even the problematization of heterosexuality, have been left to those for whom such issues have a political significance which goes beyond what they do in bed. Gay and lesbian scholarship (e.g. Snitow *et al.* 1983; Hamer and Budge 1994; Simpson 1994) continues to shape the radical direction of sexual studies, a trend that also often goes unexamined. We tend to assume that this will be so, given the more marginal status of so-called sexual minorities. Yet such commonplaces should alert us to the presence of very powerful and effective ideological processes. The 'givenness' of heterosexuality as a majority erotic choice, what is meant by 'heterosexuality', how it acquired these meanings and how it is perpetuated, the relative silence about sexual desire and its social significance, have all been left unchallenged. It is necessary to deconstruct the bases and dynamics of these assumptions, for without this what constitutes a sexual orthodoxy, even in the late twentieth century, will go unchallenged.

The often contradictory sets of ideas that surround sex and sexuality in the sexualized world we inhabit reflect a confidence in modern scientific thought that has eradicated old irrational ideas of dark fear or original sin, replacing it with an ordered and orderly set of ideas and practices in which 'norms' are not defined in terms of a universal doctrine or religious beliefs. The 'either/or' configuration of the binaries suggest a derivation from a body or bodies of knowledge that are self-contained and against which explicitly classificatory and implicitly normative judgements are made. Far from being morally confusing, such polarities allow the largely unchallenged co-existence of sexual pleasures and sexual dangers, of control and abandon, and of regulation and freedom. The shaping of 'hearts and minds' inherent in the capitalist labour process and made explicit in the work ethos that Max Weber and Antonio Gramsci and later, Edward Thompson, so vividly described, was paralleled by a process of shaping and directing sexual desire (Thompson 1967; Gramsci 1971; Weber 1974). This entailed a remystification of sexual desire, which both drew on and was legitimated by a rational scientific discourse. Such endeavours were not confined to state regulation, nor to the construction of institutionalized family and gender relations. In a twinned process, physical manifestations of sexual desire were opened up to unprecedented scrutiny, while the sex *act* was morally reordered according to its social rather than individual consequences. Those manifestations of desire which were deemed to have negative consequences for the maintenance of the patriarchal bourgeois hegemony – women's sexual autonomy, same-sex desire, expressions of youthful sexuality and auto-eroticism – were marginalized and even outlawed.

A critical examination of the sources of ideas – both positive and negative – about sex and sexuality will involve an exploration of the connections between the establishment and maintenance of the primacy of heterosexuality, and the bourgeois hegemony, connections which, it will be argued, are shaped by the inherent instability of both. There is a danger in retaining claims of a derivative relationship in the context of late modernity, in which such connections appear at least to have been weakened if not dissolved. Superficially at least, there has been a waning of the emphasis on the negative social consequences of expressions of sexual desire outside the close confines of the ordered reproductive framework of monogamous heterosexual marriage. In the post-permissive watershed of the mid-twentieth century, there has been an apparent erosion of the 'anxiety-making' (Comfort 1968) that characterized modernist discourses on sex and sexuality. With the increasing promotion of the positive potentials of expressions of sexual desire, the tolerance of sexual pleasures as a means to an end have been replaced by the positive promotion of such pleasures as an end in themselves. This shift has been dependent on, and has contributed to, the progressive disengagement of the primary association of sex with reproduction. Since the late 1960s, there has been a gradual if heavily conditional erosion of the category of pathological perversion that surrounded non-heterosexual desire. Yet the positive promotion of sexual desire entrenched more deeply genitally organized heterosexuality as the norm, while erotic alternatives, though viewed more benignly, retained their marginal status. Moreover, sexual pleasure is not for everyone. Its dangers for young people continue to be reiterated in ongoing dilemmas about sex education and the provision of contraception. Auto-eroticism remains a second-order form of pleasure, while women's quest for sexual self-determination remains problematic. More recently still, in the context of late modernity, the hegemonic security of heterosexuality has been challenged, and its 'fault-lines' exposed. On the one hand, the 'naturalness' of heterosexuality has been challenged by the possibilities of the disengagement of sexual desires from gender identity offered by queer theory.

On the other, the aura conferred on sexuality as the 'centre of our beings' has been somewhat tarnished by the omnipresence and commodification of sex and its pleasures. The flexibility in the proliferation of lifestyle choices associated with the discourses of late modernity similarly erodes the exalted and 'special' status of sexuality, reducing it to one among many indices on offer in the reflexive project of self (Giddens 1991). The suggested fluidity in the relationship between the individual and society and between agency and structure in late modernity, poses a particular challenge to the ideas about sex and sexuality which ordered our sensual experience as individual and social beings.

There is an anomaly here that needs to be addressed. On the one hand, profound changes have evidently occurred in sexual mores that have both shaped and reflect the ways in which sex and sexuality are woven into social and individual consciousness. 'Sexualization' in this sense might be equated with 'modernization'. Yet such a conclusion is both facile and incomplete. The co-existence of contradictory notions about sex and sexuality suggest the retention of fears and anxieties about, as well as a hierarchical ordering of, expressions of sexual desires.

In order to explore both the scope and conditionality of the processes by which the parameters of modernist sexuality have been shaped, the primary emphasis will not be on sexual behaviour but on the processes by which the accepted parameters of sex and sexuality have been shaped. Some chronological ordering of what follows is inevitable. Yet within the summaries of social contexts and sexual mores, there will be a emphasis on recurrent themes: the primacy of heterosexuality, and its related fragility, the differing manifestations of fears and anxieties engendered by deregulated sexual desires and their differential ordering by gender and sexual preference.

This sociology of sex and sexuality will therefore address the following questions: What is the relationship between the construction of the heterosexual orthodoxy and the bourgeois hegemony? What connections can be made between the characterizations of sexuality and the maintenance of a stable social order? Was the role of the medical profession in the early policing of sexuality an inevitable consequence of the shift to a secular scientific moral order? Can we, at the close of the twentieth century, now lay claim to a new sexual orthodoxy, one which derives from the context of late modernity – an orthodoxy which reflects the lack of fixity in social categories, and the emergence of reflexivity as the integument between the individual and the social? Do these enabling contexts render redundant the notion of 'sexual orthodoxy'?

# 1 *The* **specialness** *of* **sex**

On the occasion of my first interview as a lecturer, the candidates had been requested to present an outline for an additional course they would wish to teach on the syllabus. In fulfilling these requirements, I presented a course entitled 'A Sociology of Sex and Sexuality'. Although this represented a small component of my overall teaching profile, most of the interview was devoted to questions from the panel about the difficulties associated with teaching a course on sex. Some typical remarks ('Do you foresee problems talking about sex to a mixed group?', 'Won't there be problems of embarrassment for some of the younger students?') laid emphasis on the problematic nature of speaking about sex. Similarly, the 1994 BSA Conference, dealing for the first time specifically with sex and sexualities, attracted unprecedented media attention, which ranged from the trivializing to the openly ridiculous. More recently still, a nationwide billboard campaign advertising '18–30' holidays with the word 'sex' written in two-metre high fluorescent letters was withdrawn after public and official complaints. (In the latter case, it was claimed to be the cause of minor traffic accidents.) These anecdotes, drawn at random over a short time span, reflect and reinforce the 'specialness' of sex – a combination of anxiety and fascination that does not rely for its impact on material reality, but which resides in, and is perpetuated through, a collection of shared ideas. The duality of the social and the individual in sex is further illustrated in the conflation of morality with *sexual* morality. An 'immoral' act is almost invariably a sexual act; immorality in the printed word, in cinema or in visual imagery is likewise predominantly defined in terms of the sexual content. There is an immediate recognition that sex, even at the unfocused and commodified level in the anecdotes above, has a significance which is profoundly social, whether this manifests itself positively or negatively.

This distinction between positive and negative social significance is not linear and often contradictory. In the company of young people, particularly in a context characterized by an imbalance of social power, talking about sex may be difficult and embarrassing, even when officially sanctioned, as in sex education. Yet in other, less immediately relevant contexts, sex has become an almost obligatory motif in representations of our daily lives – what we eat and drink, however mundane; our presentation of self through clothes, make-up; even the cars we choose to drive. In medical and paramedical discourses, what we do sexually is increasingly dissected, explored, pronounced upon, so that good sex is becoming synonymous with good health. In more popular arenas, discussions about sex have been promoted from the back to the front pages of those chronicles of consumption and lifestyle, the monthly magazines. The latter-day descendants of the sexologists – the sex experts – flourish in symbiosis with these bibles of lifestyle, where from television studios, videotapes and self-help manuals, the message is presented and reinforced. Sex is 'natural' and, therefore, 'healthy'. Through good sex we experience pleasure and express our individuality. Good sex is the bedrock for getting and keeping your man (or woman), while simultaneously our ability to give 'good sex' is an indicator of our right to membership of the world of success.

So there is sex and sex: on the one hand, a source of fear and embarrassment; on the other, a source of infinite happiness and fulfilment. Distinctions are made only through the contexts from which the discourses emerge; the positivity and negativity of the 'sex' promoted or discouraged left largely implicit. This covertness is not a consciously conspiratorial strategy imposed by the thought police. Its effectiveness lies in the presence of a series of 'taken-for-granted' notions that are the meat and drink for any sociological enquiry. First, that sexual desire is a fundamental human characteristic, like thirst or hunger, and because of this fundamental status it is potentially problematic. Misdirected or allowed unfettered expression, this primary human characteristic, unlike thirst or (to a lesser extent) hunger, carries with it a sense of latent uncontrollability. Second, this consensus, even at an unconscious level, renders it acceptable, even desirable, that expressions of sexual desire be the subject of regulation and prohibition to degrees which would not be tolerated in relation to, for example, dietary habits. Third, the fears and anxieties about the negative latencies of sexuality can be alleviated by the presence of officially sanctioned 'normal' expressions of sexual desire – heterosexuality – expressions that are further monitored within a discourse that focuses on acts and outcomes rather than feelings. Yet, alongside these at least potentially negative commonalities, there are others which operate to relieve the sense of siege and pessimism. Despite the still-present 'pockets' of anxiety, in general there is the sense that there has been, and continues to be, a relaxation of 'old' attitudes which emphasize the dangers, whether individual or social, of sexual desire. The characteristics that previously marked the unruliness of sexual desire – epitomized in the modernist notions of normal and perverse – are increasingly and approvingly mobilized as indices of individuality and choice.

A sociologist's initial response to this broad sweep overview of sex in our society might be the following: that sex is at once an act of individual intimacy and of social significance, and that these underlying assumptions and the contradictory picture they comprise raises one's historical as well as sociological curiosity. An immediate subset of ideas follow, which, like the former, represent the central and abiding concerns of all sociology. Do we understand the notion of change as a linear process, as a relentless movement forward, shedding in this momentum all unwanted vestiges of the past? If the content of talking about sex has changed (from sex as the great danger to sex the great pleasure), what of the form (the problematic nature of sexuality)? More detailed and empirical questions follow: How do we know what we know about sex? How did the experts come to be experts? What might an historical dimension tell us about the prioritization of some knowledges over others? Such scepticism leads to the more detailed exploration of the 'commonsense' assumptions.

## 1.1  Words and meanings

A fundamental starting point would be to look at the words 'sex' and 'sexuality'. These are used in a confusing variety of contexts and with an ease that suggests that their meaning is fixed, shared and unproblematic. But a moment's pause suggests otherwise. Biological sex is allocated by the possession of definitive physical and physiological 'markers': externally, genitalia, penis, testes, vagina, clitoris; internally, verifiable uterus, ovaries, vas deferens, prostate gland. Non-macroscopic yet equally discernible chromosomes and hormones, again (though now less definitively) provide biochemical support for these categories. Yet the meanings given to these anatomical distinctions have a social origin.

In a fascinating and meticulous historical account, Thomas Lacquer (1990) charts the social contexts in which these now taken-for-granted categories emerged, and what they replaced. The two-sex model of humankind, defined by the indicators listed above, is, historically speaking, a recent one. In the medieval period, self-definition as male and female would not rest on possession of a vagina or penis. This does not mean, of course, that external physical characteristics were ignored. From the earliest endeavours to represent our humanity, the genital variations between individuals were chronicled. These, however, were not translated into mutually exclusive gender differences. There was only one sex (the prototype now defined as 'male') and the visible differences in the manifestations of this 'one sex', while significant, did not constitute the basis for a separate, let alone 'opposite', sex. The sex organs of all humankind possessed the same fundamental constituents. In half of humanity these organs were internal, in the other half external. The lack of externality of female sex organs was not an indicator of distinction but of incompleteness. Arguably, the distinction between completeness and incompleteness carries a significance of equal social importance. While there are obvious limitations to such a broad sweep of historical relativity, not least because of the questions it raises about the significance and intersection of cultural as well as historical relativism, the relevance of Lacquer's central point remains. The notion of there being two sexes, of opposite polarity, is of recent historical origin, and the social and political significance of sexual difference has its origins in the social, not the natural. Lacquer's work contributes equally to a problematization of a distinction between received understandings of 'the natural' and 'the socially constructed' – that one does not stand in opposition to the other, but there is a derivative relationship between conceptions of both. This work suggests that given a different trajectory of the social construction of scientific knowledge, the oppositional nature of biological sex might not have prevailed.

But how have the connections been made, connections which are of such import, between the possession of particular organs – which, as human physiology will illustrate, share very similar response characteristics – and expressions of sexual desire? For the anxieties or the celebrations which accompany social attitudes to sex and sexuality do not have as their centre the intrinsic qualities of bodily parts, but their deployment in expressions of sexual desire. Yet such expressions cannot, in the commonsense view, even in the writings of some scholarship, be seen to be synonymous with 'sexuality'. For if sexuality were simply defined and understood as the mode of expression of sexual desire, then the largely intact connection between sex and gender would be severed, and the grounding of sexuality in behaviour alone would be challenged. It is has been suggested that sexuality is a 'fictional unity . . . an invention of the human mind' (Weeks 1986: 15) and 'a term of conception and systematization, specific and historical' (Heath 1982: 11). Such representations alert us to the socially constructed element in the concept of sexuality – that sexuality is not some mystical given, the result of a biological script. Yet the umbrella of social constructionism can itself mislead understandings if left undeveloped beyond that of posing a challenge to biological determinism. An understanding of sexuality simply as a fiction leaves unexplored the parameters of the concept and the processes by which these are constituted. The categories of hetero- and homosexuality are illustrative of ways of thinking which hone and shape polymorphous desire into fixed categories, which have as their reference point physical acts that define individual sexual identities. So sexuality is both a fiction and a reality, an artificial creation and a lived experience.

The issue at stake, then, is not so much what does or does not constitute 'sexuality', but how do we make sense of its ascribed constituents? To describe some social phenomenon as a 'social construction' is to give a name to an end-point. What is required is a detailed and coherent account of how we got to that point, of what and who was involved in this process and why. To reiterate, we can say all these things (to paraphrase Marx); the point, however, is to account for them.

It has been pointed out in a number of texts and arguments that 'sexuality' is a nineteenth-century production. This argument is sustainable if we understand sexuality as either 'read off' from what one does physically with one's genitals, or as an ascribed or chosen identity, defined through and by a variety of possible signifiers – dress, mannerisms, lifestyle, erotic object choice – interpreted and illuminated not physically but psychologically. That the word itself appeared first in the nineteenth century is significant, as it emerged out of and represented a way of thinking about sex which made it possible to place all the complexities of erotic behaviour under one broad umbrella. The term, in other words, conveyed the core of the idea: that sexuality was something you had, something almost tangible, which had a form and a clear-cut boundary. Moreover, the concept and its deployment reflected the focus of concerns about the social consequences of sexual desire in the context of modernity. Similarly, the use of the word 'sex' has been shaped alongside that of 'sexuality'. The limitation of the word to the genitals and the genitals alone, encapsulated in the notion of 'having sex', is consistent with the positivist discourses of modernity. 'Having sex', in this context, is the rational organization of sexual desire into the conjoining of genitals for a given outcome – reproduction and (a modicum of) ordered pleasure. Yet within the persistence of anxieties there is a suggestion of wider meanings associated with the notion of 'having sex'. For what we have, in addition to the conjoining of genitals for a purpose, is an individual sensual experience, with a greater or lesser degree of affective involvement. It is this which is the more interesting and persistent and, it will be argued, the most problematic element in the construction of ideas and meanings of sex and sexuality.

## 1.2   The problematization of sex: positive pleasures

We can sculpt and remould the external physical accoutrements of our sex and we can order and redirect object choice and appearances, mannerisms and lifestyles. In other words, we can deal with the *external* manifestations of our sexuality. Yet a totally 'free market' in 'having sex' in this wider understanding is a dangerous proposition. The capacity to explore and push back the boundaries of our sensual capacities, with the conscious choice about the optionality of emotional 'extras', or the reordering of erotic primacy, is a profoundly revolutionary notion. The use of the word sex in the biological sense conceals the experience of our potential to exercise those elements of our humanity which, it is feared, fall beyond the reach of Foucault's (1977) 'disciplinary power'. The use of the notions of 'danger' and 'fear' are deliberate, for they point to sets of ideas about this human capacity which have a long history, but which are not now openly articulated. The idea of the specialness of sex has, it will be argued, more to do with these covertly articulated ideas about human behaviour. The specialness suggests a process by which these capacities have been recognized and given a particular form through expressions of anxieties about the consequences of such a free market. It must be emphasized, and will continue to be emphasized, that what lies behind this notion is not an argument for the existence of some essential human capacity, a view which underpins much of the 'drive' theory of sexuality. What is being suggested is that certain ideas about sex and sexuality have a long history. Though the terms in which these have been expressed reflect the social and cultural milieux in which they are articulated, there are common themes which stretch back into Antiquity. These common themes developed a particular potency under the influence of Western Christianity, where the origins of many still current ideas can be located, and where, in particular, many of the features of modernist sexuality can be located.

In popular imagination, seeing sex as a 'problem' was a nineteenth-century phenomenon. Images of a stern, frock-coated paterfamilias and swooning gentlewomen co-exist with Dickensian figures of fallen women in dark alleyways, the victims of corrupt sexually exploiting men. These images were then and remain now of powerful ideological value. They both convey and reinforce the peculiar moral significance of sex on the one hand, while emphasizing the degree to which sexual liberalization has occurred on the other. The focus on the nineteenth century as the century of sexual repression serves also to encourage a view that in preceding epochs populations revelled in a sexual Elysian field, free from all anxieties and inhibitions. Images of the joyously sexual peasant or the decadent aristocrat seeking bizarre sexual outlets to alleviate boredom carry similar messages, as do the representations of the Classical world free from the Christian emphasis on self-denial and abstinence. Such popular views serve to reinforce the orthodoxy that fears and anxieties about expressions of sexual desire are the product of the nineteenth century, the counterpart of which is the understanding of a succeeding trajectory of liberation from outdated prejudice. Yet, arguably, the themes which characterized the sexual orthodoxy of the nineteenth century – anxieties about unregulated sexual desire, the characteristics and manifestations of women's sexuality, and the consequences of non-procreative erotic practices and same-sex desire, which were vigorously and publicly expressed and reflected in institutionalized campaigns and statute law – were as effective as they were because they found resonance with unease, which had a longer history.

Foucault's (1985) work on sexual ethics in Classical Antiquity offers some insight into both conceptualizations of sexual desire and its negative as well as positive consequences. There was in Classical Antiquity no outright condemnation of the pursuit of sexual pleasure grounded in its intrinsic perilousness; rather, the emphasis was on the proper use of pleasure. Foucault points out that the concept of pleasure (*aphrodisia*) entailed the unification of desire, the source of pleasure and its experience. The three factors were related and indivisible. The essential activities for the maintenance of human life – eating, drinking and copulation – were the sources of *aphrodisia* and it was considered expected (one hesitates to say 'normal') to seek out such pleasure. The pleasurable consequences of the act led humans to seek to repeat the experience. This need for recreation of the experience was *desire*. Yet there was an ethical problem inherent in this conceptualization of desire and pleasure: 'The ethical problem that was raised was not which desires? which acts? which pleasures? but rather by what force is one transported by the pleasures and desires' (Foucault 1985: 43). The problematic resided in the degree to which one was the master of these desires. 'Sexual promiscuity', to use a modern term, was not defined in terms of numbers of sexual partners or experiences, but of the degree to which one exercised control over oneself in such encounters. The aim of self-control was to maintain the active role. Bearing in mind that these were rules by men for men, inappropriate sexual behaviour for men was *passive* sexual behaviour – denying oneself the rightful male role, as the active player in the drama of pleasure (ibid., p. 47), rather than adherence to heterosexual acts, was the proof of virility. The critical distinction in the ethics of pleasure was between the subjects and objects of sexual activity. 'The first were men, naturally, but more specifically they were adult, free men; the second included women, of course, but women made up only one element of a much larger group [women, boys and slaves] . . .' (ibid.). It is worth emphasizing that these restrictions did not indicate anything intrinsically bad in sex itself, or that pursuance of pleasure was associated with a 'fall from grace'. Pleasing the pagan gods meant aspiring to attain the highest level of humanity one could achieve. The pleasures of the flesh were an integral part of humanity and so could not, in themselves, be wrong, nor should they be denied or avoided. Recognizing, not denying, the capacity for pleasure and exercising dominion over the acts, the sources and the desires, were the signs of elevated and ethical humanity. Sexual pleasure was functional not just in encouraging reproduction, but in restoring the holistic unity of the body through the assuaging of desire.

Yet within this alternative conceptualization of pleasure and desire there were elements which, Foucault argues, prefigure the more restrictive concerns of early Christianity. First, there was evident in Greek and later Roman writings an underlying anxiety about the negative effects of excessive sexual activity, a latent uncontrollability that resulted in physical and intellectual debilitation (Foucault 1985: 15ff.). Second, monogamy, fidelity and sexual constraint were, from the first two centuries A.D., deemed increasingly desirable. In a famous analogy, Pliny (A.D. 79) praised the elephant as one who mated only five times in a two-year mating season, and then only with one mate: 'Adultery was unknown to them' (Ranke-Hienemann 1991: 17). This story, Ranke-Hienemann has noted, appeared repeatedly over the succeeding six centuries in Christian tracts on the same issues. There was a distinction, though, which Foucault notes. While increasingly recommended as a positive quality, sexual continence and fidelity were not, in pagan philosophy, enshrined in law and custom, as they were to become under Christianity. Sexual promiscuity was not discouraged on the grounds of the transgression of universal laws and therefore offences against all, but sexually promiscuous behaviour was indicative of the loss of individual sovereignty, where one became the slave not the master to one's desires. Finally, despite the less differentiated choice of erotic partners, there was a concept of perversion of the 'natural order'. This order did not have as its centre the elevation of heterosexuality, nor the primary distinction between hetero- and homosexuality. Neither was there any sense of same-sex desire being an offence against nature. A natural sexual act was one in which the male was always, regardless of the status or sex of his partner, the active not the passive participator. This active status was the defining feature of virility. Individuals who by their behaviour subverted this 'natural' role, were distinguished by external features and bearing, even dress, and their 'sexual perversion' manifested itself visibly in physical and mental degeneration. In their constant reiteration of the naturalness of active masculine sexuality, the distinctiveness of female sexuality was rendered insignificant through silence. The sexual ethics of Classical Antiquity enshrined masculine sexuality as the prototype for all sexuality, in ways which reflected the cultural superiority of men and the sensual invisibility of women.

## 1.3 The problematization of sexuality: negative desires

The sexual ethics of Imperial Rome began to erode the unity of pleasure by emphasizing the moral desirability of conjugal love and, in the context of conjugality, of sexual continence and fidelity. Additionally, there was a demotion of the ethical significance of the love of boys. As Foucault (1990: 189ff.) points out, this decline in ethical significance did not mean a decline in the *practice*, but 'of a decline in the interest one took in it: a fading of the importance it was granted in philosophical and moral debate'. Roman sexual culture began to distinguish more clearly between two sorts of love: *eros*, which is characterized by 'virtue, friendship, modesty, candour, stability', and *aphrodisia*, which emanates from a baser desire driven by the attraction of sexual parts – as Foucault puts it, 'like a dog to its female' (ibid., p. 201). There are two significant issues here. First, the qualities of *eros* are considered and lauded as virile, masculine and therefore finer, ethically. Second, there is a notion that such 'pure' love is not deemed possible between men and women. This did not mean that sexual desire, even pleasure, was not associated with heterosexual communion. Rather, as Foucault argues, that there was a waning of the notion of disembodied 'pure' love, exemplified by *eros*, and a 'more detailed correlation between the sexual act and the body; a closer attention to the ambivalence of its effects and its disturbing consequences' (ibid., p. 238).

It was this shift in conceptualization of pleasure and its consequences that laid the ground for more stringent policing of desires in the context of Early Christianity. Foucault does not suggest a fluid continuity between the two traditions, but rather suggests that the new forms of problematization, suggested by the tensions between pure love and physically driven desire, created conditions for anxieties about sexual expressions of love and desire.

> It seems more and more necessary to distrust it, to confine it, as far as possible, to marital relations – even at the cost of charging it with more intense meanings within that conjugal relationship. Problematisation and apprehension go hand in hand; inquiry is joined to vigilance.
>
> (Foucault 1990: 239)

These distinctions were developed and refined under the influence of Stoicism, which in turn impacted on the sexual ethics of Early Christianity. Early Christianity inherited from the Stoics the demotion of pleasure from the highest pursuit of humankind, replacing it with the elevation of chastity and self-denial. This central belief provided the basis for the elevation of celibacy as the purest form of human existence. As universal adherence to such a principle was not consistent with the survival of humankind, the compromise lay in the vigorous promotion of sexual continence, where the desire for pleasure was replaced by the desire for procreation. The focus on procreation in turn simultaneously valorized heterosexuality and monogamy. In the contexts of the changing political and social contexts during the first few centuries A.D., this transformation of old sexual ethics also valorized conjugality indirectly.

Under these influences, desire was *re*-problematized as an obstacle, rather than the pathway, to the attainment of higher levels of humanity. Yet the influence of Christianity in reshaping the ways in which sex was problematized cannot be underestimated. It is significant that the first message in the Bible contains the most powerful condemnation of sexual desire and pleasure, drawing on the most basic human insecurities about rejection and inner-loneliness to drive home the message. Arguably, the story of The Fall is a striking example of Foucauldian self-surveillance at work. At first sight, the story would seem to be one of the dominion of external authority over the inner self; the possession of the power of expulsion from Eden is sovereign power at its most effective. Yet the dramatization of the negative consequences of succumbing to sexual desire could operate as a powerful internal monitor of individual behaviour. For not only was submission to temptation a personal damnation, but, in the story of The Fall, the damnation of all humankind.

This conferred on expressions of sexual desire a compelling social significance, for in temptations of the flesh lay the fate of all souls. Moreover, sexual temptation was represented as actively corrupting, and not integral to the individual. The imagery of the serpent is illustrative of two key components of this new construction of sexual desire and pleasure. First, it represented the 'otherness' of sexual desire. Whereas Classical sexual philosophy represented desire as the unifying force of the well-integrated self, this imagery presented sexual desire as a *dis*integrating force. The otherness represented by a different and external entity disengages sexual desire from the inner being and confers upon it alien and threatening capacities. Second, a profoundly human characteristic was represented by an animal, one which was very far removed from the human form, and already carried within it negative and life-threatening connotations. This representation of sexual desire by a reptile disengaged expressions of sexual desire from claims to higher humanity. Sex now represented the beast in us.

The story of The Fall represents desire as an inherently human characteristic through which one experienced temptation, but, unlike the Classical doctrine, it was a temptation which individual mastery was inherently unable to resist. The only defence against the eternal fate The Fall represented was not to expose oneself to temptation; in other words, to avoid, ideally, any experience of sexual desire. The strict adherence to this doctrine remains the most highly valued expression of holiness, but its second-order rendering was more practical. In this more attainable version of complete chastity, the inherent temptation of the act of sex could be offset by demeaning sexual desire, tolerating it only as a means to an end – that is, reproduction. This shift of focus and of primary purpose profoundly moved the boundaries of understandings of sexual pleasures and sexuality itself. On the one hand, the elevation of procreation carried with it an elevation of genital heterosexuality, while demoting all other sources of sexual pleasure, whether auto-erotic, non-genital or same-sex. On the other hand, there was, in such ordering, an imposed economy of desires. The positive associations of sex with pleasure in which the purpose was the proper management of the inner self was replaced with a grudging tolerance because of its purpose – that is, procreation.

This gave new significance to sexual acts. If they were positively defined in terms of their outcome, then acts without an outcome would be wilful waste. Gilman (1989) argues that there was a further significance in the Old Testament story of The Fall and the use of the serpent to epitomize temptation. In Classical sexual ideology, the sexuality of women appeared not to be considered worthy of particular attention, except in so far as it was, along with that of slaves, characterized as passive and in need of guidance. This more covert expression of sexual misogyny was replaced by a more persistent focused and judgemental message about women's sexuality, which retained some of the old, while promoting new, prejudices. With the demonization of *all* sexual desire, the characteristics of women's sexuality received more attention. The early Christian beliefs which were reflected in the Old Testament laid more emphasis on the susceptibility of women to temptation: 'It was the serpent, not Eve, that precipitated the Fall. The serpent represents pleasure, Eve the senses and Adam, reason' (Gilman 1989: 28). It was she to whom the serpent spoke and she who was susceptible to his blandishments. This suggests that the characteristic shared by both women and the animal kingdom was the inability to resist the thoughtless sensuality of nature. In pagan belief, 'sexuality' was one positive and visible illustration of the materiality of humanity. In Old Testament sexual iconography, these positive connections were reversed. Sexual desire was now depicted as an unreasoned force differentially possessed by women, which threatened the reason of men.

Yet the significance of women's sexuality was not dismissed in this construction. The story of The Fall is suggestive of ambivalence and unease about the quality of women's sexuality and thus, by implication, about the consequences of according women sexual autonomy. For Eve, like her counterpart the serpent, was a tempter. Women's sexuality is not just separate and different, but is by nature a direct threat to the inherent moral supremacy of men. This association prefigures also the later imagery of the 'polluting woman', the carrier of disease. 'Death has a traditional association with the sexual, specifically with the beautiful female . . . female beauty, the sexually attractive female, is merely a mask for death and decay, for Eve, the murdering prostitute' (Gilman 1989: 73). So even in the infancy of Western sexual culture, women were simultaneously more biddable and actively corrupting. Female and male sexuality is thus accorded a moral differentiation in a process that implicitly links immorality and nature.

The characterization of woman as the conduit for the fearful consequences of submission to pleasure, by virtue of her sensuality, adds an ambiguity to women's sexuality that was to become an enduring theme. For women simultaneously represent the ability to experience pleasure through the senses, while at the same time representing the fatal consequences of submission to temptation. In the Christian reworking of this earlier anxiety about sensual excess, which posed a threat to the mastery of the (male) self, the danger now lay unequivocally in the sexuality of women.

New Testament sexual iconography retains these underlying themes but presents them as reversible. Christ and the Virgin Mary together represent the possibility of redemption. Representations of Christ in medieval paintings from infancy to adulthood emphasize his genitalia, the mark of manhood, and of his sexuality. Similarly, the Virgin Mary is illustrative of the possibility of chastity and purification of women's moral turpitude, while simultaneously promoting her reproductive potential. The path to salvation lay in motherhood. This promise of redemption from The Fall is a promise also of deliverance from the dark side of our humanity – our animality and specifically of our animal (sexual) desires. The presence of Mary Magdalene emphasizes this message – the redemption of the prostitute, the personification of polluting and uncontrolled women's sexuality.

Even in these early stages, then, we can recognize the features of a domain that could meaningfully be termed 'sexuality', a term that was not appropriate to the former ethics of pleasure. The de-pleasuring of sexual desire, and the disruption of the unity of *aphrodisia*, redefined meanings attached to the sexual act, whereby the act itself became positively valued for reasons external to the self. The emphasis on purpose and outcome, rather than the holistic experience of sexual desire, elevated something we might now want to call sexuality as an act-centred rather than pleasure-centred concept. Early Christianity provided a domain in which universal prescriptions operated. Internally generated 'management of self' was replaced by the more coercive regulation of an external authority, which used as its terms of reference practices, not feelings, and thus increasingly concerned itself with the body corporeal. To borrow a Foucauldian term, in this new domain of ethics – and arguably in the genesis of sexuality – the body became the object of a new gaze.

## Conclusion

This chapter began with an account of the imputed characteristics of sex and sexuality in familiar contemporary contexts. Emphasis has been placed on the contradictory elements that persist in even apparently positive promotions of sexual desire: the disorderly potentials of its unregulated expression and the persistent ambivalence about women's sexuality both encapsulated a sense of fear which, it has been suggested, accounts for a greater part of the continuing specialness of sex. In the context of the late twentieth century, this specialness is in one respect anomalous: Given the ubiquity of sex in contemporary surroundings, how can this argument of specialness be sustained? The brief account of pagan and early Christian preoccupations with sex provide some important insights into both the origins and persistence of the contemporary contradictions. My aim has been to illustrate, taking fears about sex as the focus, how this theme presented itself in the earliest origins of Western sexual thought. The association of fear with sex and sexuality is not universal in the sexualized settings of modern industrial societies. Yet the shadowy presence of this association remains in relation to non-orthodox expressions of sexual desire, in the context of anxieties about youthful sexuality, in the unresolved ambivalence about women's sexuality and in the persistent primacy of heterosexuality. Behind these hierarchically ordered categories – indeed, in the logic of their persistence – there is a sense of an essential force, of something to be controlled and regulated: an aspect of humanity which has the capacity for disrupting the orderliness of both the individual and social being. It is this twinned capacity which is made evident in the apparently contrasting ideas of Classical Antiquity and early Christianity.

The disruptive potential in the pagan view lay in the possibility of the fragmentation of the unity of desire through an erosion of individual sovereignty of the male subject, in the loss of mastery of self. The capacity for sexual desire was deemed the property of the (high-ranking male) individual, yet evidence of the proper management of this was necessary for the maintenance of his social supremacy. In the sexual preoccupations of early Christianity, the disruptive potentials were placed centre stage in the moulding of human desires. In the process, self-dominion was replaced by a paternalistic authority with universally applicable definitions, which subordinated pleasure to purpose in a severely limited and highly contextual legitimation of sexual desire. The use of these contrasting and some might say culturally remote historical examples is not meant to convey the presence of an extra-cultural essentiality in sex, but the persistence of commonalities within sexual ideologies in differing historical and cultural contexts and their influence in shaping the expression of anxieties. The problematization of sexual desire and the apparent need for its differential ordering is a preoccupation which, these examples suggest, have a long pedigree. It may take very different forms, and may even, given a superficial comparison between this century and the last, have been dissolved.

Yet the broad sweep of comparison between the end of the twentieth century and the origins of Western sexual thought suggests the presence of deep-rooted and unresolved tensions between notions of danger and pleasure, temptation and constraint, reason and unreason. The differences in the presentation of these tensions, suggested in the snapshot of history provided above, invite a more detailed exploration of the shaping of late twentieth-century sexual ideologies. In particular, the ways in which the tensions are shaped and influenced by the predominant frameworks for social regulation, whether formally through legal statutes, or informally through the more diffuse process of moral orderings, which marginalize some aspects of sex while actively promoting others. In what follows, the informal route will receive more detailed attention, though there are necessarily interconnections between the two. Specifically, this more detailed exploration will begin with the influence of anxieties associated with modernity and the 'civilizing process', and the ways in which these were both reflected in, and shaped by, accompanying preoccupations with sex and sexuality, which could be seen to constitute a recognizably modernist sexuality.

# 2 Sex *and* modernity

Modernity is associated with the 'industrializing process', characterized by urbanization, population increases, secularization and the rapid development of a highly complex division of labour (Kumar 1978). These processes were at least as revolutionary in their effects as the development of technology which both drove and accompanied industrialization. They had a profound influence on the spatial and social geographic organization of the citizens of urban environments, disrupting traditional frameworks for self and social meaning and creating in their place more appropriate matrices for the integration of self and society. Commentators of modernity illustrate the ambivalence about the dual processes of loss and creation and their human consequences. On the one hand, modernity can be seen as

> An age of the breath-taking pace of development, of the multiplication of material wealth, of the ever-increasing mastery of humankind over its natural environment, of the universal emancipation from all, real or imaginary, restrictions which constrained and hampered human creative potential for an interminably long part of history.
>
> (Bauman 1987: 112)

Yet the extent and pace of this development had a cost which somehow devalued and disempowered humankind: 'Reason's coming of age ... subjects human life to the impersonal logic of rationalised anonymous administration systems – historical processes in short, which tend to make human life mechanised, unfree and meaningless' (Wellmer 1985: 43). This human cost is usually conceptualized in terms of the fleeting, impersonal and objectified relations between individuals or groups, a pure form of alienation, which is rightly located, in the final instance, in the social relations of production. Yet for such changes to be accomplished in an historically short time span, changes had to be wrought in more than the mechanics of production or the location of populations. For a revolution to achieve its goals, it must bind hearts and minds as well as physical bodies to its cause.

Max Weber (1974) was clear about this in his study of the connections between religious beliefs and the spirit of capitalism. As Weber illustrated, the spirit of capitalism referred to a way of thinking about economic activity that combined the mechanics of rational action with the structuring of ways of thinking, of ordering and giving precedence to certain priorities of human existence. For Weber, and others since, a singular feature of the spirit of capitalism was ascetism – the conscious denial of pleasure. But there was a form to this denial that was distinctive – it was a worldly ascetism. This distinction meant that the denial of pleasure was not absolute in the sense one might associate with a monastic existence. The denial took place not outside, but within a world increasingly suffused with rationality. Thus the 'denial' frequently took the form of reordering of aspects of human behaviour rather than outright prohibition. The reordering entailed, first, the restructuring of parameters that defined, for example, profligacy. What constituted profligacy in the Calvinist context was very different from a similar judgement in the context of, for example, the Court of the Sun King. Second, reordering involved the reshaping of motives against an authority whose claim to legitimacy lay not in its location in tradition but in its expertise and detachment from any subjective interest. The motives promoted involved the primacy of externally defined purpose and outcome over internally experienced satisfaction. And what might, *pace* Weber, be termed the 'spirit of modernity', exerted an influence that went beyond material existence. The shaping of parameters and motives also impacted on emotions and affective aspects of human existence.

## 2.1   Norbert Elias and the civilizing process

> One of the many brilliant observations of Elias's study [*The History of Manners*] was the idea that the successful culmination of the process consists of the historical episode of suppression being forgotten, pseudo-rational legitimation being supplied for newly introduced patterns and the whole historical form of life being 'naturalised'.
>
> (Bauman 1987: 114)

Elias begins his *History of Manners*, first published in 1939, with a lengthy exploration of the cultural and historical meanings of 'civilization', which he views as both an expression and symbol of social formation and unity. The dynamic of the historical process was the concept of *civilité*, the basis for the ordering of social behaviour, which first became evident in the second quarter of the sixteenth century. He makes extensive use of Erasmus's (1530) *De civilitate morum puerilium* to illustrate the distinctions between *civilité* and the former patterning of social behaviour that are associated with a knightly feudal warrior nobility, encapsulated in the concept of *courtoisie*. The importance of this detailed background is, first, that it indicates and emphasizes that forms of social regulations on behaviour have a long history, and that observation and regulation of behaviour cannot be related to modernity. Second, Elias's account in its entirety represents a prolonged argument for the necessity of locating regulation of behaviour, and affective behaviour in particular, within specific historical and social structures. Finally, rather than approaching civilization as a single entity, Elias's work emphasizes the necessity to view it as a process:

The civilisation which we are accustomed to regard as a possession that comes to us apparently ready made, without asking how we actually came to possess it, is a process or part of a process in which we ourselves are involved. Every particular characteristic that we attribute to it – machinery, scientific discovery, form of state or whatever else – bear witness to a particular structure of human relations, to a particular social structure and to corresponding forms of behaviour.

(Elias 1982: 59)

Given this emphasis, then, the differences between and changes in forms of social regulation should not be interpreted in a 'before and after' dichotomy implicit in the notion that 'now we are civilized, but then they were not'. The relationship between forms of regulation of behaviour and the social structures in which they are embedded and which they reflect, keeps firmly in focus the notion of civilization as a reflexive process. At the same time, Elias makes clear the shift involved in the emergence of *civilité*, a concept which he associates closely with the dawn of the Modern Age, and which, over succeeding centuries, provided a 'measuring stick' for the emergence and ascendence of the bourgeoisie over the feudal aristocracy.

The shift in the hierarchical ordering of social power is, for Elias, indicated by changes in the ways in which people relate to one another – literally see one another:

The new stage of courtesy and its representation, summed up in the concept of *civilité* is very bound up in this way of seeing . . . in order to be really courteous by the standards of *civilité* one is to some extent obliged to observe, to look about oneself and to pay attention to people and their motives. In this, too, a new relationship of men to men, a new form of social integration is announced.

(Elias 1982: 78)

This observation of oneself and others, which is evident from the mid-sixteenth century onwards, is related, Elias argues, to the project of moulding oneself and others. It is also related, he implies, to the structural changes associated with the dawn of the Modern Age – the increasing and specific forms of interdependence engendered by the expanding division of labour in society in specific Durkheimian terms: 'The old social ties are, if not broken, extensively loosened and are in the process of transformation. Individuals of different origin are thrown together. The social circulation of ascending and descending groups and individuals speeds up' (ibid., p. 79).

Interdependence and the increasingly evident unprecedented distinctions between individuals was reflexively related to this notion of observation of self and others, as new and more dynamic forms of sociation emerged. The emphasis on 'behaviour', no longer enshrined in the unwritten assumptions of tradition and fixed hierarchies, now took the form of more detailed monitoring of visible minutiae. This new conceptualization of behaviour can be read as one index of the emergence of the notion of the 'social individual' as we understand and experience it in the Modern Age. To put it perhaps too baldly, the centrality of the individual as the pivot and legitimation for social regulation supplants that of tradition. 'The coercion exerted by people on one another increases, the demand for "good behaviour" is raised more emphatically' (ibid., p. 79). By the mid-seventeenth century, the pace and urgency of this process lessened as a new social hierarchy asserted itself. Yet there was an escalation of the regulatory content of the rules and their effects, which arguably reflected the increased density of social relations associated with the industrializing process. 'Not abruptly, but very gradually, the code of behaviour becomes stricter and the degree of consideration ex-pected by others becomes greater' (ibid., p. 80). In the less differentiated, more stable hierarchical society, the yardstick of acceptable behaviour was the degree to which it transgressed the boundaries of one's place in the ordered hierarchy. By the seventeenth century, there was a shift in emphasis regarding such behaviour, which heightened concerns about giving offence to others. This became the central normative script for the new treatises on social behaviour, and one which operated both as a more subtle and more effective form of control:

> It is immediately apparent that this polite, extremely gentle and com-paratively considerate way of correcting is, particularly when exercised by a social superior, much more compelling as a means for social con-trol, much more effective in inculcating lasting habits than mockery, or any outward threats of physical violence.
>
> (Elias 1982: 82)

These treatises on manners, though not new in themselves, were new both in their content and their effect. Yet, the notion of civilization as a process is underlined by Elias, who illustrates how forms of behaviour con-sidered proper in the sixteenth century were the source of shame and em-barrassment two centuries later. Feelings of shame and embarrassment – affective responses – figure prominently in Elias's account. One root source of such feelings is, he argues, the increasing awareness of selves in relation to others, in the context of the fragmentation of the old fixed hierarchical order. The increasing awareness of our fellow human beings produces, reflex-ively, an increased awareness of self. This arises from and feeds the sense of others' observation of us – one's visibility – the conscious awareness of which heightens the social and personal significance of our actions. This significance was, from the mid-sixteenth century onwards, increasingly rep-resented in the form of publicly articulated advice and correction.

A further significance of enshrining new forms of social integration in manners in the more detailed manifestations discussed above, is the empha-sis placed on the need to distinguish 'human' from 'bestial' tendencies. Elias uses changes in the social mores surrounding meat-eating to exemplify this: Before the onset of the civilizing process it was considered acceptable, even pleasurable, to carve meat from the full carcass of the animal in the presence of the diners. However, 'In the course of the civilising process, [people] seek to suppress in themselves every characteristic they feel to be "animal", [and] likewise they suppress such characteristics in their food' (ibid., p. 120).

Accordingly, Elias charts a gradual process by which the carcasses of cooked animals were first served skinned and dismembered, then served cut up in sections, before being carved out of sight of the diners. Such detail suggests a wider social significance for this disassociation from bestial tendencies – the concern to distance wider aspects of human behaviour from other drives and instincts that might likewise indicate an unacceptable affinity with nature. 'Behind the change in eating techniques between the Middle Ages and Modern times appears the same process that emerged in other incarnations of this kind: a change in the structure of drives and emotions' (ibid., p. 127).

Thus the same acts became associated with different feelings and emotions, in particular an increase in taboos regarding acts symbolic of these. The taboos, Elias argues, expressed themselves increasingly over the centuries, in feelings of shame, disgust, distaste or displeasure. Such affective responses were engendered by and shared between individuals *qua* themselves and others, in the form of what might be termed a 'moral universe of manners'. The ways in which these taboos were communicated changed over time but were related, as their genesis was, to changes in the structure of society. Thus, there was a decline in public pronouncements of these rituals and taboos, which over the succeeding centuries came to be communicated and inculcated at a more individual and private level – specifically, Elias says, from elders to children in the home – while there was a continuance of the moral and normative education of inferiors by superiors in the public arena.

> Later it becomes more and more an inner automatism, the imprint of society on the inner self, the super-ego . . . the social standard to which the individual was first made to conform by external constraint is finally produced more or less smoothly within him, through a self-constraint which may operate even against his conscious wishes.
>
> (Elias 1982: 129)

These insights from Elias, drawn from examples of public manners and behaviours, are germane to an exploration of the relationship between the characteristics of modernity and those of sexuality. Of particular significance is his emphasis on the historicity of feelings of shame and embarrassment, particularly in relation to bodily functions, both of excretion and those related to sexual behaviour.

Before the influence of *civilité*, special levels of shame and embarrassment were not accorded to bodily functions. They were, to a degree, proscribed, but tended to be so in relation not to what was being done but in whose presence. Thus certain activities witnessed by social equals or superiors were more proscribed than the same activities in the presence of social inferiors: 'there were people before whom one is ashamed and others before whom one is not' (ibid., p. 138). Before the mid-sixteenth century, Elias argues, the social mores did not distinguish between the functions of eating, excretion and sexual behaviour. None was seen more reprehensible nor more in need of regulation than any other.

> Neither the functions themselves, nor speaking about them or associations with them are so intimate and private, so invested with feelings

of shame and embarrassment as they later become . . . The different standards of Erasmus's time becomes clear if one reads how common-place it is to meet someone *"qui urinam reddit aut alvum exonerat"* (urinating or defecating)'.

(Elias 1982: 135)

Shifts in conceptualization of intimacy and of the relationship between shame and privacy are vividly illustrated by Elias in relation to the desocial-ization of the bedroom and of nakedness. There would be little disagreement that in the contemporary Western context, the bedroom is an 'inner sanc-tum' of intimacy, to which we would tend only to admit those from whom we have the least 'secrets'. Yet Elias illustrates to us how in medieval Europe the bedroom was as public a sphere as our kitchens are today. People would share the same bedroom and bed with little distinction made on grounds of sex and age. Only in the seventeenth century did the idea of dressing for bed arise. Before this it was considered unusual to sleep clothed; covering the body was considered shameful, as it indicated the possible presence of de-formity. Sharing one's bed with strangers was likewise not considered ex-traordinary or unacceptable. Similarly, appearing in the public street naked is today an arrestable offence of public disorder, yet Elias presents the follow-ing cameo of medieval community life:

'How often', says the observer, 'the father wearing nothing but his breeches, with his naked wife and children, runs through the street from his house to the baths . . . how often have I seen girls of ten, twelve, fourteen, sixteen and eighteen years, naked except for a short smock, often torn . . . running from their houses at midday to the baths. How many completely naked boys of ten, twelve, fourteen and sixteen run beside them'.

(quoted in Elias 1982: 164)

As with sleeping arrangements and nakedness, sexual behaviour was not considered to be especially intimate in the modern sense, nor was it the source of heightened embarrassment and shame it would later become in bourgeois society, in which 'the exclusion of such functions as sleeping, undressing and dressing was enforced with special severity, the mere men-tion of them being blocked by relatively heavy prohibitions' (ibid., p. 165). Sex was a part of social life, and again using the works of Erasmus, Elias illustrates how sexual behaviour was not distinguished from other expres-sions of sociality. Children were to be equipped with the appropriate be-havioural norms associated with sexual matters in the same way as they were taught appropriate behaviour in other spheres. There was no notion of the need to conceal such areas from children, nor of any sense of embarrassment addressing the idea of adult sexuality. Until the late sixteenth century, 'in keeping with the different state of restraint of feelings produced in the in-dividual by the structure of inter-personal relations, the idea of strictly con-cealing these drives in secrecy and intimacy was largely alien to the adults themselves' (ibid., p. 175). Accompanying couples to the marital bed and celebration of the consummation were customs that persisted well into the

seventeenth century. As with other human practices associated with intimacy, sexual activity was not just moved 'behind the scenes' in the later
stages of the civilizing process, but arguably was accorded *the* special place
in the internal ordering of affective and emotional life in the course of the
civilizing process, so that by the nineteenth century, 'The relations between
the sexes are isolated, placed behind the walls in consciousness. An aura of
embarrassment, the expression of a socio-genetic fear, surrounds this sphere
of life' (ibid., p. 180).

There is a further dimension to the civilizing process, which again is
related to the specific changes associated with modernity. In the early stages
of *civilité*, prescriptions relating to social behaviour were directed towards the
members of the higher echelons of society. It was considered neither necessary nor appropriate, given the rigidity of the social hierarchy, to direct the
behaviour of the 'lower orders'. With the increase at both the functional and
the perceptual level of the interdependence associated with the division of
labour, concern about social behaviour shifted both in its focus and in its
mode of expression. Specifically, it produced a recognition of the full existence of those not only of equal and superior rank, but those of 'inferior' rank
as well. Thus behaviour once seen as a social offence, in that it transgressed
expectations of behaviour in specific social circumstances, came to be seen
as a 'general offence'. Likewise, shame that was once contingent on social
status now became more universal. With this universalization another shift
occurred, reflecting the gradual separation of spheres that accompanied the
advanced forms of the division of labour and the related elevation of the
notion of individual rights and responsibilities.

With the changes in social structure, and the increased sense of visibility
of selves and others outlined above, particular forms of behaviour most
closely associated with instincts and impulses came into sharper focus, and
were accorded distinctive status in sensitivity and sensibility. 'In keeping
with its different interdependence, bourgeois society applies stronger restrictions on certain impulses' (ibid., p. 152).

In keeping with the changes in social structures and the separation of
spheres, the regulation of behaviour now associated with shame and embarrassment took place, increasingly, behind the closed doors of the domestic
sphere, and the direction of expressions of bodily impulses became the focus
of social education, in particular that of children by their parents. This shift
in the domain of regulation had, Elias suggests, profound consequences:

> Precisely because the social command not to show oneself exposed or
> performing natural functions now operates with regard to everyone
> and is imprinted in this form on the child, it seems to the adult a
> command of his own inner self and takes on the form of a more or less
> automatic self-restraint.
>
> (Elias 1982: 139)

This focus on the child as a social *tabula rasa* – the 'uncivilized' nascent adult
– gave rise to a widening gap in the perception of differences between adults
and children, as well as providing the background against which an ever-
widening agenda of behaviours came under scrutiny. 'The children have, in

the space of a few years to attain the level of shame and revulsion that has developed over many centuries' (ibid., p. 140).

Nietzsche (1990: 53) said that 'Shame exists wherever there exists a mystery', a maxim which suggests a starting point for a further exploration of the by now taken-for-granted association of shame with bodily intimacy. Following Elias and Durkheim, Giddens (1972: 115) noted the emergence of internal impersonal constraints on certain aspects of behaviour associated with increasingly differentiated and interdependent social relations. Yet while in the process of modernity there is an organic interdependence which binds us together, there is also an increased affective gulf that is contained within, and operates through, a sphere of the secret self, in which certain feelings and acts are considered not appropriate for exposure in the public domain. In his essay on 'Secrecy', Simmel (in Wolff 1950: 330ff.) suggests that one of the markers of 'the social' in modernity is the shift between secrecy and openness. Aspects of social behaviour that were once open are now secret, and forms of behaviour or social processes once assumed to be instinctive and pre-programmed are now deemed to be open to conscious manipulation. He argues that the dimension of secrecy, whatever it encompasses, is essential to all forms of social interaction, but particularly modern forms. For Simmel, secrecy, whether in relation to feelings, acts or things, is logistically difficult in less differentiated societies because of physical proximity, but is also less significant sociologically. With increasing differentiation and forms of interdependence characteristic of modern society, there was an expansion of the internal space within which differences were created and maintained, and with this shift an expansion as well as a change in the content of 'secrets'.

> It seems as if, with growing cultural expediency, general affairs become even more public, and individual affairs even more secret . . . Politics, administration and jurisdiction thus have lost their secrecy and inaccessibility in the same measure in which the individual has gained the possibility of even more complete withdrawal, and in the same measure in which modern life has developed in the midst of urban crowdedness, a technique for making and keeping private matters secret, such as earlier could be attained only by means of spatial isolation.
>
> (Simmel, in Wolff 1950: 336–7)

Elias's work provides insights into the mechanics of the process of civilization and the ways in which it shaped responses to, and feelings about, the social deployment of the body and its functions, particularly in the demarcation of intimate spheres. The growing distinction between the private and public domains and the emergence of the notion of 'the individual' resulted in the decline of the passive direction of social mores. These are replaced in the civilizing process, with a more focused and nuanced regulation of affective behaviour. Intimate acts and feelings – those which in the context of modernity increasingly define identity – are most likely to be associated with shame and embarrassment. Furthermore, feelings of shame reflexively operate as internal constraints that are both the consequence and the protectors of these 'secret spheres'. The internality of these mechanisms and their consequences contribute over time to their being seen not as external constraints, but naturally ordained patterns. Yet their focus lays emphasis on, and consequently imbues with anxiety, behaviour which is the source of sensual pleasure.

> Society is gradually beginning to suppress the positive pleasure component in certain functions more and more strongly by the arousal of anxiety; or, more exactly, it is rendering this pleasure 'private' and 'secret' . . . while fostering the negatively charged affects – displeasure, revulsion, distaste as the only feelings customary in society.
>
> (Elias 1982: 142)

## 2.2   Civilization and the repression of sexual desire

Published a decade before Elias's work, Freud's (1929/1961) essay 'Civilisation and its Discontents', similarly dealt with the impact of civilization on the shaping of feelings and behaviour, but in ways which reflected the more pessimistic overtones of earlier commentators on modernity. As Bauman (1987: 113) suggests, Freud:

> . . . depicts modernity as a time when the 'reality principle' attained domination over the 'pleasure principle', and when people, as a result, trade part of their freedom (and happiness) for a degree of security, grounded in a hygienically safe, clean and peaceful environment. The trade off may be profitable, but it comes about as a product of the suppression of the 'natural' drives and the imposition of patterns of behaviour which ill fit human predispositions and offer only oblique outlets for instincts and passions.

Freud's pessimism about civilization echoes that of Max Weber in relation to 'disenchantment'. While acknowledging 'the whole sum of the achievements and the regulations which distinguish our lives from those of our animal ancestors and which serve two purposes – namely to protect men against nature and adjust their mutual relations' (Freud 1961: 89), these achievements are bought at a cost – 'what we call our civilisation is largely responsible for our misery' (ibid., p. 86). The negative consequences for humanity are, in this essay, the inhibitions on expressions of love and the continuing process of containment of sexual desire.

Love is one of the foundations of civilization, being the original driving force behind any social intercourse with others (ibid., p. 117). Yet, there is a complication in this pre-modern state, which parallels that of the pre-rational importance of mysticism in the integration of human society. Freud was suggesting that there is a psychic danger in this simple romanticism. On the one hand, sexual love offers a source of pleasure with the widest and deepest dimension for humanity. Yet there is a 'worm in the bud' of this promise. The possibility of these exquisite pleasures is muted and haunted by a fear of the loss of the object of love and the font of pleasure. The possibility of this loss increases with the complexity and differentiation of social formations associated with the civilizing process. The perception of, and response to, this circumstance is to inhibit expressions of love and commitment to one individual, while at the same time extending the affective sphere to encompass an ever-widening circle of fellow humans. Freud calls this strategy 'aim-inhibited love', which in its immediate application represents friendship, and in a wider one encourages affective attachments to community, national identity and humanity in general. The basic human need of love, which lies at the heart of civilization, thus produces what for Freud is the most important characteristic of civilization – the regulation of social relationships, in which the needs of the individual are partially subsumed under the needs of the community. 'The liberty of the individual is no gift of civilisation. It was greater before there was any civilisation, though then, it was true, it was for the most part of no value, since the individual was scarcely in the position to defend it' (ibid., p. 95).

Genital love and 'aim-inhibited love' – friendship and its wider social and cultural expression – are distinguished in the context of civilization. Genital love provides the foundation for new families, and friendships promote cultural development because they escape the exclusivity of the former. But while the relationship between love and civilization is initially defined by its positive consequences for humanity, the avoidance of fear of loss and the regulation of social relationships, civilization progressively, disrupts this harmony. The expansion of social formations that increase the extent and quality of cultural life, broadly conceptualized, comes into conflict with the scope of expressions of erotic love.

Thus there is, for Freud, a irreconcilable tension between civilization and sexual pleasure, a tension which is characterized and shaped by three constraining parameters: the sexual expression of love between parents and children, the denial of children's sexuality and the curbing of the erotic object choice of the mature adult. In his 1912 essay, 'On the universal tendency to debasement in the sphere of love', Freud (1986: 45ff.) sees 'psychical impotence' in both men and women (though, unsuprisingly presenting in different forms) as a 'universal affliction' of civilization. This psychical impotency is, in simple terms, the inability of both men and women to experience sexual pleasure fully. The causes of this are integrally associated not just with the more diffuse temporal category of 'civilization', but specifically with the characteristics of Western culture. Cultural norms intervene in the capacity of men to experience sexual pleasure: they cannot develop full potency except with, as Freud puts it, 'a debased object' – a woman with whom he will be comfortable introducing the 'perverse components' necessary for complete sexual pleasure. Choosing a mistress or even a wife from 'the lower classes' is, for Freud, the 'consequence of the need for a debased sexual object, to whom, psychologically, the possibility of complete sexual satisfaction is linked' (ibid., p. 254). Similarly, women's 'psychical impotence' is the consequence of, first, as with men, the incest taboo and suppression of infantile sexuality and, second, the imposition of virginity and sexual passivity in maturity. This notion of 'debasement' associated with sexual pleasure is not, as might be interpreted, solely an indication of Freud's misogyny. While phrases such as 'debased object' are undeniably offensive, and arguably dangerously so since they resonate with wider misogynist prejudices, it is worth bearing in mind that Freud was giving a scientist's account of ways of thinking which prevailed in relation to sexual pleasure which he had observed first hand and from secondary sources, either historical or anthropological.

The conceptualization of sex as degrading, defiling and polluting was, Freud argued, derived from the incest taboo and the prohibition of extra-familial expressions of sexual desire which applied to both men and women. The ongoing sense of dissatisfaction and craving for stimulation which, for Freud, inevitably accompanies civilized sex and which is frequently the cause of sexual neuroses, likewise lies in the frustration of the original sex aim, the parent, for whom all subsequent sexual experiences are a poor substitute. Sexual desires in Freud's view are, and remain, animal desires – support for this contention lies in the anatomical placing of the genitals *inter urinam et faeces*. 'The genitals themselves have not taken part in the development of the human body in the direction of beauty: they have remained animal, and thus love, too, has remained in essence just as animal as it ever was' (ibid., p. 259).

If the logic of civilization is to release humanity from the despotism of nature and enable a degree of self-monitored autonomy, then a distance has to be maintained between humanity and animality. Thus civilization cannot do otherwise than curtail expressions of sexual pleasure. The evident persistence of sexual dissatisfaction – epitomized in 'psychical impotency' – supports the presence of the suppressed components of human sexuality, those which provide the (forbidden) routes to full sexual pleasure.

Yet there is a redeeming consequence of this repression, for the energies and creativeness that would otherwise be employed in experiencing the full gamut of human sexuality are, Freud says, deflected into the 'noblest cultural achievements' (ibid., p. 259). There is thus a symbiotic relationship between the suppression of sexuality and civilization: one is not possible without the other. As civilization progresses, 'The tendency on the part of civilization to restrict sexual life is no less clear than its other tendency to expand cultural life' (Freud 1961: 103–104).

The original denial of incestual desire, of youthful sexuality and of 'animality', the prohibitions which enabled civilization, became embedded in cultural frameworks and expressed in value judgements. In the Western cultural trajectory, sexual pleasure was increasingly associated negatively with animality, while chastity became a desirable quality, particularly in women. The ascendence of patriarchal dominance expressed itself sexually in a narrowing heterosexual matrix of active male and passive female sexuality. The 'animal' pleasures of sex, frustrated by the constraints of the civilizing process, become subordinated to the advantages of ascetic sexuality, characterized by sexual continence, monogamy and rational sex:

> Heterosexual genital love, which has remained exempt from outlawry is itself restricted by further limitations, in the shape of insistence on legitimacy and monogamy. Present day civilisation makes it plain that it will only permit sexual relationships on the basis of a solitary, indissoluble bond between one man and one woman, and that it does not

like sexuality as a source of pleasure in its own right and is only prepared to tolerate it because there is so far no substitute for it as a means
of propagating the human race.

(Freud 1961: 105)

The acculturalization of sex, associated with the repressive influence of
civilization, becomes the dynamic for a process whose continued presence is
ensured by its being the source of psychic security. What began as a process
of releasing human potential has become an embedded system of denial of
the promise of sexual diversity and of universalizing prohibitions on expressions of sexual desire. Freud's account of the negative effects of civilization
on expressions of human sexual desire thus bears a striking resemblance to
Weber's account of rationality.

## 2.3 Sex and rationality

In his account of rationalization and its association with occidental capitalism,
Weber emphasized the ambiguity of its effects. For Weber, a defining quality
of humanity is the ability to make choices between a number of possible
routes to a given end. Freedom is in this sense synonymous with rationality,
in that:

> To act as a free person therefore means to act purposively . . . The
> deliberate calculation of the opportunities for and consequences of
> purposively orientated action, conditioned by means available in each
> case, manifests at the same time both the rationality and the freedom
> of that action.

(Weber, quoted in Lowith 1982: 45–6)

But the freedom which is realized in this activity is at the same time compromised. 'The "freer" the actor's decision . . . the more motivation itself,
*ceteris paribus*, falls remorselessly within the category of "means" and "ends"'
(ibid., pp. 44–45). The choices do not take place in an ideological vacuum.
For the promotion of rationality itself was an ideological endeavour that
reflected the principles of Puritan discipline. Thus the choices of means
could not simply be defined in terms of the ends. Choices of means were
made in a context that valued certain choices over others in their own right,
as well as prioritizing certain characteristics of the end. For Weber, as Sayer
points out, ascetic discipline entailed 'elimination from everyday life of what
is not godlike', and 'the primary ungodlike factors were actually the average
*habitus* of the human body and the everyday world' as well as 'the spontaneous enjoyment of life and all it had to offer' (Weber, quoted in Sayer
1991: 123). The measure of success of rationality is the extent to which its
terms of reference and logic has permeated all aspects of social life. As the
demystification associated with modernity progressively undermines old certainties, humankind increasingly seeks a replacement for the old ordering
framework, one which gives some order and meaning to actions. The new
framework which provides this psychic security is rationality. Thus, looked

at historically, as each dimension of social life is subjected to one form or another of intellectual bookkeeping, and 'old' ideas are challenged and discarded, another natural home for rational action is created. Rationalization breeds more rationality.

This is the 'iron cage' so familiar in relation to Weber's analysis of bureaucracy. Yet, as Derek Sayer points out, a cage is the antithesis of freedom. The original meaning of the 'iron cage' was the 'house of steel', a translation which for Sayer has a more persuasive message. For one can escape from a house of steel, but there is a safety in inhabiting it which offers a tempting security, one which, as Weber noted, becomes increasingly difficult to escape from:

> It is as if knowingly and deliberately, we actually wanted to become men who require 'order', and nothing but order, who grow nervous and cowardly if this falters for a moment and who become helpless if they are uprooted from their exclusive adaption to this order.
> (Weber, quoted in Lowith 1982: 55)

The inescapability of rationality lies in its creation of a dependency. As Sayer suggests, a metaphorical translation of *ein stahlhartes Gerhause* is 'the shell (also *Gerhause*) on a snail's back: a burden perhaps, but something impossible to live without' (Sayer 1991: 144). This interpretation emphasizes the importance of the subjective in Weber's analysis of social action: we are not automatons but actively engage in our own 'imprisonment'.

On the one hand, rationalization in its subjective understanding offered unprecedented release from magical, unpredictable and even despotic mechanisms for the direction of social action. On the other, the mechanism which defined rationality and through which a sense of individual autonomy was achieved contributed to a progressive loss of that autonomy. Thus, the means are subverted from their original purpose (service to humankind and their needs): humans themselves become servants, the ideas the masters. This, for Weber, is the paradox of modernity and the source of the pessimism he equates with disenchantment. The real tragedy of civilization was that the process that crafted 'freedom' simultaneously contributed to its mutation.

In accounts of the ambiguity of modernity, the impact of ways of thinking about sex and sexuality received little attention. Yet given the central dynamic of both the worldly asceticism and the spirit of modernity, sexuality was a prime candidate for attention. In a world which increasingly valued containment of feelings and desires, however worthy, the potential disorderliness of sex and sexuality, as the least mediated outlet of emotions and feelings, became the source of unprecedented anxieties. These anxieties were not reflected in outright prohibition of sex. They were, though, through the twinned processes of shaping of motives and sculpting of boundaries of meaning, to reorder ways of thinking about sex, what is prioritized and what is marginalized, in a corresponding modernist sexual orthodoxy.

In a brief address paid to the problem which the essential irrationality of the erotic posed for worldly asceticism, Weber listed the contexts in which erotic impulses were contained within purposive frameworks of reproductive marital alliance, and in doing so implicitly acknowledged that modernity had put in place frameworks for rationalizing the 'irrational'. The 'rationalizing process', which arguably civilization constituted for Weber, entailed the routinization of sexual desires, which primarily required the sublimation of 'the ineradicable connection of animality' with sexual life. For in the erotic relation, 'the lover realises himself to be . . . freed from the cold skeletal hands of rational orders, just as completely as from the banality of everyday routine' (Weber quoted in Gerth and Mills 1970: 347–8).

The denial of the erotic in the promotion of sexual ascetism is paramount in this process, since erotic desires are the 'powerful deadly enemy . . . a constant deadly sophisticated revenge of animality' (ibid., p. 348). But the erotic is a constant temptation, since it represents 'the gate into the most irrational and therefore the real kernel of life' (Sayer 1991: 125). The mechanics of rationalization – the purposively ordered motivations for social action subjectively experienced – require the promotion of marriage for the personal and emotional advantages it offers in the context of fragmented traditional orders. The routinization of sexual pleasure is advanced in the marital state, and 'given to man to live according to the rational purposes laid down for it, to procreate and rear children and to mutually further one another in the state of grace' (Gerth and Mills 1970: 349). In exchange for the 'primal naturalist and *un*-sublimated sexuality' that characterized pre-modern life, one is offered the emotional security and predictability of routinized sexual pleasures. The Christian and – particularly in relation to rationalized sex – the Puritan sexual ideology promoted the positive outcomes of this exchange, offering a source of psychic security in a world where traditional certainties had been dissolved, while promoting the promise of individual autonomy in the ordering of social action.

The discussion of the mechanisms of rationality – the ordering of social action in relation to means and ends, and the loss of freedom that this inevitably entails – illuminates the shaping of sexual desires and of what constitutes sexuality in the context of modernity. The discussion also provides insights into the role of subjectivity in this process. For freedom of choice – the positive promise of rational action – implies the active participation of the individual actor. Yet the framework within which choices are increasingly made operate to shape social meanings and contain individual autonomy through an internalized value system. The original logic for the routinization of sex – inner-worldly ascetism – has become redundant, but its effectiveness remains evident in restricted and aim-directed sexual desire, which stripped of its original context is experienced as 'natural'. The primacy of genital heterosexual sex is the 'snail's shell', which offers protection from the alternative, the unnerving promise of erotic diversity.

## Conclusion

In the optimistic interpretation, modernity entailed the triumph of reason over superstition, and the developing human capacity for reasoned behaviour represented the advances offered by rational action for individual freedom of expression. Why, then, was it the case that sexuality in the apotheosis of the age of reason suffered from the imposition of constraints, the closing down of possibilities for erotic self-expression? This chapter began by suggesting that in addition to the parameters of modernity more usually addressed – technological progress, spatial and social reorganization of populations and the triumph of reason over superstition – there was an additional element less often recognized, the shaping and directing of moral sensibility. The suppression of the irrational which was the corollary of modernity led to a renewed focus on the disruptive potential of sensual pleasure. Elias's history of manners traces the process by which social shame and embarrassment were engendered in the civilizing process, and why these feelings came to be particularly associated with bodily functions. More pertinently, he suggests ways in which, paradoxically, modernity conferred upon sex qualities which imbued it with enduring fascination. Fearful and mysterious, sequestered in privacy and increasing prudery, its ordinariness made special, it was increased rather than reduced in mysticism. Elias's work illuminates a dimension of modernity that is rarely discussed and that has a particular saliency for many of our taken-for-granted ideas about sex, intimacy and shame. They are also suggestive of the persistence and reworking of pre-modern ideas discussed in the previous chapter – the continued presence of heterosexual reproductive sex and the specialness of sex, now expressed through heightened feelings of shame.

Freud's two essays provide a striking account of the disenchantment of sexual desire, encapsulated in the notion of 'psychical impotence'. He clearly implicates the process of civilization in the denial of the potential of sexual diversity, which is the inherent characteristic of humanity. For Freud, civilization restricts the choice of the end-point of sexual desire to 'the opposite sex, and most extra-genital satisfactions are forbidden as perversions . . . that there shall be a single kind of sexual life for everyone disregards the dissimilarities, whether innate or acquired, in the sexual constitution of humans' (Freud 1961: 104).

In the work of both authors there is an argument that civilization restricts sensual pleasures. The review of Weber's argument about rationality and the rationalizing process suggests the mechanisms which lie behind this central theme of repression. For the ascendency of rational action to be effected, the erotic kernel of life had to be marginalized and rewritten in a script of sexual asceticism, which transformed the irrationality of polymorphous sexual desire into routinized sexual practice. The rationalization of desire and of disruptive potential of 'the greatest irrational force of life: sexual love' (Gerth and Mills 1970: 343), was to be achieved through the routinization of sexual desire. The discussion of the chapter overall provides a backdrop to an understanding of the making of a modernist sexuality, in which the parameters of normal and perverse, of healthy and pathological, established 'civilized sex' as heterosexual coitus.

# 3 Enlightenment pleasures *and* bourgeois anxieties

There is a popular tendency, when thinking about sexual manners and sexual ideologies, to assume that anxieties about, and sexual mores relating to, expressions of sexual desire have relaxed with the progression of civilization. The examples used in the previous chapter suggest a process that is both the more complicated and less linear in its genesis and appearance. While the evidence abounds to support this complexity, there is a persistence of the notion that sexual repression is associated with 'the past', and that, in parallel with the dissolution of traditional social structures and the ascendence of secularism over religion, there has been a slow yet consistent process of sexual liberalization. This evolutionary view, which parallels the 'modernization thesis', operates in a narrow historical framework, drawing much of its supportive evidence from the contrasts between the sexual mores of the late nineteenth and mid to late twentieth centuries. The high-profile sexual prudery of the bourgeois-dominated world of the late nineteenth century is often accepted as the epitome of sexual repression and therefore the gauge by which all subsequent relaxation of rules is measured. The stark contrasts drawn between the prudish silence of 'Victorianism' and the cacophony of sexual discourses in the late twentieth-century Western context lend further credence to the notion of 'later is better', or, at least, 'more liberated'. A model which lays emphasis on patterns of linear change deflects attention from ideological continuities contained within the orthodoxies of both repression and liberation, thus disabling a more critical examination of change.

The unproblematic acceptance of a progression from repression to liberalization gives legitimacy to – even closes off from critical scrutiny – such important features as the primacy of coitus as *the* outlet from sexual desire, the unconscious acceptance of heterosexuality as the epicentre of the erotic, the asexuality of children, and the gender-specific quality and direction of sexual desire. Critical approaches that seek to isolate themes of continuity, rather than rely solely on contrasts, reinforce the importance of the connections between specific historical contexts and accompanying sexual ideologies.

Chapter 2 illustrated, using the work of Elias and Freud, how the civilizing process is integrally related to the heightened regulation of affective and in particular sexual behaviour. This chapter will trace in more detail the construction of recognizably modern parameters of acceptable sexual desires and of the social frameworks and belief systems which shape and mould them. Specifically, it will address the evolutionary model of repression to liberation through an account of the principles of Enlightenment sexual orthodoxies, which, it will be argued, both stand in contrast to, and share commonalities with, the successive beliefs and mores of bourgeois sexual culture. It will begin by reviewing the changes that Enlightenment thought wrought in ways of thinking about sex, while illustrating the ways in which 'old' anxieties were refined and reworked. Attitudes to, and concerns about, sex and sexuality in the nineteenth century will similarly be outlined and developed. It will be argued that despite the manifest distinctions between the apparent celebration of sexual pleasures of the eighteenth century and their suppression and denial in the succeeding age, there are core ideas about expressions of sexual desire which, within this progression, are stabilized and reinforced.

## 3.1   The promotion of pleasures

Enlightenment thought shaped the prevailing ideas about sex in the eighteenth century in ways that both challenged and reinforced prevailing orthodoxies. It specifically challenged the formerly negatively charged associations between sex and sin in their positive promotion of sexual pleasures. However, the frameworks within which these were promoted both retained the centrality of heterosexuality while further shaping and reinforcing the male-centred bias in constructions of sex and sexuality.

The most radical element in the promotion of sexual pleasure, and one which represented a clear break from the influence of Christian ideas, was the reversal of the consistent association of sex with animality. Before 1700, the animal world was, to all intents and purposes, seen as inanimate – that is, animals were not accorded any acknowledgement of their senses and non-human creatures were valued only in terms of their usefulness to humanity. Any associations with animals, other than to make use of them, was considered to be profoundly demeaning. Accordingly, bodily functions shared with non-human creatures were devalued by association. The distinction between the human and animal worlds was not only of philosophical but also moral importance. For although the devaluing of animality placed humanity in an elevated position, it was a fragile ascendency, given the manifest physiological commonalities between humans and animals. Sexual impulses were particularly singled out and the use of such words as 'bestial' and 'brute' carried quite specific sexual connotations. Such views were prominent in the earliest Christian teachings, where penalties for the sexual crime of bestiality were strictly enforced (Salisbury 1991).

> Lust, said a sixteenth century moralist, made men 'like . . . swine, goats, dogs and the most savage and brutish beasts in the world'. In the bestiaries and emblem books a remarkably high proportion of the animals which appear are meant to symbolize lasciviousness or sexual

infidelity... The sexual impulse of man was usually conceived of as thrusting up from below.

(Thomas 1983: 38)

Enlightenment sexual ideology, on the other hand, valued nature positively and with it the connections between humans and the 'natural world'. 'Rejecting Calvinist notions of original sin, and the corruption of the flesh, [Enlightenment thinkers] argued that nature was good and that proper behaviour should seek to realise human nature rather than to deny, fight and conquer it' (Porter 1982: 4).

The materialist and humanist themes of Enlightenment thought were fuelled by the advances in technologies of scientific enquiry. The invention of the microscope and refinements of the telescope both affirmed the existence of spheres within and beyond the known visible world. Expeditions of exploration into new lands and cultures further questioned previous certainties about the superior status of humanity in the world of nature. The division between humankind and nature was not unbridgeable, as had previously been proposed; rather, the two were integrated harmoniously in a moral and physical universe. Thus all forms of behaviour formerly negatively associated with 'nature' now became important and positively valued indications of humanity. The pursuit of sensual and particularly sexual pleasure were elevated within this now positively valued membership of the natural world: 'These naturalistic and hedonistic assumptions – that Nature had made men to follow pleasure, that sex was pleasurable, and that it was natural to follow one's sexual urges underpinned much of Enlightenment thought about sexuality' (Porter 1982: 4).

This valorization of sexual pleasures complemented the growing emphasis on companionate and intimate conjugality (Stone 1977), where sexual *intercourse* was promoted not just for relief of lust but as an important form of social bonding. Speaking about sex became, under these influences, not just acceptable but desirable.

Manuals appeared, discussing sexual techniques, compatibility, venereal diseases, fertility, birth limitation and reproduction. Above all, sex therapy burst upon the scene. The most famous exponent was James Graham, who set up his headquarters first at the 'Temple of Hymen' at the Adelphi in the Strand, and then later at St James's. Graham lectured to fashionable crowds about the invigorating properties of happy sexuality and gave instructions as to how it could be made more successful and enjoyable.

(Porter 1982: 7)

This open and frank discussion about and representations of sex in print is evident also in the proliferation of pornographic and erotic literature and pamphlets. In his fascinating book on the subject, Roger Thompson (1979) points out that there is a long history of popular consumption of erotica, even in periods characterized by sexual guilt and prudery. It was expected that gentlemen had in their possession, or were familiar with, from a relatively early age, a number of Classical Greek and Roman erotic texts, either in the original or translated. Among them were the works by Ovid, Petronius and Plautius. Nor were such texts confined to consumption by the privileged stratum of society, or to adults only. Schoolboys were expected to be conversant with all the works of Ovid, and references to Ovid or Plautius in the cheap and available 'Chap Books' indicate a wider and less restrictive readership (Thompson 1979: 4).

Despite this longstanding tradition of the availability of explicit sexual texts, their content was nevertheless subject to moral and regulatory scrutiny. In pre-Civil War publications:

> Several translations of classical and continental works showed marked prudery . . . the Anonymous translator of the *Decameron* (1620) omitted or silently altered all the racier tales in his 'version of more decorum than fidelity'. Two topics plainly embarrassed the bowlderisers: over explicit descriptions of physical passion, and homosexuality. The first diluted into mere sentimentality. The second is either omitted, or the whole situation is altered into a heterosexual one, sometimes with bizarre results.
>
> (Thompson 1979: 10)

Interestingly, Thompson distinguished between the pornographic (aimed at sexual excitement), the obscene (aimed at shocking or offending), the bawdy (aimed at making people laugh at themselves or others) and the erotic (aimed at more lovingly and romantically intimate sexual pleasures) (ibid., pp. ix–x). While all were to some extent represented in Enlightenment works on sex, he argues that there was a recognizably English preference for the obscene and the bawdy, of which many home grown versions were produced. Erotica and uncompromisingly pornographic (in Thompson's terminology) material tended to originate in France and Italy. While the Restoration was characterized by an explicit challenge to openly repressive Puritanism, it nevertheless retains, Thompson argues, an evident ambivalence about what might be termed 'honest' celebration of sex. British writers, he says:

> Excelled at making sex shocking as they failed to make it either exciting or funny. They could disgust; they could not excite or amuse. Their response to sexuality was smut, or burlesque, or rage, or outrage . . . For all their libertine philosophising and summonsing to merriment, they seem profoundly inhibited and uncomfortable about the subject. They cannot treat it in a matter-of-fact balanced way; they cannot laugh about it without sniggering or describe it joyously, straightforwardly, even innocently. Their reaction is disproportionate, discordant, distorted and disassociated . . . Shame is the spur.
>
> (Thompson 1979: 212)

Whatever misgivings might have been held privately about this exhortation to the celebration of sex, these were not publicly visible. Dress, particularly women's dress, emphasized their active sexuality, and in ways which belied the strong masculinist theme within this public expression. Prostitutes did not work in dark back streets in poor areas, but walked and openly consorted in fashionable areas. Sexual shows and clubs were commonplace and sex in public was accepted (Porter 1982: 9). 'The Georgian sexual economy was public and permissive in its fashions, its street life, its gossip and not least its erotica' (Porter and Hall 1995: 106). Dividing lines between the sexually respectable and disreputable were not clear-cut, as they were to become in the next century. 'Respectable' men kept mistresses; 'respectable' women were mistresses and took lovers. Women were not deemed impure and fallen if they were, in modern parlance, sex workers. Sexual libertinism was not considered pathological but evidence of a well-balanced stable man and, to a lesser extent, woman. Neither was this openness and indulgence in sex cause for official intervention. The Bawdy Courts – popular courts comprised of property-owning citizens – which since before the Norman invasion censured sexual misdemeanours such as adultery and fornication, began to decline by the end of the sixteenth century (Addy 1988).

There was, then, sufficient evidence for a distinctive 'Enlightenment sexuality' distinguished by two factors: the valorization of nature as the underwriter of sexual pleasure and a publicly evident celebration of sex and erotica, which openly confronted the ecclesiastically directed sexual ethics that had prevailed previously. Yet there were features within this apparent liberation and celebration that moderated and circumscribed the depth of its radicalism.

## 3.2 The ordering of pleasures

Enlightenment thinking openly and successfully loosened the hold of Christian prejudices and anxieties about sexual behaviour. Yet this radicalism did not challenge the male-defined primacy of heterosexuality, orthodoxy or the ambivalence about women's sexuality. The enthusiasm for expressions of sexual pleasure was tempered by an emerging emphasis on the physical dangers of sexual excess, and the elevation of conjugal and procreative sex (Porter and Hall 1995: 65–106). In both the medical and quack literature, boundaries of acceptable sexual practices were drawn in relation to what was deemed 'natural' and 'healthy'. Specific anxieties were expressed about masturbation and the sexuality of the young. 'In sexuality, as in matters of child rearing, personal freedom and government, Enlightenment belief in liberty and indulgence had well-defined limits, its own pressures and intolerances, contours and chiaroscuro' (Porter 1982: 15).

There were three 'well-defined limits' to the sexual radicalism: it was male-defined and male-centred; it was a classed radicalism; and it was increasingly defined in terms of heterosexual coitus. From the vantage point of the late twentieth century, eighteenth-century ideas about sex were unremittingly masculinist in language, imagery and, arguably, intent. In their recent meticulous account of Enlightenment sexual knowledge, Porter and Hall (1995) illustrate the complexities, if not the tensions, in Enlightenment sexual ideology. Using the most widely available sexual treatise of the time, Nicholas Venette's *Tableau de L'Amour Conjugal*, Porter and Hall illustrate the degree to which the celebration of sexual pleasures was male-orientated.

The text itself has a fascinating history, first being published in 1686, with the first English translation traceable to 1703, and continuing to be re-published and revised throughout the eighteenth and nineteenth centuries (Porter and Hall 1995: 64). The author was, to quote the frontispiece of the twentieth English edition, 'an eminent surgeon and member of the Royal Academy of Paris' (Venette 1750/1984). The contents range through details of male and female sexual anatomy and physiology, through discussions about the correct age of marriage and the attributes of women 'naturally prone to the Act of Copulation':

> A woman, hot in constitution and vehemently desirous of commerce with man, is easily distinguished by those versed in the nature of the sex. However, it may not be amiss to observe, in order to inform the ignorant, that the breasts of such a woman are generally very small, but at the same time conveniently plump and hard: there is a profusion of hair about her privities (which have a high situation, near the navel)... The hair of the head is short and inclined to curl; her voice is shrill and loud; she is bold of speech, cruel and oppressive to those of her own sex, and unsteady in her devotion.
>
> (Venette 1984: 56–7)

The greater part of the text is devoted to detailed descriptions of, and advice on, the methods by which sexual pleasures and procreation can be advanced. While Venette is unambiguous about the equal capacities of men and women to this end, he makes distinctions between the quality of expression of sexual passion that accord with the notion of a male-centred bias. 'Both men and women taste excessive pleasure in mutual caresses; and it is difficult for me to determine which receives the most' (Venette 1984: 117). This even-handedness notwithstanding, he proceeds to make a strong argument in favour of men:

> No doubt but our privy parts are more sensible than those of women, being all nervous; or, to explain myself better, nothing but nerves: whereas women's parts are fleshy and consequently less sensible... we have also a firmer mind, and stronger fancy than women. The filaments of our brain are more stretched and hard, and when we love, it is with greater force and spirit. Women, on the contrary, are of a more inconstant mind, and weaker fancy. The fibres of the brain are soft, and more flexible; and though they sometimes appear to love more ardently, yet they do not feel as much pleasure in caresses as we.
>
> (Venette 1984: 118–19)

Porter and Hall (1995: 76) confirm this impression with the view that 'Venette operated within sexual stereotypes... His vision was phallocentric (the merest glance at a penis, he reveals, will make a woman go wild with desire), and it is certainly male-orientated. He devotes chapters to the choice of a bride, but not a husband, thereby endorsing social reality'. Though, as Porter and Hall warn, 'we must never mistake texts for people' (ibid., p. 105). Given the popularity of this text and its longevity of existence, it is reasonable to conclude that the messages it contained about the centrality of male-defined and -directed celebration of pleasures found an appreciative audience.

While women were enthusiastically 'embraced' in the new sexual mores, their real equality – or to use David Evans's (1993) term, their 'sexual citizenship' – in this new world was highly equivocal and circumscribed. The recognition and celebration of women's sexuality followed a script driven by male sexual fantasy, and cannot be taken to infer, automatically, a shift in wider sexual and civil equality. As Mary Woolstonecraft so passionately argued in the late eighteenth century, women for the most part remained in a gilded cage of social expectations and attendant promise of security of male 'protection' (Taylor 1984: 3–4). Any evidence of deviation from the feminine behaviour that accompanied this was considered to be 'masculine'. Eighteenth-century women in the upper echelons of society who played out these sexual roles compromised rather than complemented their acceptance as intellectual equals (Thomas 1959: 195–261; LeGates 1976: 21–40). Limitations on the promise of the democratization of pleasure also extended to the lower orders:

> The Enlightenment mentality was also frightened of plebian sexuality. Just as one didn't talk about atheism in front of the servants, so eroticism wasn't for them either. The title of one of the more widely circulating pornographic magazines makes this point clearly: *The Covent Garden Magazine; or Amorous Repository, Circulated Solely for the Entertainment of the Polite World (1774)*. In part, the fear was that sexual licence would slide into general disorder and anarchy. But the far greater fear was that the masses were fast breeders; they would outrun their ability to look after their own offspring, and also the nation's capacity to absorb them.
>
> (Porter 1982: 16)

The conditional sexual licence also operated to delimit acceptable forms of sexual practice. For it was during the eighteenth century that the practice of sodomy was refined in both its meaning and moral content. Randolph Trumbach (1991) argues that before 1700 acts of sodomy with young men did not constitute a challenge to the accepted paradigms of masculinity, and were not, therefore, seen as 'contrary to nature'. In the small aristocratic circles of the seventeenth century:

> The love of boys certainly did not exclude the love of women; the love of boys was seen as the most extreme act of sexual libertinism, and it was often associated, as well, with religious scepticism, even republican politics . . . The unconventionality of the minority of rakes [sexual libertines] who were sodomitical was therefore frightening to society at large, but they were not held in contempt. It was, instead, that they were held secretly in awe for the extremities of their masculine self-assertion, since they triumphed over male and female alike.
>
> (Trumbach 1991: 130–31)

Two shifts occurred in the eighteenth century. First, the act of sodomy came to be associated with a sexual 'type', a personage; second, that act became negatively associated with bestiality, in ways which echoed the twinning of sodomy and bestiality in early biblical texts, where the division between man and animals, between reason and nature, was emphasized and elevated. Although Enlightenment thinking valorized the connections between reasoned man and nature, 'nature' came to be conceptualized in gender-specific terms. Thus sexual acts between men and women were legitimately 'natural' by their connections with procreation, whereas those between men and men became marginalized and decried as offences against nature. However, the 'offence against nature' might rather be understood as an offence against the boundaries of socially accepted masculinity. While pre-1700 sodomy was not, as Trumbach (1989) reminds us, to be understood as legitimate, it was within the bounds of acceptable 'natural' masculine sexual behaviour, if a little extreme in its expression. These boundaries narrowed from 1700 onwards, not so much through outright condemnation and outlawry of the practice, but through a shift in the social meaning attached to it. This shift was indicative of a process by which one's sexual behaviour became more a signifier of the 'social self', rather than an adjunct of a more eclectic and private eroticism. In sexual behaviour, as in many other spheres of life, there emerged a blurring of the old boundaries between the private and the public – or, to be more accurate, between the meanings of the 'individual' and 'the social'. Individual erotic practices came to carry with them more clearly defined social meanings, particularly if the individual was male, possessing a greater level of 'social power'. Thus it was that the erotic practices of men that transgressed the social norms attracted greater opprobrium than those of women. As Trumbach (1989) and Faderman (1981) among others have indicated, women who had sex with women troubled the water of social order less; only those women who overtly took on the masculine role or sexual trappings (dressing as men, or using dildos) attracted the appellation of 'unnatural'.

The final sense in which there was a qualified celebration of sex in the eighteenth century was an increasingly anxious preoccupation with masturbation. Albeit encouraged by the activities and overheated writings of quack 'physicians' anxious to promote their patent remedies, tracts that warned, in terrifying detail, of the physical and mental debilitation produced by 'habitual self-abuse' found a ready audience, even in the mid-eighteenth century. These anxieties were expressed through concerns about the effects of masturbation in the young, in parallel with the emerging sense of the child as a distinct entity (De Mause 1976; Aries 1979). The seriousness with which this practice was viewed, even in the early eighteenth century, is evident in the content and the prolific circulation of two famous treatises. *Onania; or, the Heinous Crime of Self-Pollution, And all its Frightful Consequences, in Both Sexes consider'd &c*, whose author is listed as 'A physician in the country', was in its sixteenth edition in 1737, and a later, equally widely circulated text, *Onanism: or, a Treatise upon the Disorders produced by Masturbation, or the Dangerous effects of secret and excessive venery* by M. Samuel Tissot, first published in 1760, and appearing in English in 1766, was still available well into the nineteenth century.

This strong undercurrent of conservatism within the radicalism reinforced and reproduced in new forms the ascendence of heterosexuality, the problematization of the sexuality of women, the young and the lower classes. The emphasis on refinement within expressions of sexual desire conferred upon sexual freedom a normative and stylized framework, which arguably cemented into a new scenario many of the 'old' anxieties already discussed.

As Porter has argued, Enlightenment sexuality was, above all, 'refined' sexuality. Sex was celebrated, encouraged and publicly evident, both in indirect and direct ways. The positive approval of the 'naturalness' of sexual pleasure stood in contrast to, and overtly challenged, the predominance of the negative self-denials of Puritanism and indeed of all mainstream Christianity of the period. Yet its true radicalism was compromised by the classed and gendered parameters that reflected the dominant political and cultural ideologies of the period. Porter further suggests that the emphasis on refined sexuality prepared the way for a reversal of the celebration of the 'natural joys of sex', where refined and stylized pursuance of sexual passions slowly metamorphosed throughout the eighteenth century into a level of prudery and a conscious eschewal of the respectability of openly pursuing and speaking of such pleasures. Such a reversal was in part a rejection of the overweening hedonism of Enlightenment thought, and a weariness with the endless incitement to hedonism which 'characterises much of Georgian culture' (Porter 1982: 21). 'Above all, sex with sensibility seemed to solve that constant problem of the English Enlightenment: how individuals could indulge their own selfish passions without danger to the social order' (ibid., p. 20).

## 3.3 The bourgeois watershed

> The history of the Victorian age will never be written: we know too much about it.
>
> (Strachey 1948: 6)

The nineteenth century was a century of change with special qualities. The end-point of a prolonged and steep rise in population, and with it a parallel urbanization, rapid technological developments in production, the accompanying disruption of traditional work organization and practice, it was, truly, the century which saw the culmination of 'The Great Transformation' (Kumar 1978). But it was a transformation that was inherently unsettling, uneven and unpredictable in its consequences for those at its centre.

At the beginning of the century, though numerically in the minority, the bourgeoisie made up in power and wealth what they lacked in numbers. They lay at the centre of the changes, self-consciously aware of their distinction from the old aristocracy on the one hand, and the rapidly expanding working class on the other. This central position gave them the advantage of realizing the full promise of the century, but their ascendency of position and access to the promise of modernity did not carry with it the social or political certainties of their predecessors. 'What the bourgeois had in common was the negative quality of being neither aristocrats nor labourers, and of being uneasy in their middle class skins' (Gay 1984: 3).

Durkheim has immortalized (while not inventing its features) the concept of 'anomie' – the despairing insecurity experienced in the face of sudden change in social or personal circumstances, irrespective of whether the changes are for good or ill. Such negative responses result from the disruption or removal of predictable internal or external guidelines for existence. While the bourgeoisie were the prime movers of these profound upheavals, they were also at the vortex of its psychological consequences. One response to this position, as Durkheim's work on this issue illustrates, is the drive to create new predictabilities, to impose a new order and new moral imperatives.

Collectively, then, the nineteenth-century bourgeois mood was a mixture of helplessness and confidence: 'endemic excitement was controlled by social devices and private defences . . . Everything was being called into question: religious teachings, political principles, and, very emphatically, sexual morality' (Gay 1984: 67).

Nineteenth-century sexuality conjures up images of sexually repressed, even asexual women; of the stern passionless black frock-coated paterfamilias; of excessive prudishness about and denial of the body and all its functions, coupled with the dark undercurrents of guilty (male) sexual excess; of the proliferation of pornography and of prostitution; of 'fallen' women clutching the illegitimate and shameful results of their seduction. Such familiar cameos have been challenged in the meticulous work of Peter Gay (1984, 1986) and, from a different disciplinary stance, by Michel Foucault (1979). In Volume 1 of *The History of Sexuality*, Foucault (1979) dismantles the 'repressive hypothesis', replacing the notion of repression with one of a mechanism for social regulation in which disciplinary power replaced sovereign power as the dominant instrument for the management of populations. The effectiveness of this new regulatory power depended on the distinction of domains of human behaviour that become the objects of knowledge: family limitation, women's sexuality, infantile sexuality and non-procreative sex. Out of these 'objects of knowledge' were forged 'subjects of power', who embodied the potentially disruptive elements in the management of populations, and who became figureheads for the created fields of knowledge and for the management of pleasure: the Malthusian couple, the masturbating child, the hysterical woman and the sexual pervert.

The imposition of disciplinary power instigated not just a moral hierarchy but an ordering of pleasures. The work of Foucault draws attention to a further complexity in the Victorian sexual orthodoxy that questions assumptions of its unproblematic effectiveness:

> The primary concern was not the repression of the sex of the class to be exploited, but rather the body, vigour, longevity, progeniture and descent of the class that 'ruled' . . . it has to be seen as the self-affirmation of one class rather than the enslavement of another; a defence, a protection, a strengthening, and an exaltation that were eventually extended to others.
>
> (Foucault 1979: 123)

Here, Foucault emphasizes the lack of coherence of the bourgeois class, which drew from a variety of lifestyles, incomes, origins, even religious beliefs. What bound the class together was not the unitary beliefs or backgrounds of the individuals, but their shared position as the 'buffer' between the working class and the former ruling aristocracy. There was thus a need – made more urgent by the insecurities of the rapidly changing world in which they increasingly became the central figures – to create and maintain a unitary ideology, which was to represent shared notions of morality and respectability.

These features illuminate the presence of the frequently reiterated 'hypocrisy' of Victorian sexuality – the distance between 'profession and practice' (Gay 1984). This underlying class insecurity is one complexity in the story of bourgeois sexuality. The other is evident behind another frequently recognized contradiction in bourgeois sexual orthodoxy – the differential construction of women's sexuality. We take for granted, in retrospect, that the major focus of Victorian sexual morality was focused on, and expressed through, the 'social evil' of prostitution. Prostitution was discussed in such diverse venues as popular journalism, serious weekly reviews, medical tracts and publications from evangelical organizations devoted to the rescue of fallen women. The universality of anxiety about this issue suggested a variety of motives, which included genuine commitment to philanthropy, the need to establish and promote public health endeavours, as well as the question of national security. But there was the suggestion of other, less high-minded preoccupations: the added attraction of salacious interest, of vicarious titil- lation. For prostitution provided a forum within which to express, covertly, anxieties about, and fascination with, the characteristics of women's sexuality.

The backbone of Victorian sexuality was the successful promotion of a version of women's sexuality, an ideal of purity and sexual innocence well fitted to the separation of spheres that underpinned the patriarchal power base of the new ruling class. This conferred an urgency on the construction of an orthodoxy that distinguished between the two figures of the madonna and the whore. 'Woman was believed either to assist or to exacerbate male sexual control and her sexual identity determined whether or not she was seen as a respectable and responsible member of society' (Nead 1988: 6–7). Yet the reality of the matter stood in contrast to the ideological construction. The figure of the sexual madonna, the self-effacing angel in the home, bore little resemblance, as Peter Gay (1986) points out so vividly through his use of private diaries of middle-class Victorian women, to the living and loving women of the period. Gay has emphasized that there was no clear agree- ment in just how this sexuality was to be constructed. There was, he says, a running controversy throughout the nineteenth century regarding the ques- tion of women's sexuality, its extent and characteristics. The debate was not confined to Britain, but involved physicians and other experts in France, Germany, Sweden and the USA. The positions taken ranged from the extremes of denial of Dr William Acton, whose vociferous affirmation of women's sexual anaesthesia have been at the centre of subsequent disagreements between historians of the nineteenth century (Harrison 1967; Marcus 1970; Smith 1970; Hall 1992), to Dr Auguste Debay's *Hygeine et Physiologie du mariage* (1848), which while acknowledging the sexuality of women nevertheless accorded it a passive status.

There was, therefore, no consensus on the nature of women's sexuality. Within the proliferation of improving and advisory literature of the day, the majority laid emphasis on the 'lesser' sexuality of women or denied it outright. However, there was a suggestion of a consensus at a less consciously expressed level, which points to undercurrents in these contestations and anxieties that have a longer pedigree: 'Behind men's blustering claims to a monopoly of sensuality, or, at least, to their undisputed superiority in that department, there lurked a lifelong ineradicable anxiety, men's fear of women' (Nead 1988: 168).

While the anxieties were focused on women, the underlying concern was the maintenance of male sexual ascendency in the new economies of pleasure and of reproductive sexual activity. The motivation for this endeavour arguably lay in two directions. First, there was a paradoxical challenge to male hegemony, which gathered pace in the latter half of the nineteenth century. Legislation which enshrined married women's property rights, and which accorded them at least in principle wider access to education; the political organization of women in which they campaigned against the sexual double standard; changes in the demands of the labour market, which offered a wider social stratum of women the opportunities for a measure of economic independence; and the increasing numbers of women who actively resisted the notion of the marital hearth and home, all contributed to an increased sense of defensiveness and fear among bourgeois men. Although the most strident expressions of anxiety were expressed under the guise of concerns about public health and morality, with the 'fallen women' of the streets as the focus, the pervasiveness of debates about, and commentaries on, the sexuality of women in the promotion of a new moral order – or as Gay's title has it, 'the education of the senses' – belies a deeper insecurity about the maintenance of male sexual dominance in the face of these changes. As Gay mischievously but pointedly suggests:

> The pervasive sense of manhood in danger is, of course, the counterpart to that notorious nineteenth century fiction, women lacking all sexual appetites. This now appears as a reaction formation, as powerful as it was unconscious . . . To deny women native erotic desires was to safeguard men's sexual inadequacy. However he performed, it would be good enough. She would not – could she? – ask for more. Dr Acton's reassurances to timid men about how to face their young, and they feared, possibly demanding brides are thus a valuable clue to the distressing preoccupation of his culture.
>
> (Gay 1986: 197)

There is no sense in which the Victorian orthodoxy can be taken as indicative or representative of all classes any more than it can be taken as a literal representation of what was actually done and felt. It was a profoundly powerful ideology, in the strictest sense of the word, which was manufactured by, and largely for, the bourgeois. It was a deeply classed sexuality that was being promoted, one which was calculated to distinguish the bourgeoisie not just from its inferiors, but also from the debauches of the decadent and waning aristocracy, whose sexual excesses served as a buttress to elevate the moral and sensual economy and self-control of its successors. The manufacture of the partial fiction that was bourgeois sexual morality also depended on, as has already been argued, the mobilization of its counterpart, the spectre of the 'dark angel', the sexuality of working-class women. Yet this spectre was itself a complex figure. On the one hand, it gave voice to a fundamental fear associated with the unseen presence of disease – an ever-present possibility but, like death, not to be dwelt on. On the other, it was the object of compelling cultural fascination, almost obsession, which was characterized by barely disguised prurience (Dickens 1861; Mearns 1883/1970; Sims 1889/1984; Hardy 1891/1965; Keating 1972; Stanley 1984). The numerous accounts of the lives of the poor represent them as lesser beings that were closer to animals, lacking in civilized human qualities, and these more general judgements carried with them intimations of the characteristics of their sexuality – in language reminiscent of pre-Enlightenment thinking. As with the issue of prostitution, the specifically sexual anxieties were approached obliquely through concerns about overcrowded living, and particularly the sleeping arrangements of the urban poor. Fears associated with the latent bestiality in sexual desire were resurrected in the context of these unfamiliar surroundings. According to the contemporary social commentaries, those who inhabited the 'rookeries' of urban settings lacked the essential property – reason – with which to tame and control the dark side of humanity. Thus the sexuality of the lower classes was spoken of as barely distinguishable from animals. The enthusiasm with which these attributes were dwelt upon supports the notion of continuing fascination that went beyond philanthropic concerns. Yet this 'bestialization' of working-class sexuality again bore little resemblance to reality. The real lives of the labouring classes were as much of an unknown territory as the cultural habits of the colonized countries of British imperialism.

In her study of the papers of the London Foundling Hospital, Barrett-Ducrocq (1991) provides some illuminating insights into the courtship and sexual mores of the urban working classes, in her detailed examinations of letters written to the Board of Governors requesting acceptance of the illegitimate children of single working women into the hospital. Though such accounts were undoubtedly laundered to ensure their acceptance as 'respectable', the reiteration of similar circumstances surrounding the conception of the children is more than suggestive of well-established sexual and social mores, which, Du Crocq argues, retain many traditional formats, as well as suggesting more commonalities with, than distinctions from, the dominant sexual morality. There is ample evidence for a protocol of courtship, which precedes sexual relations, and of the requirement, at least verbally expressed, of the sexual act as a precursor to marital intentions (Barret-DuCrocq 1991: 98ff.).

As Mort (1987) has argued, the promotion of bourgeois sexual morality was integrally related to a wider project of moral and cultural reformation of the industrial urban working class. Unbridled sexuality was both a concern in itself and a metaphor for the wider social pathology of the body social. Concerns about the social consequences of the mismatch between the massed and numerically dominant labouring classes and the promotion of middle-class values, fuelled an aggressive discourse of sexual morality in which, increasingly, there was an interlocking of the domains of the moral and the healthy.

A less openly articulated component of the discourse of Victorian sexuality, but one which in particular from the mid-century onwards was a persistent presence in the construction of healthy and rational sexuality, was the privileging of heterosexuality. This was not spoken of in such terms, but was evident in the obliquely mobilized yet effective marginalization of all non-procreative sex, which drew into focus male and to a lesser extent female homosexual practices.

The increased attention paid to homosexuality, and particularly male homosexuality, suggested the continuing marginalization of non-procreative sex. Randolph Trumbach (1989: 150ff.) has argued that 'modern' character-izations of male homosexuality can be traced from around 1750. The marginal, even deviant status of non-procreative sex was underpinned and embodied within the figure of the 'sodomite' – a person defined primarily in terms of his sexual behaviour and preference. The categorization of unacceptable expressions of sexual desire as synonymous with deviant individuals expedited the imposition of new and more stringently regulatory legal statutes in the decades to come.

> In 1810, in London . . . two men were sentenced to death and seven others were imprisoned for sexual relations. Six of the latter were required to stand on the pillory where they were pelted by thousands of spectators with dead cats, mud and offal until they were almost completely buried.
>
> (Faderman 1981: 153)

Weeks (1990) reminds us that since 1533, 'the penalty for the abominable vice of buggery', whether with men, women or animals, was death. The death penalty was finally abolished in 1861 in England and Wales, and in 1889 in Scotland. But, Weeks (1990: 15) argues, this was not a preliminary to the liberalization of the law but of the tightening of its grip: 'By Section 11 (The Labouchere Amendment) of the 1885 Criminal Law Amendment Act, *all* male homosexual acts short of buggery, whether committed in private or in public, were made illegal'.

In 1898, the Vagrancy Act also criminalized homosexual 'soliciting'. These acts were illustrative of shifts in relation to male homosexuality. First, they extended the meanings of male homosexuality beyond the practice of buggery and, second, they signalled an intensification of the recognition of the radical possibilities of homoerotic behaviour. Both factors were consistent with the growing concern to map out and contain the legitimate boundaries of accepted sexuality, defined in terms of male/female, penetrative procreative monogamous sexuality. 'Deviant' sexual behaviour in men, as in working-class women, was particularly threatening, as both possessed sexual appetites which, if uncontained, could prove socially chaotic.

From the nineteenth century this marginalization began also to apply to women. Commentary on lesbian sex in medical journals, literature and popular journalism became more frequent and changed in its tone. Vicinus (1989) suggests the less tolerant and more uneasy and judgemental attitudes reflected the challenge lesbian women, by their more open demands for rights of sexual affirmation, posed to the basis of male regulation. Gender-challenging behaviour in women drew the same response as that of men. Thus it was that by the mid-nineteenth century lesbian women, along with 'fallen women' and homosexual men, came to be labelled sexual deviants, whose activities sinned both against nature and society. 'Nature', the final arbiter against which behavioural norms were constructed, was not now a primarily philosophical concept, as it was in the eighteenth century. 'Natural-ness' had become embodied in a physical form, the finality of the distinction between natural and unnatural underpinned by expanding understandings about, and attention to, physical manifestations of morality. The collapsing of three distinct sexual entities – the homosexual male, the lesbian woman and female prostitute – under the umbrella of 'sexual deviancy' suggests the extent to which they represented, in different ways, the troubling and dis-ruptive potential of 'uncontrollable, independent and active sexuality' (ibid., p. 185). They also represented a challenge to the central pillar of the bourgeois sexual orthodoxy: the pre-eminence of a masculinist sexuality.

The insecurity that Gay has argued was endemic in the bourgeoisie, despite their continued ascendency, was arguably reflected in the crescendo of anxiety about the physical and mental dangers of 'self-abuse'. Lesley Hall has amply illustrated the extent to which a preoccupation with masturbation escalated throughout the nineteenth century and beyond (Hall 1991, 1992; Porter and Hall 1995). Hall points out that this fixation – even obsession – was not driven solely by the commercial interests of the quack practitioners who marketed the excruciatingly constrictive devices to contain inadvertent erections, nor by more 'orthodox' medical practitioners:

> Such implements were not necessarily imposed – as has often been suggested in sensational discussions of the Victorian horror of mastur-bation – by doctors on victimised patients, or by anxious and punitive parents on their children. The horror associated with deliberate self-abuse and even involuntary nocturnal emissions was widespread, and such ferocious remedies, savouring of the punitive, may even have been acceptable because they fed into the sexual guilt of 'victims': they seem to have been applied by mature male sufferers.
>
> (Porter and Hall 1995: 139)

Mastering self-abuse was arguably the last summit to conquer in the need to monitor and contain the 'uncontainable' – the sexual beast within whose presence was signalled by involuntary erections and nocturnal emissions, which posed a threat to the newly rationalized sexual drive.

Attitudes to children's sexuality share many of the same assumptions and anxieties: those related to social class, gender, the mobilization of 'na-ture', and the increasing role of the pathologizing process in the mapping out of acceptable sexuality. The natural was increasingly characterized as requiring monitoring and control, and nowhere was this more evident than in relation to children's sexuality. Arguably, it is the attitudes to children and sexuality where the tensions and anxieties, as well as the contradictions of modernist sexuality, are most clearly evident. The logical trap, Jordanova (1987) points out, within Enlightenment views of children's sexuality was reflected in the later construction of children as being both asexual and sexually corruptible, both innocent and dangerously impure:

> The state of childhood may be seen as pure, innocent or original . . . Children may be analogised with animals or plants, thereby indicating that they are natural objects available for scientific or medical investigation. Children could be valued as aesthetic objects valued for their beauty and physical perfection – but they could equally be feared for their instinctual animal-like natures.
>
> (Jordanova 1987: 6)

Superficially, the response to these doubts and fears was the separation of sexuality from childhood, accomplished through what Foucault (1979) has called 'the pedagogisation of children's sex'. The monitoring and controlling of the distressing presence of 'sexual nature' was to be accomplished through the attentions of medical experts, and more indirectly through legal frameworks which distinguished children as a separate social category:

> Concern over and surveillance of the sexual emotional and physiological immaturity and lack of autonomy of those defined as within childhood, has been progressive, resulting in a process whereby 'childhood and sexuality became separated [and] their boundaries rigorously policed'.
>
> (Evans 1993: 212)

Such concerns were reflected in the development of regimes which involved deliberate and mechanical intervention to prevent even the possibility of 'self-abuse'. Brutal mechanical contraptions designed to 'discourage' masturbation or other auto-erotic activity were marketed commercially (Hall 1992). Yet, as with women, ideas about children's sexuality were more complex and contradictory than they first appear. Peter Gay has argued that nineteenth-century children came by sexual knowledge in the same ways as many do today, through observing animals, from each other and from what Gay calls 'platonic libertinism' – the evidence of sexuality which abounded in the streets and, to a lesser extent, in the respectable homes. Jonathan Gathorne-Hardy (1973) provides first-hand accounts of the sexual initiation of middle-class children by their maids and nannies, corroboration of which comes also from Freud's reminiscences and 'Walter' in Marcus's *The Other Victorians* (Marcus 1970: 339).

A Royal Commission in 1871 found that in three London hospitals there were 2700 cases of venereal disease among girls between the ages of 11 and 16 years. The sexual use of young girls was indirectly sanctioned, as twelve was the age of consent. Girls of this age could be procured for the (substantial) price of £20, a valuation which gave some clue to the social class of the purchasers (Pearsall 1969: 360).

That virginity was highly prized erotically was reflected in the still popularly held notion, despite medical advice to the contrary, that sex with a virgin was a cure for syphilis. The eminent artists, Ruskin and Carroll, created tableaux of their fantasy versions of pre-pubescent 'purity', child pornography veiled in an artistic form (Pearsall 1969: 430–46; Gilman 1989:

271–3). Like other contradictions regarding sex in this period, this preoccupation was gendered and classed. The girls who were its focus, specifically pre-pubescent girls, were mostly, though not exclusively, children of the urban poor. Men who escaped prosecutions for these illicit attentions were those with the most social power. 'Magistrates were very keen on men who took an unnatural interest in children, provided that they were not well-connected, were not famous, or were not clergymen' (Pearsall 1969: 434).

The tensions between the promotion of women's sexual purity and its contradiction in practice have already been outlined. In relation to children, such contradictions were magnified and exaggerated. Notwithstanding the bourgeois promotion of childish purity and innocence, representatives of the same class involved themselves in highly stylized eroticization of small girls. In painting, verse and prose, thinly veiled in sentimentality, little girls were sexualized and salivated over. In the mainstream of medical science and sexual and moral educators, tracts were written and devices marketed to prevent the harmless exploration by children of their own sexuality; while men of the same class were sanctioned in their literary or literal defloration of children of the same ages. The professed innocence of children, unprotected by legal statute until the very end of the century, provided the barrier behind which innocence could be violated.

## Conclusion

The striking feature of the preceding account is the co-existence of, on the one hand, direct contrasts between promotion of pleasures and anxieties and, on the other, the progressive strengthening of underlying and structuring parameters of what constitutes sex and sexuality. It is these themes that provide 'threads of continuity' across the distinctiveness of the different epochs. These threads of continuity, which will continue to be developed in succeeding chapters, already exhibit a recognizable form, which, given the associations discussed in this and the previous chapter, might be termed 'modernist sexuality'. If this category has one defining feature, it is reproductive and therefore by definition, heterosexual. As has been illustrated, the refining process began before the nineteenth century, but was closely associated with the major preoccupations of bourgeois ideology. Although under this influence, there persisted pre-modern anxieties that bound sexuality with morality, the biblical twinning of sex with sin had become more refined in its presentation. Now the concerns were reflected in, and accredited to, notions of 'natural' and 'unnatural'. Nature was differentially mobilized in the eighteenth and nineteenth centuries, but the apparently divergent attitudes to the pleasures of sex occluded shared anxieties. The increasing focus on sexual practices led to the creation of a sexual centre of heterosexuality and a hinterland of practitioners of non-procreative sex. These separate sexual spheres were populated by 'figures' who represented sexual ideals to be strived for: the monogamous heterosexual conjugal couple, the innocent child, the sexually dependent and pure woman. The counterpart to this process was the emergence of marginal figures, as necessary for sexual regulation as their ideal counterparts: the prostitute, the sexually precocious child, the sexually perverse adult and the sexual independent who transgressed increasingly narrow gender boundaries. Behind this process lay other less clearly articulated ideas about sex and sexuality, which are equally to be associated with sexual modernity.

The body-centredness of sexuality and the emphasis on its desirable or undesirable physical consequences was consistent with a rationalizing project, where the rational was contiguous with the controlled and contained, the sensual ascetism increasingly associated with civilization; the irrational with the surrender to disorderly sexual desires. In such a view, pleasure cannot be part of the rational equation – the direction of specified actions to a specified end. Ephemeral and unquantifiable, the pursuit of sensual pleasure cannot guarantee predictability of outcome. A focus on practices, ordered positively and negatively, promoted an economy of sex where expressions of sexual desire, deemed superfluous to the project of reproduction and mastery of desire, were considered wasteful both in the moral and physiological sense. Directly or indirectly, 'sexuality' became a process within which accepted 'means' were directed towards a delimited 'end'. Conceived in this manner, sexuality became more amenable to systematic analysis, in a period in which scientific approaches to the investigation of human behaviour were increasingly being deployed.

# 4   *The* **science** *of* **sex**

The principal feature of the science of sex was that it made sex an *object* of study. As has already been suggested, sex was accorded a distinctive status in ecclesiastical moral doctrines and in the development of interactive social existence associated with the civilizing process. This distinctiveness reflected what were felt to be innate qualities, which rendered it inimical to human volition and control, a view reinforced by the imposition of prescriptive rules about expressions of sexual desire. The science of sex marked a shift in the ways in which anxieties about sex were expressed. Making sex an object of study had a number of consequences. First, there was a focus on behaviour, more easily observed, classified and measured than feelings and desires. Second, there was an implied if not conscious denial of subjectivity and of moral judgements. This was an endeavour committed to enquiry not regulation. Finally, the establishment and growth of a body of specialized knowledge fostered a new body of specialist 'keepers of knowledge' – the scientists of sex. Though having a more narrow professional base than branches of orthodox medicine, sexology nevertheless followed similar patterns of development. Initially, the endeavours of the scientists of sex were somewhat fragmented and idiosyncratic, devoting attention to pathologies and the establishment of parameters of the normal and the abnormal; but from the early twentieth century, the science of sex focused increasingly on the observation and classification of 'normal' human sexuality. For this second generation of sexologists saw themselves as the only effective vanguard to break through the pruderies and ill-informed prejudices that were the fall-out from sexual Victorianism. In a sense, then, the scientists of sex were men (and they were, with one exception, *all* men) with a mission – to lighten the darkness of sexual ignorance. Yet there are other less benign consequences. Foucault's analysis of disciplinary power lists three strategies through which the power/knowledge axis is constructed: classification, observation and normative judgement. These stages are all clearly visible in the emergence of a science of sex. In the increasingly secularized world of mature Western capitalism, the objectivity of science was to assume the role of moral arbitration. The process of scientific enquiry was thus accorded a standing of authority unmatched except for that of priests or deities, and the servants of science inherited directly or indirectly the mantle of moral arbiter.

## 4.1   Origins and originators

It is tempting to conflate a science of sex with the medicalization of sex, suggesting that sexology and the associated anxieties were a direct product of the medical profession in the nineteenth century. While it is the case that the development of a science of sex is a late nineteenth-century phenomenon, and that some members of the medical profession were actively involved in its generation, the two cannot be so simply and causally conflated. Similarly, there is rather more complexity to the science of sex than the phrase suggests. It was a unified endeavour in that both early and late sexologists consciously pursued a classificatory and objective methodology in which moral judgements were represented as irrelevant. Yet in both early and late sexology there was clear evidence of a prescriptive content, which was reflected, in the first expressions of secular concern about sex, through an emphasis on negative (as well as positive) physical consequences. Precursors of the more well-known anxieties about such consequences in the late nineteenth-century sexological pronouncements are evident in the widely circulated quack literature of the eighteenth century. While the emergence of masturbation as the principle sexual *bête noire* is more usually associated with the nineteenth century, there was a vigorous and wide circulation of treatises on 'the heinous crime of onanism' in the previous century. Robert MacDonald argues that:

> The anonymous pamphlet named *Onania: or, The Heinous Sin of Self-Pollution, And All its Frightful Consequences in Both Sexes consider'd, &c.*, made its appearance in the beginning of the eighteenth century, ran to at least nineteen editions, and popularised a theory that had a powerful effect on Western society for the next two centuries.
> (MacDonald 1967: 423)

The number of editions, and the extent to which each was increased by the contribution of readers' 'confessions' and anxieties, suggests that the pamphlet and its contents found a ready audience. In 1758, a second major contribution to 'masturbation anxiety' made its appearance, *L'onanisme, ou Dissertation physique sur les maladies produites par la masturbation*, written by a Swiss named Samuel Tissot. Translated into English, German and Italian, it was 'scarcely out of print for the next seventy years . . . with the last edition printed as recently as 1905' (ibid., p. 426). Anxieties about sex and particularly masturbation in the eighteenth century must be interpreted in context. The medico-sexual treatises and pamphlets, Roy Porter (1989) argues, reflected two principle features of eighteenth-century discourses on sex that are 'concomitants' rather than opposites. The Enlightenment period has been represented as 'the golden age of sexual liberty' and more recently as a period of:

> ferocious male libertinism, leading to intensified exploitation of vulnerable female servants, teenage prostitutes, on the one hand, while on the other it was a period characterised by the excitation of new sexual fears, especially anxieties about masturbation (mainly in young males),

about puberty in teenage girls, about nymphomania, hysteria, enervation – all these fears being intensified by the irrefutable sanction of disease.

(Porter 1989: 146)

The pre-eminence of the idea that pleasurable sex was healthy produced an emphasis on the *physical* consequences of sex, both positive and negative. These, in their turn, provided a fertile ground for the manufacture and subsequent allaying of anxieties by both quacks and orthodox medical men. Anxieties about venereal diseases (syphilis and 'the clap') were widely discussed, in ways that often failed to distinguish adequately between more or less benign symptoms, an obfuscation that ensured a ready market for literature that diagnosed and treated sexual 'disorders'. Yet these 'anxiety-makers' cannot be equated with their nineteenth-century counterparts. There was a long tradition of quackery in the provision of love potions and seductive aids, and this role continued in the eighteenth century.

The activities of the extraordinary doctor James Graham would raise eyebrows even in the most sexually *avant garde* of the late twentieth century. Educated in Edinburgh, it was Graham's contention that maximizing sexual pleasure was a necessary precursor for good health. Accordingly, in 1780, he opened the 'Temple of Health' at the Adelphi in London. In this establishment, he constructed, and hired out for fifty pounds a night, the 'Celestial Bed':

> 12ft long by 9ft wide, supported by forty pillars of brilliant glass . . . the super-celestial dome contains the odiferous, balmy and etherial spices; odours and essences, which is the grand reservoir of those reviving invigorating influences which are exhaled by the breath of the music and the exhilarating forces of electrical fire, is covered of the other side with brilliant panes of looking glass.
>
> (quoted in Porter and Hall 1995: 109)

The aim of this dazzling edifice, was not, however, just to maximize sexual pleasure, but to encourage procreation. 'Superior ecstasy which the parties enjoy in the Celestial Bed is really astonishing and never before thought of in this world: the barren must certainly become fruitful when they are agitated in the delights of love' (ibid.).

This remarkable exponent of sexual health represented, Porter suggests, the 'convictions of the moderate Enlightenment', namely that unlicensed libertinism was not only individually unhealthy, but was responsible for the social ills of the late eighteenth century. In this there was a fine, but necessary line to tread between 'asserting the physical "naturalness" of libidinous sexuality and at the same time sermoning and even legislating to restrain its misuse' (ibid., p. 172).

The high profile of anxieties about masturbation in a climate that positively valued sexual pleasure suggests that it lay at the interface of the notions of 'nature as instinct' and 'nature as normative', illuminating the tenuous relationships between the two. The concept of self-control mediated in this tension, a concept for which masturbation was the antithesis: evidence for the triumph of the 'beast within', the sexual personification of the dark side of nature.

Against such a background, the 'sexologists' of the eighteenth century operated as much as the 'Doctor Ruth's' of their time as they did the harbingers of a sexual doom. In this crucial respect, the distinction between this century and the next is evident. The mind/body fusion of eighteenth-century sexual orthodoxy was ruptured in nineteenth-century discourses, which desensualized the body – treated it as a machine to be managed and serviced, kept under check, and protected from the ravages of 'the beast within'.

Nineteenth-century developments in a science of sex were, at least in the first half of the century, closely associated with fear about epidemic diseases – cholera, typhoid, consumption (tuberculosis) and syphilis – connected with the rapid expansion in both the size and social composition of the cities. There was, from the 1830s, a 'transformed social field' (Mort 1987) through which anxieties about the social and moral consequences of urbanization and industrialization were expressed. Ideas of morality and immorality were shaped against the habits and morals of the key figures in this transformation: the urban labouring poor and the newly ascendent bourgeoisie. The role of the medical profession in this was central but not unambiguous. Mort (1987: 27) points out that the medics had a particular motive for centring themselves as the moral arbiters and mouthpieces in this 'environmentalism' and becoming the front men for what he calls 'state intervention into working class culture'. The consequence of these two factors was to ensure the centrality of the medical profession in the moral overseeing of urban populations; which, in its turn, conferred upon the profession as the century progressed, the role of moral arbiter on all behaviour perceived to impact negatively on urban social order. From the beginning of the nineteenth century, health and morality were negatively conflated, and this association was reflected in and shaped the constructions placed on sexuality in the emerging medico-moral writings. The negativity of the construction was strengthened by reference to that apotheosis of unhealthy and immoral behaviour – the conditions of the urban poor. In their role as the moral arbiter, 'The medical men acted as powerful ideologues for the professional gentry and sections of the industrial bourgeoisie, laying claim to the middle class monopoly over the issues of health and hygiene' (ibid., p. 42).

In this regard, they were to speak in the language of the bourgeoisie, driven to distinguish themselves and their values from those of the decadent aristocracy on the one hand and the bestial poor on the other. The result was not only a negative construction on sexuality, with an emphasis on the dangers rather than the pleasures, but also an emphasis on the deadly results of sexual over-indulgence and sensual voluptuousness.

Notwithstanding their 'natural' role as mouthpieces for the new bourgeois values, the profession as a whole showed no great enthusiasm for writing about sex in a scientific context. In the one area that was arguably tailor-made for this purpose, birth control, leading members of the medical profession were not just silent, but openly and vehemently opposed (Peel 1964; McLaren 1978; Hawkes 1991). In the second half of the nineteenth century, from the more stable vantage point of a profession now in control of its inner factions, and with the added legitimacy of being at the centre of the rapidly expanding medical knowledge, some practitioners began reluctantly to acknowledge the need for arbitration in ways that reinforced the connections between sexual behaviour, morality and public health:

> It is only reasonable to suppose that our familiarity with the details of the question [of moral education], and our being frequently brought into contact with those who have committed offenses against morals, place us in a very advantageous position for ascertaining the real facts upon which alone a correct judgement can be placed.
>
> (Beale 1887: 161)

Moreover, they saw it as their reluctant duty to extend their remit as public health educators into sexual matters. In the words of R. T. Trall, MD, the author of *Sexual Physiology and Hygiene: An Explication, practical, scientific, moral and popular of some of the fundamental problems of sociology*, this book, which was to sell 80,000 copies, was:

> In style, arrangement and application addressed to the popular rather than to the professional reader. Its sole object is to instruct the masses of the people on those subjects which have hitherto been to them, in great part, a sealed book . . . The public has too long ignored as indelicate, or as too intricate and mysterious to be comprehended except by those who are educated in all branches of the medical profession, the subjects which lie at the foundation of their earthly being.
>
> (Trall 1903: 5–6)

Mason (1994) argues that the reluctance, even repugnance, with which the medics of the day approached any discussion of sex or even intimate examinations had less to do with a 'general fastidiousness' than with the unwelcome associations of sexual 'medicine' with the despised 'quacks'. Sexual advice literature remained widely available, evidence of sexual anxiety in the lay public, and also of the lucrative living still to be made fanning those anxieties. The most frequently quoted exemplar of these is *The Functions and Disorders of the Reproductive Organs in Youth, in Adult Age, and in Advanced Life, Considered in their Physiological, Social and Moral Relations*, written by the infamous William Action MRCS in 1857. As Marcus (1966: 13) points out, 'This book is entirely about men and male sexuality. With the exception of two extremely short but significant passages not a word is said about women'. The first deals with the effect of conception and childbirth on women's sexual excitement:

> If the married female conceives every second year, during the nine months which follow conception she experiences no great sexual excitement. The consequence is that sexual desire in the male is somewhat diminished, and the act of coition takes place but rarely. And, again, while women are suckling there is usually such call on the vital force made by the organs secreting milk that sexual desire is almost annihilated.
>
> (Acton, quoted in Marcus 1966: 30)

The message is clear. The concerns about the dampening down of sexual desire with maternity are those of the consequences for the male. The second passage refers more explicitly to the nature and quality of women's sexuality.

> I should say that the majority of women (happily for them) are not very troubled with sexual feeling of any kind. What men are habitually, women are only exceptionally. It is too true, I admit, as the divorce courts show, that there are some few women who have sexual desires so strong that they surpass those of men ... I admit, of course, the existence of sexual excitement terminating even in nymphomania, a form of insanity which those accustomed to visit lunatic asylums must be fully conversant with: but with these sad exceptions, that there can be no doubt that sexual feeling in the female is in the majority of cases in abeyance ... and even if roused (which in many cases it never can be) is very moderate compared with that of the male.
> (Acton, quoted in Marcus 1966: 31)

Almost any historian or commentator of the sexual mores of this period has an opinion about Acton and his works, most particularly on his views on women's sexuality (Marcus 1966; Smith 1977; Gay 1984; Peterson 1986; Hall 1992; Porter and Hall 1995). These range from taking Acton's now famous statement that women are seldom troubled with sexual desire as being the last word on Victorian sexual orthodoxy to arguing, like Mason, that this view of women's sexuality was neither typical of Victorian sexuality, nor of the views of Acton himself. Mason points out, first, that writings about sex abounded with comments on women's sexual desire and the role of the clitoris, coupled with the still prevailing view that orgasm was necessary for conception to take place. Second, Mason argues that Acton's other works, particularly on prostitution, acknowledge the presence of a strong sexual desire within women, and that his pronouncement on their near-anaesthesia sexually was aimed at relieving the anxiety of middle-class men about impotency and its relation to masturbation. In support of Mason's interpretation, two further points might be made. First, this book was published in 1857, a time when it has been argued that the medical profession was still in the thrall of its clients, rather than the other way round (Mason 1994: 181). In a highly competitive climate, there must have been a temptation to err on the side of reassurance about the sexual anxieties of the day. Second, this was a period characterized by late marriage, raising further anxieties over what to do with unallayed sexual desire, and the consequences of either celibacy, masturbation or use of prostitutes on their reproductive futures. For if we go beyond the more well-known passages, Acton acknowledges that some women have equal passions to men. But, of course, such women are 'loose, or at least low and vulgar women' who 'give a false idea of the condition of female sexual feeling in general'. The false idea gives young men 'the erroneous notion' that they will have to perform sexually in marriage 'beyond their exhausted strength, and for this reason dread and avoid marriage' (Acton, quoted in Marcus 1970: 31). Here we see a cycle of anxieties that is self-fulfilling. Marcus suggests that our interpretation of the veracity of Acton's views should take account of a fantasy element in this period, which seamed together views of 'what should be' and 'what was'.

The first half of the nineteenth century was marked more by an increasing emphasis on the dangers of sex in which the physical and moral were conflated, rather than the predominance of objective scientism. Towards the end of the second half of the century, through the efforts of a handful of individuals who were not representatives of their parent professions, sex became an object of study. The work of these genuine pioneers was to be both profoundly radical and, at the same time, instrumental in remoulding a sexual orthodoxy.

## 4.2   Scientists of sex

> The . . . emergence of sex as an object of study was one of the major features of the social sciences of the period and stands as a central moment in the constitution of modern sexuality.
>
> (Weeks 1989: 141)

The ground-breaking work of the eminent forensic psychiatrist and physician, Richard von Krafft-Ebing, was arguably the exemplar of the science of sex, in that it represented a dispassionate objectivity that retained a normative element. Krafft-Ebing collated explicit details from hundreds of case studies cataloguing 'sexual perversions' ranging from benign fetishistic attachments to cannibalism and necrophilia. The text was for the specific use of the medico-legal practice of forensic science, to provide a baseline for distinguishing between 'normal' and 'abnormal' sexual behaviour in the legal context. *Psychopathia Sexualis: With Especial Reference to Antipathetic Sexual Instincts. A Medico-Forensic Study* (1897) was first published in English in 1899. In the Introduction, the author wrote:

> It is not intended to build up in this book a system of the psychology of sexual life . . . the object of this treatise is merely to record the various psycho-pathological manifestations of sexual life in man to reduce them to their lawful conditions.
>
> (Krafft-Ebing 1899: iv)

The demand for such records illustrated 'the importance of the subject [sexual life]' and the 'sad lack of scientific knowledge' to allow legal and medical experts to make informed (and dispassionate) judgements. This first scientific text was created by and for experts among whose 'exalted duties and rights' was a 'search for truth'. Thus, 'A scientific title has been chosen and the technical terms are used throughout in order to exclude the lay reader. For the same reason, certain passages are written in Latin' (ibid., p. vii).

Written for the eyes of professionals only, it remains difficult still to gain access to a full English translation. The work is distinguished from previous medical writings on sexual behaviour by its cool detachment. Whether the description is of a erotic attachment to velvet cloth, or sexual intercourse with dead bodies, the tone remains the same; these activities are described, one after the other, with little comment except the extent to which they are acquired or congenital disorders. Yet there are, behind the sexual portraits of Krafft-Ebing's 'cases', sets of assumptions about the sometimes fine dividing line between the normal and the pathological. Much that is either explicitly stated or implied about the bases for these distinctions is in keeping with broader parameters of the 'normal' of this period, particularly those which relate to the status of homosexuality, to auto-eroticism including masturbation, to the nature and extent of women's and children's sexuality, and to the dangers of sexual excess. A relatively new focus, emanating from the specialism of the author, emphasized the relationship, in the context of modernity, between aberrant sexual behaviour, *nervous* diseases and *mental* disorders:

> Exaggerated tensions of the nervous system stimulates sensuality, leads the individual as well as the masses to excesses, undermines the very foundations of society and the morality and purity of family life. The material and moral ruin of the community is readily brought about by debauchery, adultery and luxury. In such periods of civil and moral decline the most monstrous excesses of sexual life may be observed, which, however, can always be traced to psycho-pathological or neuro-pathological conditions of the nations involved.
>
> (Krafft-Ebing 1899: 6–7)

Biologically determined coitive heterosexuality was seen as the norm. Any deviation was considered, to a greater or lesser degree, pathological: 'were it not so, the whole world would be a bordello, and marriage and the family unthinkable. At all events the man who flees women, and the women who pursue sexual gratification are abnormal phenomena' (quoted in Gay 1984: 154). Men who desired or who had sex with men were exhibiting not moral but psychological degeneration as a result of faulty development. Such a view is consistent with Krafft-Ebing's later support for Magnus Hirschfeld's campaign for the decriminalization of homosexuality in Germany (Wolff 1986: 43).

Krafft-Ebing's work is illustrative of the role of science in the search for the 'truth' about human sexuality, consciously shirking none of its multifarious expression, simultaneously avoiding value-judgements, while making it clear that these 'truths' are not for public or lay consumption. In many respects, this work occupies a position on the cusp, prefacing the devotion to using the insights of science to expand the boundaries of 'the normal' evident in the work of the younger contemporaries of Krafft-Ebing: Havelock Ellis, Iwan Bloch, Magnus Hirschfeld and Sigmund Freud. Ellis himself was to say of Krafft-Ebing that:

> His great service lay in the clinical enthusiasm with which he approached the study of sexual perversions, with the firm conviction that he was conquering a great neglected field of morbid psychology which rightly belongs to the physician. He accumulated without any false shame a vast mass of detailed histories, and his reputation induced

sexually abnormal individuals in all directions to send him their auto-
biographies, in the desire to benefit fellow sufferers.

(Ellis 1899: 70)

Ellis began his six-volume work, *Studies in the Psychology of Sex*, in 1899,
the result of his commitment to the detailed study of sex. A study of this
magnitude of what he saw as a crucial element of humanity was necessary
to end a silence that encouraged unhealthy obsession and the promulgation
of misguided and crazy viewpoints. In the preface to Volume 1, he argues
that:

> The question of sex, with the racial questions that rest on it, stands
> before the coming generation as the chief problem for solution. Sex lies
> at the root of life and we can never learn reverence for life until we
> know how to understand sex – so, at least, it seems to me. Having said
> as much I will try and present such results as I have to record in that
> cold and dry light through which alone the goal of knowledge can be
> truly seen.

(Ellis 1899: xiv)

This quote illustrates much of what needs to be said in relation to Ellis's
work. Born in 1859, training first as a teacher and then in medicine, he was
a contemporary and intellectual colleague of Eleanor Marx, Edward Aveling
and the leading British Marxist, Harry Hyndeman. As one of the pioneer
sexologists, he worked closely with, and was mutually influenced by, Iwan
Bloch and Magnus Hirchsfeld, and to a lesser extent Freud, as well as acknowledging his debt to Krafft-Ebing. Weeks (1990: 61) commented on the
approach to Ellis's study: 'The two principles Ellis employed were a form of
cultural relativism as applied to moral attitudes, and biological determinism
as applied to essential sexual characteristics'.

Ellis's work lacked the reformatory zeal of Hirschfeld's and the somewhat discursive and disarming style of Iwan Bloch. It was often long-winded,
gentle and persuasive, while not shirking from explicit descriptions when
deemed necessary. Unlike Krafft-Ebing's work, this was a text clearly written
for the (educated) lay person, each discussion following the same format. As
Weeks has indicated, descriptions of sexual behaviour that Ellis's readers
might have approached with misgivings or worse, he found a cultural precedent for, while validating their 'naturalness' through reference to the sexual
behaviour of animals. This is a familiar strategy in scientific writings of the
period, and one which Ellis freely deploys in relation to auto-eroticism,
sexual inversion, gender differentiated sexuality, and to the genital/coital
imperative. The term 'natural' has not disappeared from this discourse, but
is now valued differently. Though used as a reference point, its deployment
differs from that of Enlightenment thinking in that 'nature' does not offer
the ticket to sensual freedom, nor is it associated primarily with the dark
force as earlier in the nineteenth century. Instead, it now has a *positively*
normative role. Constraints on sexual activity – boundaries between the
normal and abnormal, the acceptable and unacceptable – are drawn by reference to the interplay between nature on the one hand and human cultural

variation on the other. His treatment of 'variations' from these positively valued norms represent a cautious balance between open radical challenge and the maintenance of the classificatory boundaries deemed necessary for scientific endeavour. For example, like Krafft-Ebing, Ellis distinguished between congenital and pseudo-sexual inversion, a particularly troublesome sexual variation for a discourse so infused with the primacy of masculine assertiveness and of heterosexual norms. Accordingly, Ellis devoted an entire volume to 'sexual inversion' (which after its publication in Britain was speedily withdrawn as lewd and grossly indecent, and its publisher, not Ellis, tried and found guilty of the offence). His sympathetic treatment of sexual inverts was qualified by his distinction between 'congenital' and 'acquired' sexual inversion ('inversion' being the term Ellis, and other sexologists, used for same-sex desire), where the former was deemed acceptable by virtue of its status, whereas the latter was the consequence of the corruption of weak persons. His ambivalence about sexual inversion, despite his underlying humanist compassion, is evident:

> The congenital invert should neither be accepted as equal or better, nor crushed beneath a burden of shame . . . Inversion is an abberation from the usual course of nature. It bears, for the most part, its penalty in the structure of its own organism. We are bound to protect the helpless members of society against the invert. If we go farther and seek to destroy the invert himself, we exceed the warrant of reason.
>
> (Ellis 1899: 356)

The extent to which Ellis was a 'man of his time' is also clearly underlined by his treatment (or lack of it) of *women* sexual inverts – to whom, in a substantial volume, he devotes only a few pages. His treatment of heterosexuality in women similarly treads the line between sexual liberalism and adherence to prevailing norms. Margaret Jackson has argued that the six volumes of Ellis's work carry within them two main themes: first, that biology and nature have accorded not only heterosexuality but an imbalance of sexual power relations between men and women in such relationships primacy and legitimacy; and, second, that under the auspices of 'nature', 'even the most violent and dangerous forms of sexual perversion are ultimately rooted in "innocent and instinctive impulses" and thus, it is implied, harmless and acceptable' (Jackson 1994: 109). While this perhaps oversimplifies Ellis's position on the subject of sexual perversions, it nevertheless directs attention towards the lack of challenge to the male-defined orthodoxy. In particular, Jackson singles out the legitimation of masculine ascendency in courtship, which Ellis sees as a form of conquest by the male over the female – a pattern valorized by nature. The emphasis of this patterning and of its primacy in the ordering of human sexual behaviour enshrined the existent heterosexual norm.

> Although it seemed to hold out the promise to women of sexual liberation, it promoted as 'natural' the form of heterosexuality and sexual pleasure which eroticized male dominance and female submission . . . It reinforced the coital imperative, blocking their search for alternative

forms of heterosexual intercourse which were safe and pleasurable and carried no risk of pregnancy.

(Jackson 1994: 119)

Ellis's position as Britain's first scientist of sex was matched by two leading continental figures: Magnus Hirschfeld and Iwan Bloch. Born in 1868, trained in philosophy and then medicine, specializing in neurology, Hirschfeld placed the study of sexuality in general, and of homosexuality in particular, in the mainstream of science. He founded the first Institute for Sexual Science in 1919, which was dedicated to research into sexuality under the disciplines of biology, pathology, sociology and ethnology, but included the practice of social, psychological and forensic medicine. Provision was also made in the Institute for advice on sexual difficulties and marital problems (Jackson 1994: 175). His activities were tirelessly campaigning as well as scientific, and in addition to massive works on sexual inversion also studied transvestism, which, for the first time, distinguished between homosexuality and cross-dressing' (Weeks 1990: 129).

> The fact that his great predecessor Professor R. von Krafft-Ebing had recognised that homosexuality was not an illness but a sexual variation, had opened up a new approach on this 'taboo' subject. [Hirschfeld] states loud and clear that this variety of human love is part of human sexuality, and both its causes and its manifestations need to be scientifically investigated . . . In this he anticipated Kinsey by more than forty years.

(Wolff 1986: 34)

Iwan Bloch, a contemporary and colleague of Hirschfeld, published his English translation of *The Sexual Life of Our Time and its Relations to Modern Culture* in 1908. Although in many ways Bloch can be 'read' as a sexual enthusiast and radical liberal, and by his own admission is 'an ardent advocate of "free love"' (Bloch 1908: 281), the freedom he supports is not that of unregulated sexual expression, but a 'sexual union based on intimate love, personal harmony and spiritual affinity' (ibid.). He devotes a substantial section of his book to detailed descriptions of earlier nineteenth-century preoccupations – impotence, masturbation, sexual hyperaesthesia, sexual aesthesia and inclinations to sexual perversion – and is ambivalent about 'auto-eroticism' and what he calls 'its baser form, masturbation'. Like Ellis, Bloch guardedly validates such forms of erotic expression through natural precedents, but expresses concern about the possibility that such pleasures, if overdone, will eclipse the importance of, and motivation for, heterosexual coitus. Similarly, he exhibits the still-prevailing uneasiness about the characteristics of women's sexuality. While on the one hand he emphatically denies the inferiority of women to men, he nevertheless retains the notion of implicit inequality through the differential analysis of their sexual characteristics and potentials. There are also elements in Bloch's work which are reminiscent of much older anxieties about their erotic capacities:

> How much more woman is sexually than man is can be observed in asylums, where conventional inhibitions are withdrawn. Here, according

to Shaw's observations, the women greatly exceed the men in fluency, malignancy and obscenity; and in this relation there is no difference between the shameless virago from the most depraved classes in London and the elegant lady of the upper circles . . . In all forms of acute mental disorders, according to Shaw, the sexual element plays a more prominent part in woman than in man.

(Bloch 1908: 86)

The issue of men who desire men posed a problem for these scientists of sex, however much they apparently challenged the prevailing orthodoxies. In their search for scientific and physiologically centred truths, the presence of recognizably physical and mental *men* (rather than the drooling degenerates of the earlier characterizations) must have jarred the certainties about the security of such frameworks. The existence of homoerotic desire raises questions regarding the central pillars of the science of sex, usually not specifically outlined, but clear in their presence by implication: the centrality of the reproductive logic for the arrangement and experience of coital sex and the resultant 'truth' of heterosexuality, ideas which are integral to patriarchal constructions of sexuality. Thus, Bloch, the sexual enthusiast and liberal radical medical scientist, speaks of the 'riddle' of homosexuality. He is quite happy to acknowledge the *principle* of equality, politically and physiologically, between homosexual men and their heterosexual counterparts. He is clear that homosexuality is not, as Krafft-Ebing originally stated (yet was later to rescind), a sign of physical and consequently mental degeneracy. However, he sees homosexuality as a remnant of earlier civilization – within an evolutionary model – which is now at the very least a sexual anachronism:

Both for the species, and also for the advancement of civilization, homosexuality has no importance, or at least, very little. It is obvious that as a land of enduring 'monosexuality', it contradicts the purpose of the species. Equally obvious is that the whole of civilisation is the product of physical and mental differentiation of the sexes, that civilisation has, in fact, a heterosexual character.

(Bloch 1908: 534)

On the subject of lesbianism, less still is said – only some two pages are devoted to 'true' tribadies, who are, he says, less in number than homosexual men or 'urnings'. He acknowledges, however, that women are more inclined, by nature, to find close physical relationships with women easier. Thus the challenge the obvious existence of the lesbian poses to this 'equal yet different' discourse of sexual modernism is diminished. The dominance of the heterosexual norm is illustrated by the notion of 'pseudo-homosexuality', a neat sidestep in logic that manages to maintain the centrality of the norm, while (as a good scientist) not ignoring the evidence to the contrary. Pseudo-homosexuality is assigned by Bloch externally defined causes: physical abnormalities (hermaphrodism), insufficient opportunity for intercourse with the opposite sex, disillusionment or disgust with men (as in female prostitutes), psychical hermaphrodism (cross-dressing), and 'noble friendships' between men and especially women (Bloch 1908: 539–54). In all these cases,

and particularly in the notion of *pseudo*-homosexuality, there is the suggestion of second-best choice to the ideal.

The early scientists of sex focused on the observation and classification
of physical manifestations of human sexuality. While they acknowledged
the connections between the physical and the psychological, it was, causally,
a one-way street. Malfunctioning physical mechanisms or abused physical
capacities *led to* mental pathologies: a *corpore sana* ensured a *mens sana*.

## 4.3   Freud and the radical challenge of the subconscious

The work of Sigmund Freud turned this equation on its head. Born in 1856
in Moravia (Austria-Hungary) into a large extended middle-class family, he
eventually trained in medicine, specializing in neuroanatomy and neuropath-
ology. His very earliest intellectual interests were, as he put it, 'directed more
towards human concerns than towards natural objects' (Freud 1986: 14).
This preoccupation, in association with the focus of his medical training
under Charcot, marked a distinction between his contribution and that of
the sexologists discussed above. His contribution to the science of sex derives
from the period beginning in the last years of the nineteenth century, when
he began to explore the subconscious dimension of the mind in his search
for an explanation of the range of neurotic manifestations in his patients.
Freud's hypothesis was that neurotic behaviour was not evidence of a physical
pathology, nor of moral turpitude, but of an inadequately 'tamed' subconscious where sensual childhood desires and traumas impeded the socializing
influence of the super-ego. The tensions between these primitive desires and
their gratification and the demands of civilized and socialized existence was,
for Freud, the mechanism through which sexual identity and the socialization
of sexuality was accomplished. Pathological forms of sexual behaviour or
identity were the results of unresolved desires that escaped the civilizing
process, and manifested themselves in neurotic or aberrant behaviour or in
the content of dreams. The potential for a radical challenge to the hitherto
assumed naturalness of heterosexuality in Freud's work lay in his distinction
between the sexual object (the person from whom sexual attraction proceeds)
and sexual aim (the act towards which the instinct tends) (ibid., p. 46).
There is no 'taken-for-granted' relationship between the two:

> . . . we have been in the habit of regarding the connection between the
> sexual instinct and the sexual object as more intimate than it in fact
> is. Experience of the cases that are considered abnormal has shown us
> that in them the sexual instinct and the sexual object are merely sol-
> dered together – a fact which we have been in danger of overlooking
> in consequence of the uniformity of the normal picture, where the
> object appears to form part and parcel of the instinct.
>
> (Freud 1986: 59)

In long footnotes in successive editions he develops this idea. Inversion, he says, cannot be understood as innate unless we 'are to accept the
crude explanation that everyone is born with his sexual instinct attached to

a particular object' (ibid., p. 51). In a 1915 footnote, he adds the following in relation to the problematic of homosexuality and the non-problematic 'norm' of heterosexuality:

> By studying sexual excitations other than those that are manifestly dis-played, it [psychoanalysis] has found that all human beings are capable of making a homo-sexual object choice and have in fact made one in their sub-conscious ... psychoanalysis considers that the choice of an object independently of its sex – freedom to range equally over male and female objects – as it is found in childhood, in primitive states of society and early periods of history is the original basis from which, as a result of a restriction in one direction or the other, both the normal and inverted types develop ... Thus from the point of view of psycho-analysis the exclusive sexual interest felt by men for women is also a problem which needs elucidating and is not a self evident fact based on an attraction which is ultimately of a chemical nature.
>
> (Freud 1986: 56–7)

Three radical possibilities are suggested by these assertions. First, they render the notion of 'natural' heterosexuality, defined by erotic choice, mean-ingless. Second, there is a denial of the physical origins of sexual object choice. Third, the resolution of sexual desires into one category or another is the out-come of negotiation in a social context, not the invisible and unconscious hand of biological drives. These possibilities, as well as the limitations in their subsequent development, are illustrated in Freud's work on infantile sexuality and its resolution in adult gendered sexual identity.

Infants are born with the ability to experience sexual satisfaction. Crucially, in relation to the promotion of the coital 'norm', this potential is not genitally focused, but is originally derived from feeding and excretion, and the later reproduction of these earliest sensual pleasures through auto-erotic activities. As they grow older, children's sexual curiosity leads them to see the genital difference between boys and girls. Faced with the evidence of castration, boys seek to identify with the one person who is safe from the fate – their father – and in emulating his example retain their first love object, a female, into maturity.

> [The sexual aim] of males is more straightforward and the more under-standable, while that of females actually enters upon a kind of invo-lution. A normal sexual life is only assured by the exact convergence of the two currents directed towards the sexual object and the sexual aim, the affectionate current and the sensual one ... It is like the com-pletion of a tunnel which had driven through a hill from two directions.
>
> (Freud 1986: 127)

The passage of women is more fraught, more complicated and less satisfactory. First, they resist accepting the 'reality' of castration, resulting in possibile neurosis and homoerotic attachments to women in maturity. Freud argues that to 'join up the tunnel', the little girl must abandon her 'mascu-line' autonomous sexuality manifested through clitoral masturbation. This, along with the abandonment of her first love object, her mother, is the price to be paid for mature womanhood and vaginal coitally defined sexuality. In her libidinous 'castration', her active polymorphous sexuality is silenced. In 1931, Freud recognized some implications and shortcomings of his explanation of women's acquisition of heterosexuality:

> The account of how girls respond to the impression of castration and the prohibition against masturbation will very probably strike the reader as confused and contradictory. This is not entirely the author's fault. In truth, it is hardly possible to give a description which has general validity. We find the most different reactions in different individuals, and in the same individual the contrary attitudes exist side by side.
>
> (Freud 1986: 380)

In this later revision of his views, Freud suggests that the evidence of women's sexuality collected since his original essay implies that the possibility of bisexuality (defined as non-coital heterosexuality) is greater in women than in men. Second, he can find insufficient explanation for the dual erotic roles of the vagina and clitoris in adult women; and third, he acknowledges the overall lack of clarity in the theory. There are two possible explanations for what amounts to a silencing of the radical potential of Freud's sexual theories. The first and more obvious is that Freud as a 'late Victorian' could never escape completely the orthodoxies of his time, particularly those which were the principal supporting frameworks of male-defined heterosexuality. The second can be found in Freud's own work, dealt with in the previous chapter. The containment of the polymorphous potential of both infantile and adult sexuality was the consequence of the course taken by Western civilization, one in which expression of desires was subordinated to social integration and order.

Notwithstanding the limitations of the full radical potential, the first scientists of sex succeeded in their aim of making sex an object of study, in the process disengaging sex from more traditional associations of measured conjugality, libidinous excesses, of titillation or of denial. These (partial) uncouplings were made possible by the licence conferred by scientific endeavour on a legitimating framework, which eased the transition from sex as danger to sex as pleasure.

## 4.4  The sexual enthusiasts

Alfred Kinsey, a trained biologist, began his study of human sexual behaviour in 1937. His first volume, *Sexual Behaviour in the Human Male*, was published in 1948, going into ten printings in the subsequent four years. The second, *Sexual Behaviour in the Human Female*, was published in 1953. He might be described as a 'true' scientist of sex, for in his eyes only a value-free approach could dissolve the confusions and prejudices around this human activity:

> Nothing has done more to block the free investigation of sexual behaviour than the almost universal acceptance, even among scientists, of

certain aspects of that behaviour as normal, and of other aspects as abnormal . . . This is first of all a report on what people do which raises no question of what they should do, or what kinds of people do it.

(Kinsey *et al.* 1948: 7)

Kinsey's view was that previous studies were statistically useless and confused moral values, philosophic theory and scientific fact. The centrality of the normal–abnormal dichotomy in the work of his predecessors was counter-productive in the advancement of the 'free investigation of sexual behaviour' (ibid., p. 7). A field biologist, whose work hitherto had involved the detailed study of the behaviour of a single species of wasp, Kinsey used the same method, taxonomy, to study human behaviour. This was consistent with his aim to 'obtain data about sex which would represent an accumulation of scientific fact completely divorced from questions of moral value and social custom' (ibid., p. 3). The frequency with which a wide variety of sexual outlets from bestiality to heterosexual coitus occurred in a sample population would indicate the frequency in the total population – in this case, white American men and women. Frequency alone indicated typicality, rather than any exogenous morality. Just as it would be scientifically meaningless to make moral judgements about the behaviour of wasps, so it was with humans. Yet while he and his colleagues distanced themselves from the moral and philosophical judgements of other studies, they elevated the legitimacy of science as the only acceptable road to truth. Scientifically established parameters of sexual behaviour are the necessary precursor to any legal or moral judgements. It is science, and only science, which can cut its way through the forest of ignorance. Nor was it appropriate for sexual knowledge to be the privileged province of scientists, priests or doctors. Kinsey believed that ordinary men and women, young girls and boys, have urgent need for informed and unprejudiced knowledge. In particular, it is the unmarried and the young who are disenfranchised in this way: 'The law specifies the right of the married adult to have regular intercourse, but it makes no provision whatsoever for the approximately 40 per cent of the population which is sexually mature but unmarried' (Kinsey *et al.* 1953: 15).

This 40 per cent, the authors say, need to know whether or not it is physically damaging to masturbate, or whether they will compromise their future sexuality by doing so. Should they indulge in pre-marital petting or extra-marital sex? Are expressions of their sexual desire normal or abnormal? The proper source of the answers to such questions are not medical books or religious tracts, but facts that are scientifically isolated from such influences by methods that ascertain the 'incidence and frequency' of sexual behaviour outside the marital and strictly procreative context. Doubts about the advisability of masturbation, pre-marital sex or choice of sexual partners could now be allayed with reference to statistical evidence of their 'incidence and frequency' regardless of social and moral context.

It followed, then, that for Kinsey sexual acts were sexual acts, from bestiality to chaste procreative non-orgasmic marital communion. His views on the subject of homosexuality, given his 'value-free' stance, are at one level unsurprising but at another were to have a considerable impact at the time (and arguably now). He rejects the categorization of individuals as homo- or heterosexual. They should rather be seen as:

> Individuals who have certain amounts of heterosexual experiences and certain amounts of homosexual experiences. Such terms are better used to describe the nature of overt sexual relations or to stimuli to which the individual erotically responds.
>
> (Kinsey *et al.* 1948: 617)

Accordingly, Kinsey and his co-workers' study sought to quantify the incidence of men whose physical contact with other men brought them to orgasm irrespective of their predominant sexual experiences or their sexual identity:

> In these terms . . . the data in the present study indicates that at least 37 per cent of the male population has had some homosexual experience between adolescence and old age . . . Among males who remain unmarried until the age of 35, almost exactly 50 per cent have homosexual experiences between adolescence and that age.
>
> (Kinsey *et al.* 1948: 623)

This finding contradicts two previous beliefs about homosexual relations between men. First, all previous studies, including those by the sympathetic Ellis and Hirschfeld, suggested the incidence of such relations to be no more than 2–4 per cent. Second, if such behaviour was so widespread (and, given the moral climate on this issue, this figure could be assumed to be an underestimate), it was not meaningful to describe such activity as either perverse, inverse or abnormal. Similarly, he found that homosexual acts between women were less frequent and less widespread, yet tended to persist for longer periods. By the age of thirty, 17 per cent of women had had sexual contact with other women to orgasm. His findings on masturbation confronted the orthodoxy in similar fashion. This was the second most important source of male orgasm, involving more than 92 per cent of the male population. Of the 5300 males interviewed, 5100 recorded masturbation in a range of frequencies – from several times per day to several times in their lives. In women masturbation was the second most common type of sexual activity, before and after marriage, and the one most likely to lead to orgasm (95 per cent). As with the male respondents, masturbation continued (indeed often began) in adulthood. Two conclusions follow: first, that masturbation, in any frequency, cannot result in physical deterioration, for otherwise the health of the nation would be seriously compromised; and, second, at least by implication, masturbation as an erotic practice of choice ranks second only to coitus for both men and women. The classification of sexual acts as normal or abnormal (and therefore healthy or unhealthy) was irrelevant and meaningless. 'Sexual outlets', as Kinsey termed them, were simply a response to sufficient physical and psychical stimulation. It follows that there is 'little evidence of the existence of such a thing as innate perversity, even among those individuals whose sexual activities society is least inclined to accept' (Kinsey *et al.* 1948: 678).

Kinsey's cool scientism cut through the tangle of prejudice and fears which had surrounded masturbation (formerly 'self-abuse') and, even more disturbingly, same-sex desire. These findings were not received with equanimity (see Pomeroy 1972: 283–386). For not only did they 'normalize' disturbing if not deviant expressions of sexuality, these were *ex post facto* pronouncements made on the basis of what people actually did, not what they should do. This was perhaps the most disturbing aspect of the Kinsey Reports, whose findings are still not common currency. Worthy of note also, as a marker in the history of attitudes to sex and sexuality, is that Kinsey was able to recruit volunteers to talk to people in white coats about their most secret desires. This suggests a further element in the progression of a science of sex, which co-existed with, perhaps even relied on, the de-repressive trend. For the work of the twentieth-century scientists of sex extended the regulatory network of discourses about sex, in a manner which reversed the Foucauldian argument about the 'repressive thesis'. Behind what might be called the 'liberalization thesis', the scientific gaze, while consciously avoiding former confusions between moralizing and enquiry, continued and extended the project of sexual surveillance. Lionel Trilling (1964) points out that there are dangers in such applications of science: first, that the lay public unquestioningly accepts the precepts and findings because it is science; and, second, that there is a slippage in any sociology between the goal of furthering understanding of selves and others, and the feeding of a 'bland tyranny', where sociological findings fostered conformity by providing 'norms' and encouraging us to live in 'unnoticeable' ways. Through more subtle channels, then, 'The act of understanding becomes the act of control' (ibid., p. 227).

The viability of this possibly unintended agenda of the science of sex is illustrated by the development of the related speciality of sex therapy, in which the pioneer figures were William Masters and Virginia Johnson, whose major works, *Human Sexual Response* (1966) and *Human Sexual Inadequacy* (1970), observed and measured the physical mechanisms of sexual intercourse, and provided, on the basis of this, a definitive text for the treatment of sexual dysfunction. They were not the first to advise about pathways to sexual pleasure. In the eighteenth century, Venette's *Conjugal Love* and the anonymously authored *Aristotle's Masterpiece* reached a wide popular readership (Porter and Hall 1995). Almost fifty years before Masters and Johnson, Marie Stopes (1918a, 1918b) shocked the still reluctant medical professionals and delighted her many supporters and readers by her enthusiastic and straightforward acknowledgement of the potential for sexual pleasures on offer for both men and women in the marital state. Despite the romanticized language and the emphasis on conjugal sex, these texts were in huge demand and indicated a continuing appetite for sexual self-help texts. During the inter-war years and after the Second World War, this appetite was legitimized in a climate that promoted marital sex as the vital ingredient for a stable home environment, a view represented by an expanding consortium of experts (Brecher 1970).

This new sexual enthusiasm differed from that of the eighteenth century. For whereas *Aristotle's Masterpiece* assumed an unproblematic possession of sexual prowess, the expert-ridden world of the mid-twentieth century could not leave sex to 'take care of itself'. Sexual pleasure had to be learned, directed and re-directed when it 'lost its way', and the apotheosis of this new sexology lies in the work of Masters and Johnson.

Superficially, the work of this couple can be interpreted as true 'sexual modernism' which confronted the central pillars of the heterosexual coital orthodoxy. Women are more poly-erotically sexual and are multi-orgasmic. The focus of women's sexuality is the clitoris, not the vagina, as measured in ease and multiplicity of orgasm. Age offers no barrier to sexual enjoyment, nor to orgasmic achievement. These 'discoveries' (which were present in the work of their predecessors) in a new climate of sexual enthusiasm confronted the primacy of the penis in sexology directly, and established a version of women's sexuality neither derivative of, nor dependent on, that of the male. Their work has thus been interpreted as 'explicit feminism', and exhibiting a bias towards the sexuality of women (Robinson 1976: 122). However, such a view ignores other elements in their approach, particularly its therapeutic applications, which were anything but radical and promotional of women's sexual autonomy.

First, there was a strongly and traditionally gendered script to their therapy. For these clinicians, sex was 'coupled' sex. During their sexual therapy sessions, they would not see individuals, only 'units'. The units comprised either an established marital couple, or an unmarried individual plus a surrogate partner, provided by the Institute if the patient was male (Szasz 1980). Provision of surrogate partners for single women attenders was not acceptable to Masters and Johnson; sexually dysfunctional women had to provide their own surrogates. Their justification for this was given in terms of traditionally gendered views of sexuality. The primary concern of men sexually was effective sexual function – potentially procreative sex, in ways which maintained their masculinity.

> As a result, the man usually regards the contribution made by a partner surrogate as he would a prescription for other physical incapacities . . . For him the restoration of sexual function justifies putting aside, temporarily, any other value requirement.
>
> (Masters and Johnson 1970: 156)

Women, on the other hand, have different requirements to overcome sexual dysfunction – a 'relatively meaningful relationship' that 'gives her permission to value her own sexual function' (ibid.). Such a relationship, they say, could not be achieved in the therapeutic time-scale of two weeks with a male surrogate partner because, 'For the sexually dysfunctional woman security of an established man/woman relationship, real identification with a male partner, and warmth and expression of mutual emotional responsibility are all of vital concern' (ibid.).

Second, there was evidence in their work of a prioritization of heterosexuality over homosexuality. They emphasized erotic equality of the two forms of sexuality, asserted homosexuality was not a disease, and were happy to treat all 'sexually dysfunctional' couples. Yet there were elements in this apparent sexual pluralism that require further comment. Despite their support for a 'different yet equal' approach to homoeroticism, they distinguished between 'dysfunctional' and 'dissatisfied' homosexuals (Brake 1982: 190). The former category was synonymous with its heterosexual counterpart, but the latter referred to those who wish to be 'converted', or 'revert' to the hetero-sexual state.

The work of Masters and Johnson has implications for much of what has been said on the science of sex. For while they in one sense were the representatives of the new sexual age of the 1960s and 1970s, on the other they perpetuated the 'anxiety-making' tradition evident throughout the sex texts of the preceding two centuries (Comfort 1968). The late twentieth-century version of this tradition was 'orgasmic anxiety'. The diagnostic cri-teria for orgasmic dysfunction illustrates the extent to which gender-specific heterosexual coitus was retained and strengthened in its position at the apex of constructions of sexuality. Orgasmically dysfunctional men were unable to climax intra-vaginally or suffered from premature ejaculation. The ability to orgasm with masturbation was not relevant to the diagnosis. The related diagnosis of 'anorgasmia', a condition only suffered by women, applied to the inability to orgasm whether by masturbation or in coition.

The terms in which these conditions were described and treated were strongly reminiscent of masturbatory anxiety of the previous two centuries. Here the distinction between Masters and Johnson and Kinsey is most evident. Whereas anxieties about sexual performance are absent in the findings of Kinsey, they have a continued presence in – even provide the logic for – the therapeutic endeavours of Masters and Johnson. While they were self-professed 'sexual enthusiasts', there is little evidence that they sought to de-fuse the anxiety or to challenge its basic premise – the primacy of the orgasm for sexual pleasure. Anorgasmia is a disease, a sexual disease for which they had the cure. Premature ejaculation, which Kinsey viewed as 'biologically efficient', is the sign of inadequate masculinity. With the orgasm as the ultimate (in both senses of the word) goal, anything is permissible. Full citizenship in the land of Orgasmia is not a matter of personal choice or of an ability to enjoy sex in any ways we choose:

> Not having orgasms can create fear of performance that propels a woman into the spectator role, dampening her overall sexual responsiveness, just as is true for a man. Anorgasmia can also lead to loss of self-esteem, depression and a sense of futility.
>
> (Masters and Johnson 1986: 472)

The parallels between this statement and those about masturbatory insanity and 'spermatorrhoea' are striking. As the inventors of both the disease and the providers of the cure, such pronouncements justify their characterizations as the 'quacks' of the late twentieth century.

## Conclusion

The making of a science of sex cannot be understood as a 'modernization of sex'. Such a notion suggests an evolutionary progression, in the process eliminating old anxieties. A more complex history of ideas and practices has been presented, in which there were reforming, even radical elements evident, but which were limited in the extent to which they challenged the under-lying orthodoxies. Arguably, in all the words written and observations made, little advance has been made in the acquisition of new knowledge about human sexuality. The significance of the scientists of sex was not that they uncovered startling new pieces of flesh we didn't know we had, nor the route to sensual experiences previously unchartered. Their work can be seen rather as the progressive expropriation of human sensual experience, sometimes driven by quite radical intentions, sometimes by professional self-interest, and all reflecting the central importance accorded to sex in the period of modernity. Nevertheless, one might expect that in the course of nearly two centuries, some erosion of the central tenets would occur. And superficially, they did. Sexual pleasure replaced sexual danger. But did it? *Some* sexual pleasures were validated, but at the cost of a comprehensive sexual demo-cracy. We ceased to be the sexual authors of our fate, as certain parts of the body and the ways we 'used' them were designated for our sexuality, while others were at first forbidden, as physically and morally dangerous, and later, in the world of Orgasmia, as erotically 'inefficient'. Discourses of physical and moral danger were replaced by regimes of sexual efficiency, a sexual mode of production in which the forces of production were labelled as more or less direct routes to the desired end – orgasm.

Evident throughout this chapter has been the primacy of heterosexual coital sex, the folly of sexual excess, and the elastic influence of nature on human sexuality. In the first stages of the construction of a science of sex, these parameters were explicitly stated in a normative and moralizing lan-guage, a framework constructed of polarities, of rights and wrongs, of the healthy and the pathological. In what has been interpreted elsewhere as 'modernization' or sexual reform, the emphasis shifted to a positive promo-tion of sexual pleasure from accredited sources. In the sexology of late modernity, the orgasm has become both the pinnacle of sexual endeavour and the legitimating motive for orgasmic activities. With the establishment of the goal, the role of sexology is to teach us the most efficient means. And the rationalization of sex does not stop there. To employ an analogy from political economy, not only are the productive forces designated, but also the appropriate social relations to maximize the efficiency of sex.

Throughout the construction of a science of sex, the central figures are the copulating man and woman. Despite the apparent extension of franchise to all sexual citizens, those whose erotic choices deviate from this orthodoxy are accorded a supporting cast status. If the science of sex had one unifying feature, it was the commitment to overturning the fear-ridden traditions that emphasized the uncontrollable and the animal – the antithesis to human reason and volition. Science provided the antidote to both fear and ignorance, by providing the tools to disentangle myth from reality. Through the objective dispassionate lenses focused on the physical secrets of the mechanics of sex, or on the depths of the subconscious, the unpredictable energies could be harnessed. The ordering and monitoring strategies can then be passed, through the conduits of the experts, to the afflicted, the 'naturally perverse'. The science of sex offers a blueprint for rationalization of the erotic, presenting us with an equation between desire and outcome. A closer look at this working model reveals a new personification of old fears about sex. The fear of sexual danger has been replaced by a fear of sexual dysfunction, manifested in anxieties about performance, in the efficient deployment of the equation of desire with outcome. The secrets of expertise now internalized by the sexual subject are the source not just of efficient pleasure but of insecurities about one's capacities, anxieties which bind the sexual subject to the expert in a circular and self-reinforcing relationship of power. The anxious is not now the sick but the perpetually inadequate, who is not the lost soul, the aberrant or the inherently perverse, but the incompetent pupil, the one who has not yet learned the lesson.

# 5 Planning sex

Heterosexual genital love, which has remained exempt from outlawry is itself restricted by further limitations, in the shape of insistence on legitimacy and monogamy. Present day civilisation makes it plain that it will only permit sexual relationships on the basis of a solitary, indissoluble bond between one man and one woman, and that it does not like sexuality as a source of pleasure in its own right and is only prepared to tolerate it because there is so far no substitute for it as a means of propagating the human race.

(Freud 1961: 105)

The science of sex shaped ways of thinking about sex that remain recognizable today. The ease with which we think about sex in a variety of sometimes contradictory ways, is testimony to the classificatory models provided and perpetuated by sexology. Moreover, it provided a context in which sex could be talked about in ways that did not involve obligatory moralizing or could be interpreted as covertly salacious. It also, and most familiarly, strengthened the distinctions between the normal and abnormal, distinctions that were not intended, primarily, as a moral judgement. Normal and abnormal expressions of sexual desire were measured against harmful or advantageous physical or psychological consequences. As we have seen, the concept of 'nature' was flexibly deployed in the emergence and maturation of sexology, where nature was variously the script or the outcome of the statistically predominant mode of sexual expression. In either case, the central position of heterosexuality was both retained and strengthened in the progressive construction of sexuality. What was once ordained by God was affirmed by the *men* of science. Coital intercourse had become synonymous with sex. Sexuality, always a nebulous term, was defined by genital contact.

Throughout these dispassionate orderings, *hetero*-sexuality, despite Freud's cautious suggestions to the contrary, was mandated by nature. A theorization of, rather than a moralization about, expressions of sexual desire made possible the promotion of sexual pleasures while at the same time continuing their regulation. The focus on the dangers of unregulated expressions of sexual desire was gradually superseded by the promotion of the advantages, both social and individual, of an informed sexual population monitored and shaped by the advice of the experts – the scientists of sex and their successors, the sexual educators and therapists. Though less central than in the 'pre-science' era, there remained in this positive valorization of sex an ordering of sexual practices and desires, which continued to hold at its centre heterosexual coitus. The concomitant marginalization of same-sex desire and auto-eroticism continued, though in a more muted form, to distinguish qualitatively between 'masculine' and 'feminine' sexuality. Yet in this process of positively promoting one form of sexual expressions over others, little attention was paid to the characteristics of heterosexual coital sex. That this was the mode of expression decreed by nature meant, presumably, that nature would arbitrate in its articulation. Such was not the case. For 'normal' sexuality, narrowly defined in the wake of sexology, was to come under scrutiny in the first half of the twentieth century.

Following Foucault's reminder that from the late sixteenth century onwards, there has been a proliferation of speaking about sex (Foucault 1979), these discourses to a degree in the eighteenth but almost exclusively in the nineteenth century were dominated by the negative individual and social consequences. Speaking about sex in the twentieth century was characterized by the gradual but systematic promotion of the positive social and individual advantages of sexual intercourse. But, as Elias (1982: 140) suggests, 'this is only possible because the individual capacity to restrain one's urges and behaviour in correspondence with the more advanced feelings for what is offensive, has been, on the whole, secured. It is a relaxation within an already established framework'. The internalization of sexual mores to which Elias refers is reflected in the conditional promotion within specific contexts – that of reproductive and marital sex. But Foucault's criticisms of the 'repressive thesis' could equally be used to reveal the extent to which within this apparent liberation there is a persistence of old and the construction of new regulatory threads. An argument which suggests that the twentieth century from the inter-war years onwards can, in a reversal of the 'repressive thesis' of the nineteenth century, be seen as a period of progressive liberalization of sexual mores, has some justification. Forms of expression of sexual desire have continued to receive attention and, since the contribution of the science of sex, from increasingly approving eyes. Yet, as Foucault said of the nineteenth century, behind this appearance of 'repression/liberalization' there were more complicated regulatory processes at work. The appearance, even experience, of this liberalization not only involved such complexities but was dependent on them.

In this and the following chapter, this idea will be developed. Two themes will be followed in which principle modes of expression of heterosexual desire were conditionally promoted – reproduction and conjugality. This chapter will explore the first of these themes, the troubled relationship between sex and contraception and the terms under which (some of) the tensions were resolved. The conditional promotion of pleasurable sex in marriage will be dealt with in the next chapter.

## 5.1   The problem of reproductive sex

The promotion of rational action as the mode of action most fitted to conditions of modernity gave a new significance to the implications, particularly the social implications, of individual choice. A principal prerequisite for rational action was the availability of a variety of possible means to ends. This condition was dependent on another – the ability of the individuals faced with a choice to make the most efficacious decision, one which was based on the primacy of the desired outcome. A facet that distinguished this model of rational action from other models of individualism was that the ability to make choices was not necessarily innate, but required the guiding presence of appropriate knowledge and the educative role of objectively motivated experts. Such a model in relation to sexual activity posed particular problems. The fostering of individual choice in the rational model created a tension between the perceived irrationality of sexual desire and the required capacity to make reasoned choices with the desired outcome. At a time when the positive advantages of heterosexual sex began to be promoted, this tension and the response it engendered is evident in the anxieties expressed in the opposition to the provision of birth control.

On the face of it, the use of birth control is a profoundly rational act – the choice of the most effective means (contraception) to a desired end (prevention of pregnancy). It additionally offered a means by which the most 'unplannable' of human activities could be directed and regulated within the context of the valorization of (contained) sexual pleasures. The increased use of methods of birth control in the late Victorian and Edwardian periods in response to economic as well as social factors, should thus not only have been welcomed but actively encouraged. The emerging view at the turn of the century, of the political and economic advantages of planning, should have further advanced the positive attributes of birth control. Yet evidence of increased use of rational means to ends – birth control – fanned old and introduced new anxieties about the consequences of encouraging and promoting the means with which to avoid pregnancy.

Demographic concerns were to give new social significance to procreative sex. During the course of the nineteenth century, the population of England and Wales had increased from 10.5 to 26 million. This trend was accompanied by a fall in family size, and was thus largely attributed to the fall in mortality rates since the eighteenth century (Henderson 1949: 35). The reduction in family size was class-specific. The Royal Commission on Population reported that in 1880 the families of social classes I and II were half the size of social classes VII and VIII. This imbalance persisted into the early twentieth century, where the working-class fertility rate was twice that of the middle and upper classes (ibid., pp. 26–9). Methods of birth control were being used increasingly among the middle class and the notoriety of the efforts of exponents of its use further publicized its availability (Peel 1963: 115).

Support for the use of birth control came from other quarters, though for less altruistic purposes. For concerns about the quality as well as quantity of the population were expressed in the context of the increasing popularity of Eugenicist arguments: the view that it was the responsibility of humanity to ensure breeding from the fittest stock to secure longevity and health, but also, on a less universal basis, to maintain national supremacy (Marchant 1916). In this context, the differential fertility rates were cause for alarm about reproductive behaviour from a variety of sources and somewhat surprising alliances: medical professionals, feminists, social commentators, Fabian socialists. For those who held such views, the notion of state involvement in planning was paramount. State planning of reproduction was a necessary starting point to avoid the disastrous consequences of unregulated breeding: 'Decay and moral collapse would be avoided when the government stepped in to assume its proper responsibility in the area of reproduction' (McLaren 1978: 191; see also Davin 1978).

There were clear views also about who were to be the focus of these official attentions. For planned reproduction not only demanded state intervention into the process of procreation, but also of child-rearing. In both, women and their performance of the role of wife and mother came under increasingly close scrutiny, legitimated by the arguments about the health of the nation's children and the strategic strength of its work and defence force (Davin 1978; Lewis 1980). By the beginning of the twentieth century, reproduction of the population could no longer be left to chance, nature, or the vagaries of individual actions. In a climate that increasingly promoted the idea of state-led planning of the population, the usefulness of methods of birth control would seem to be undeniable and unproblematic. Yet the issue of planning pregnancies was passed over and attention focused on the monitoring and education of the nation's mothers. It was not until the late 1930s that the state and the medical profession reluctantly acknowledged the usefulness of birth control for the alleviation of the dilemma in the face of persistently high rates of maternal mortality and illegal abortions.

Why this reluctance? John Peel has pointed out that technologies of birth control have not progressed significantly between the early nineteenth century and the clinical use of the anovular contraceptive pill in the early 1960s. So the question was not one of demand for non-existent methods. The obstacle to the unproblematic application of birth control to alleviate the suffering of women in large impoverished families and from the physical debilitations of sequential pregnancies was not one of availability of method but of attitude.

All those who expressed concerns about the undesirable demographic features also expressed degrees of revulsion about the issue of birth control. The opposition in the early stages of this debate was influenced by religious beliefs (that prevention of pregnancy was unnatural and therefore sinful), by the medical profession (artificial methods of birth control were harmful to health, and little distinction was made between abortion and use of birth control), to a more ambivalent degree by feminists (birth control would render women sexual slaves of male lust), and by moralists who argued that provision of birth control would encourage sexual promiscuity. Despite the variation in both the backgrounds and ideological positions of the exponents, there is a common feature: the implications of the use of birth control for sexual behaviour, particularly in relation to women. Though not a central figure in these early debates, the attitudes of the medical profession clearly articulated to a greater or lesser extent many if not all of these objections.

## 5.2   Birth control, sex and the medical profession

The prevailing attitude of the medical profession to birth control for much of the nineteenth century was one of profound negativity bordering on contempt. Exposing women to the means by which they might experience sex without the fear of pregnancy posed a threat both to family life and to standards of public morality, by encouraging unregulated sexual activity: 'Women would rarely preserve their chastity, illicit amours would be common and seldom detected, seduction would be facilitated and prostitution would be almost universal' (quoted in McLaren 1978: 82). In 1880, Dr Albutt, a member of the Medical Branch of the Malthusian League, a compendium of birth control campaigners from a variety of ideological standpoints, published a simply worded, low-cost pamphlet advising on the use of the condom, the douche and the Mesinga Ring or Dutch cap. The author and distributor were struck from the General Medical Council for 'having published and caused to be sold a work entitled *The Wives' Handbook* at so low a price as to bring the work into the reach of the young of both sexes to the detriment of public morals' (ibid., p. 132).

Birth control was also conflated, morally, with abortion – both were 'filthy expedients for the prevention of conception' (Wood and Suitters 1970: 114–15). Despite the evidence of increasing resort to barbaric and potentially lethal amateur abortive methods (Elderton 1914: 136), the opposition of the profession remained. Women who sought to prevent pregnancies by any method were illustrating their irresponsibility, 'increasing love of pleasure and distaste for home and family life' (Marchant 1916: 318).

By the inter-war years, the use of birth control, with or without official sanction, continued -- given some unofficial moral impetus by the promotion of the use of condoms during wartime for the control of venereal disease (Peel 1963: 137). Yet it still was not the state, but a voluntary organization, the National Birth Control Council, which orchestrated and organized the provision of condoms from their voluntary clinics. By the mid-1930s, demographic trends again provided an impetus. Concerns were expressed over two factors: the continuing maternal mortality rate and the overall population growth. By 1936, the population was not replacing itself, while both the causes and rates of maternal mortality were higher than that of 1911. In 1939, the *Birkett Report* found that (at a time when it was a criminal offence) abortion nevertheless accounted for between 15 and 20 per cent of all conceptions in England and Wales (Birkett 1939: 108). These alarming figures did not result in a complete reversal of their former indifference, but prompted the medical profession to review their position, a shift in attitudes which was paralleled, though gradually, in party political attitudes to the social desirability of the use of birth control (Rowbotham 1977; Doughan 1981; Leathard 1980). Yet it was the evidence that despite moral pronouncements women were planning their reproductive and therefore an important aspect of their sexual lives, that arguably provided the greatest impetus for the medical profession's reluctant acceptance of birth control into their domain of knowledge and practice. Despite continued misgivings that 'birth control does not mean sex control, but unlimited indulgence without its responsibilities and consequences' (*The Practitioner* 1923: 34), and that 'the limitation of motherhood may produce ... manifestations of nervous and psychical disturbances often seen in childless women, married or unmarried' (ibid., p. 38), the profession reluctantly acknowledged the need for their professional authority over this unsettling autonomy: 'We have to realise that a knowledge of contraception has arrived, that it's no longer a monopoly of the classes, but has penetrated deeply into the masses, and that the public look to the Medical Profession [*sic*] to see that this knowledge is directed into the right channels' (ibid., pp. 2–3).

By the late 1930s, a reluctant medical profession, and an even more reluctant state, was forced to act. The medical profession began to establish serious research endeavours into methods of birth control (Peel 1964: 140), and the second Labour government finally capitulated to pressures from within and from the local authorities and issued, in 1930, Memorandum MCW 153. This memorandum authorized local authority welfare centres to give birth control information to married woman when deemed necessary on medical grounds, though the memorandum received scant publicity and many of those to whom it applied remained ignorant as to its existence. Thus the state gave way to public pressure and to public health expedience but with the bare minimum of outright commitment. Similarly in 1930, the Lambeth Conference of the Church of England conceded in a resolution on the matter of provision of contraception that, 'Where there is a clearly felt moral obligation to limit or avoid parenthood and where there is a morally sound reason for avoiding complete abstinence the conference agrees that other methods should be used' (quoted in Leathard 1980: 47).

The nettle had been grasped and the negative consequences had to some extent been defused by the restriction of provision to married women and then only for medical reasons. This reluctance to take responsibility for actively supporting the means by which women could control their fertility has usually been attributed to concerns about the imbalance between working- and middle-class fertility rates, which, in the Eugenicist-dominated climate of the early twentieth century, endangered national and racial strength. But the groups who, in the end, were to legitimate the (conditional) distribution of contraceptives rarely expressed their opposition in these terms. The principle reason given for reluctance was the *moral* consequence of unregulated use of birth control. And the moral dimension was clearly attributed to sexual behaviour. If these misgivings were overcome in the medical profession by fears of a lack of professional authority over the grassroots expansion of birth control, the political anxieties were eroded in the climate that elevated the notion of 'planning'. If rationality was the philosophical motif of modernity, the action blueprint was planning.

## 5.3 Planned sex

The 1930s was characterized by the motif of planning – in the economy, in the provision of education and health, and in the organization of industry. From the 1890s, but particularly in the first decades of the twentieth century, there was increasing emphasis placed on the need to plan and order more and more areas of people's social and private lives. The blueprint of this endeavour can be seen in the development of scientific management of the labour process and industrial production. It was Taylor's (1911/1972) *Principles of Scientific Management* that seriously launched the application of systematic rational and scientific principles to the planning of production. These three characteristics were to be delivered by the conveyor-belt, mass-production techniques we now automatically associate with the production of Henry Ford's automobiles.

There was one striking distinction between these scientific, rational and systematic methods and those proposed more than a century before by Adam Smith in *The Wealth of Nations*. For whereas Adam Smith's emphasis was on the organization of the *task* in the process of which the workers were largely passive operatives, Taylor and his disciples' attention was extended to those without whose efforts the tasks would not be undertaken – that is, the workers. The movements of workers' bodies were monitored, adapted and finely tuned as if they were extensions of the machines with which they worked. Arguably, this principle of treating the workers as synonymous with machines was not new, indeed was central to Marx's analysis of the basis of capitalism's exploitative mechanisms. What distinguished this planning endeavour from its more openly exploitative predecessors was the legitimacy afforded by the idea of scientific management. The belief that science owed allegiance to no dominant interest and that its neutral and dispassionate application would be of universal benefit prevailed. If a more ergonomically efficient organization could be developed for a task or set of tasks, the belief was that this offered benefits both to employer and employee, as well as promoting the more general health of a society dependent on the continuing success of capitalism.

The strategy of observing and timing body movements extended beyond the production line into every aspect of factory life. These endeavours gave new significance to the bodies of the workforce. The fine detailed monitoring extended, under Ford's direction, outside the factory gates and into the workers' homes. The diets and drinking habits of the workers came under scrutiny, as did the patterns of their sexual and emotional lives. The logic of planning and the techniques associated with it meant that it was perhaps inevitable that it would infiltrate ever deeper into the domestic sphere. If the primary concern was efficiency of the organization of means and predictability of desired outcome, all possible random and unforeseeable obstacles to this must be, if possible, eradicated.

Planned activities are predictable and must be so. This predictability is ensured by the conformity to the blueprint of action, and the eradication of any aberrant activities that would either cut across or deflect the ordering of tasks. The practical application of scientific methods required the involvement of humans for its realization, experts in the appropriate field who could advise on the most desirable end and devise the most efficient means with which to achieve it. This model of organization offered the possibility for the direction of heterosexual desire, which would avoid the disturbing potential for excess that the idea of non-reproductive sex suggested. For it was this potential that conferred on birth control a mantle of disreputableness and irresponsibility. There was, even in the most enthusiastic promoters of birth control, an acknowledgement of these characteristics. Promoting contraception was equated with promoting sex. The negative aspects of this seemingly unavoidable connection were to a large degree defused in the 1930s by an emphasis on forward planning, in which motherhood was implicated alongside the economy, education and health. Under this rubric, 'Matters once left to the individual, the family or the local authority were now becoming, more and more, matters concerning the state and its institutions' (Gittens 1982: 48).

In the face of the possibly sexually irrational responses to the availability of contraception, family planning was promoted as the primary advantage. And behind the somewhat bland title there was an equal promotion of marital sexuality and the disqualification of pre-marital sex. Crucially, with this prioritizing of planned families, the equal advantage offered by contraception – the eradication of fears of unwanted pregnancies and the consequent enhancement of sexual pleasure – was silenced.

In the 'modernization' of contraception, we can see all of these features of planning very clearly. First, the establishment of a desired end (or ends) – the management of population and the related reduction of family size, and of infant and maternal mortality rates. Additionally, there was the more humanistic element, that of the improvement of the quality of life for those of child-bearing age. Second, the emergence of experts – both medical and moral (sometimes conflated), whose task it was not just to direct the use of effective means, but to devise blueprints that would both ensure the most effective end and remove from the equation, as much as possible, the presence of unpredictability, in this case misdirected sexual desire. Properly promoted, contraception offered the first means by which sexual desire and its outcomes could be rendered predictable and therefore containable. For whatever its promotion as being of universal advantage, the planning of procreation, like industrial production or the layout of cities, inevitably and crucially entails regulation and therefore control.

The measured provision of birth control by a medical profession that was by definition conservative in its attitudes to sexual morality, offered the possibility of planned sex. And as with other spheres of planned social provision, it was the professionals who arbitrated on the legitimacy of the end for which the means were to be utilized. The basis on which planned sex was made respectable was not the needs of the individual woman, but the judicious maintenance of her maternal health by the medical profession. In the political climate which promoted the notion of forward planning, contraception offered the possibility of overcoming the unpredictability of the population's procreative behaviour. The collection of pressure groups that comprised the National Birth Control Association was, in 1939, consolidated under a new name, the Family Planning Association, whose stated objectives were:

(i) to advocate and promote the provision of facilities for scientific contraception so that married people may space or limit their families and thus mitigate the evils of ill-health and poverty and (ii) to establish

Women's Health Centres where, in addition to contraceptive advice, treatment and advice could be sought for involuntary sterility, minor gynaecological ailments and marital difficulties.

(quoted in Leathard 1980: 60)

These aims were far removed from the attitudes which so vehemently opposed the promotion of birth control thirty or even twenty years earlier. The same components that had led to anxiety about the negative and undesirable effects of freer availability of birth control, which had their roots in anxieties about sexual behaviour, were now rearranged to present a positive and desirable picture of planned and plannable marital sex.

## 5.4  Family planning sex

Whether trying to induce people to smoke, to drive a car or to wear hats, advertising has stressed, and where necessary invented, the sexual rewards, and has conspicuously ignored the implications for health and pocketbook. How can we account for family planning's astonishing failure to publicise the universal predominant and immediate advantage of contraception – enhanced and unencumbered sexual pleasure?

(Stycos 1977: 287)

The desirability of an ordered management of the troubled issue of birth control finally led to its being accepted within a narrow legitimating framework, narrow in the sense that the confinement of sex to marriage, whatever the mores people adhered to publicly, was an unrealistic and unrealized ideal. Yet the name 'family planning' implicitly supported both planning and intra-marital sex. In the context of family planning, sexual pleasure was a silent partner – with the exception of Marie Stopes. In 1918, Stopes published *Married Love* and *Wise Parenthood*, which by 1927 had gone to 14 editions, selling 465,000 copies and being translated into seven languages. In addition to providing details of mechanical and chemical methods of birth control, the contents of *Married Love* in particular was distinguished by her promotion of sexual pleasure, and the role of birth control in assuring this. In 1923, she opened her first clinic in Whitfield Road, London, which was to attract 5000 women in the next five years.

Her outspoken promotion of sexual pleasure and of birth control, coupled with her obvious success despite her lack of medical qualifications (she was a Doctor of Science), did not endear her to the medical establishment. In 1922, she was accused by a prominent physician of 'experimenting on the poor', a charge which led to a highly publicized libel case the following year. The account of this trial, which became, as Box (1967), suggested, 'the trial of Marie Stopes', highlights the moral dilemmas posed by the provision of birth control. Objections against *Married Love* centred on detailed descriptions of sexual intercourse that emphasized the attainment of pleasure for both man and woman. Stopes was asked by the defending council, 'what does a girl want to know that for?' and 'would not the knowledge of contraception and sexual methods increase unpropitious behaviour?' (Box 1967:

118). The issue was the connections made between use of contraception and sexual pleasure. Council for the defence asked: 'are not the two things quite separate from each other? Why in order to teach a young girl about sex are you to talk to her of check pessaries, and why in order to teach a married woman the use of the check pessary are you to write also about sex?' (ibid., p. 171).

The misgivings about the consequences of sexual licence implied by the provision of contraception constituted a theme that was never fully resolved in the context of ordered planned parenthood. The increased availability of birth control and the successful promotion by its well-organized supporters in the first three decades of the twentieth century changed the relationship between sex and reproduction. On the one hand, there was, at least in principle, the choice for women to have 'non-reproductive sex'. While this offered a solution to the infant and maternal mortality consequent on large families and low incomes, it also meant that, for the first time, women could experience sexual pleasure freed from the fear of unwanted pregnancy. This presented two problems, which were evidenced in the arguments of the opponents of contraception.

Increased availability of contraception occurred at a time when the traditional sexual division of labour, which cast women as mothers and curators of the home, was already under pressure from changes in women's expectations about education, work experience outside the home and about their sexual autonomy. Contraception offered, in principle, a direct challenge to the idea that for so long had equated women's sexuality with their procreative instincts. In extreme forms, this took the view that women's capacity for sexual pleasure was derived from their knowledge that conception would result from the sexual act.

The second perceived problem raised by the availability of contraception was that it offered a free licence in sexual pleasure. The question of who benefited from this was to divide the first feminist movements over the Contagious Diseases Acts and the later promotion of social purity (Walkowitz 1983; Bland 1985; Mort 1987). For many feminists, the freedom of sexual pleasure was accorded only to men. This opposition to birth control was informed by the view of women's sexual passivity – that there was an essential difference between men's and women's sexual appetites. In this view, male sexual appetites were insatiable, and the removal of the fear of pregnancy would remove one more obstacle to sexual satisfaction. It would remove, also, a traditional defence for women against male sexual demands. Yet, as has already been argued in preceding chapters, the pronouncements about women's sexual passivity contained an undercurrent of anxieties, of much longer standing, about the dark uncivilizable side of women's sexuality, which were held in fragile check by their maternal instincts. These anxieties were not explicitly stated, but were implicit in the argument that suggested birth control meant sexual excess.

On the other hand, if birth control methods continued to be withheld, unregulated 'reproductive sex', which had led to 'over-breeding' among certain categories of the poor, would continue. Once again, these anxieties contained a recognition of the presence of ungovernable sensuality, which was reflected in procreative profligacy. These were the dilemmas that had somehow to be resolved or at least negotiated. In one sense they were contained by the restriction of contraception to married women, and only under specific and medically defined circumstances. Sexual autonomy was thus conditional, contained within frameworks of patriarchal control. Anxieties about unwarranted sexual freedoms implied by the sanction of contraception were muted until the 'problem of the unmarried' rekindled them. Pre-marital advice had always posed a problem for the Family Planning Association (FPA). Its brief was concerned with the spacing of births, not the sex lives of women. Although the Association held that children should be born by choice not by chance, this had to be set against its striving for organizational respectability: treating the unmarried was not respectable (Leathard 1980: 138). This view came increasingly in conflict with the evidence that young people were having pre-marital sex and evidence that illegitimate births as well as abortions, sometimes in the very young, continued to rise (Grahame 1989).

By the mid-1960s, the issue of 'the unmarried' was being debated within the FPA, but it was Helen Brook, a fiercely independent member of the FPA, who took it upon herself to resolve the question. In 1964, with the aid of private funding, she opened the first Brook Advisory Centre in Whitfield Street, London. Between 1964 and 1970, seven others followed in major cities. The centres were committed to providing not only advice and treatment on contraception and abortion, but also sexual and emotional counselling. In 1967, both the Abortion Act and the NHS (Family Planning) Act were passed, testimony perhaps to the effectiveness of more than three decades campaigning rather than the final resolution of the misgivings that continued to surround these issues. The NHS (Family Planning) Act gave official approval for provision of contraception in local authority clinics to the unmarried but, significantly, did not make it compulsory. Left to the discretion of the medical profession, and lacking unequivocal political support, provision of contraception to anyone who wasn't married or a family planner remained vulnerable to regressive regulation.

In 1984, Victoria Gillick was successful in challenging the looseness of the Act's structure, in a short but highly publicized campaign to prevent the provision of contraception to young women under sixteen without their parents' consent. Though ten months later the Ruling was overturned by the House of Lords, the success of Gillick and the terms of the debate surrounding the campaign were sufficient illustration that there persisted a view that birth control would mean sexual excess, particularly in the case of young unmarried women. The significance of the Gillick case was that it illustrated the extent to which many old anxieties remained under the facade of modernization. The idea that the provision of contraception outside the constraints of marital monogamy and in the context of youthful sexuality would result in sexual promiscuity lay at the centre of Gillick's campaign. That it was initially successful, albeit for a short term, suggests that these views were not confined to one eccentric individual. The anxieties about free access to contraception for young unmarried women suggest a perception that such conditions would encourage a sexual autonomy in women based on individual pursuit of pleasure. Put another way, the prioritization of marriage and of stable monogamy implicit in the later emphasis on age as the qualifying factor suggested that acceptable sex – that is, sex which does not give rise to any anxiety – was that undertaken within a given framework with a predictable outcome – marriage and parenthood. Despite the advantages offered by the planning motif for the ordering of heterosexual desire, the troublesome elements in the connection between freedom from fecundity and increased sexual pleasure would not go away, fuelled as they were by tensions that persist today.

In Volume 1 of his *History of Sexuality*, Foucault (1979) introduces the central theme – the isolation and examination of discourses about sexuality. Foucault emphasizes that his primary aim is not to examine the *content* of what was and is said about sex, whether positive or negative. Ignoring the fact of repression or celebration of sex and looking instead at who speaks and in what contexts discourses develop, clarifies the ordering, the prioritization and the parameters of what does and does not constitute sex. Moreover, the co-existence of apparently contradictory discourses about sex can be explained: how in one context sex can be promoted and accepted, while in another marginalized and discouraged (ibid., p. 11). The tensions which remain evident in the issue of contraceptive provision illustrate these points well. In a study conducted in 1988, three years after the Gillick Ruling was overturned by the House of Lords, a small cohort of family planning professionals practising in the inner area of a large conurbation were interviewed about their attitudes to the issue which the Gillick Ruling had raised – namely, the concerns associated with the provision of contraception for young and unmarried clients. The ways in which these concerns were expressed suggests that planning sex via the rational use of contraception is not completely successful in overcoming the chaotic potential of expressions of sexuality outside the confines of marital monogamy (Hawkes 1995).

There were a number of ways in which these concerns were voiced. First, there was the issue of age. As Jackson (1982: 49) has said: 'the desire to conceal sex from children reflects not only our ideas of what is good and bad for them, but also adult fears and anxieties about sexuality'. Jackson also points out that the connection between children and sex 'is to bring together two sets of issues which are highly emotive, that readily promote moral outrage and righteous indignation' (ibid., p. 1). While on the one hand official circulars direct local authorities to provide contraceptive advice and treatment regardless of age and marital status, the attendance of young teenage women at family planning clinics unavoidably confronts the troublesome connection between children and sex. Despite the medical framework in which family planning consultations take place, anxieties about *social* consequences were evident, expressed in the context of the age of the young women. These were further expressed in the context of their imputed sexual behaviour. The following comment from a study undertaken in family planning clinics, in which practitioners were asked about their views on these issues (Hawkes 1991), is suggestive of this:

> *Nurse #1 (28 years):* I think to a large extent that [The Gillick Ruling] gave them the excuse they had been looking for to say no, we don't

want to prescribe for the under-sixteens . . . the odd doctor will do, but I think on the whole they tend to take them in and frighten them to death about cervical cancer. They're not really interested in finding out if the girl is already having sex, they're more interested in the fact that if they're having sex and they're on the pill, they're more likely to get cancer of the cervix.

The anxiety that contraception encourages promiscuous sexual behaviour is here expressed through the prism of a medical rather than moral discourse. While there is no formal exclusion of access to the necessary contraceptive knowledge, the mystique of medical knowledge is deployed informally to impose constraints through the attachment of risk to sexual behaviour. The difficulties raised by the tacit encouragement of under-age sex in prescribing for a fourteen-year-old might be expected to be overcome once the age of consent has been reached. In pursuing the source of the reluctance to prescribe for young women, I asked the same respondent whether there was an age at which these concerns with age abated:

*Nurse #1 (28 years):* It seems to be sixteen. Sixteen seems to be the OK age. There's never any question that they [the doctors] can't prescribe for a sixteen year old. Although quite often they do go through that they do face dangers of cancer of the cervix. There are a few doctors who will talk to them, and if they still want to go on the pill they will put them on the pill, in the circumstances where the girl is already sleeping with her boyfriend. But if they're not, they will say 'go away and think about it for a few months and then see how you feel'. I mean, if they are going to sleep with them, they're going to sleep with them, aren't they?'

It would appear, then, that the legality of the sexual act of the young woman does not overcome the disquiet about her sexuality; yet once again this disquiet is not expressed through outright refusal of the request. The message conveyed to the young woman is that such expression of her sexuality is premature and potentially dangerous to her health. Sex (for the young) is presented as being medically dangerous, not morally bad. Yet the medical consequences of sexual intercourse cannot, logically, disappear after a certain age. Behind this medical concern is another threat to successful 'planned sex'. The words 'responsible' and 'irresponsible' were a strikingly consistent feature of the conversations with the professionals. In every case, the words were used in relation to the sexual and contraceptive behaviour of young women. One respondent was quite explicit in relating irresponsibility to sexual behaviour, while at the same time distinguishing between the general social and specifically family planning context of this judgement:

*Doctor #2 (45 years):* I think fourteen or fifteen year olds are completely and utterly sexually irresponsible. I mean, sexual mores at this time make it [sex] highly acceptable. I think contraception is a side issue. I don't think it makes any difference at all. I think if they thought contraception was not available they would think of highly risky manoeuvres to avoid pregnancy and find them unsuccessful.

Though at the more outspoken end of the spectrum of responses, this comment typifies, in its characterization, the view about the *source* of the irresponsibility of young women. The irresponsibility lies in young women's inability, by virtue of their age, to resist the encouragement given by the sexual mores. This suggests an uncontrollability about young women's sexuality, a quality exacerbated by the sexualized context in which young women live. For this respondent, it is these two factors, rather than the provision of contraception, which predisposes the young towards sexual irresponsibility. A selection of extracts from other respondents develop the theme:

> *Nurse #3 (48 years):* I wish it was like Mrs Gillick says, that because we tempt them . . . and all this . . . I think it's nothing to do with the case. It's society, society tempts these girls sexually.

The 'temptation' of young girls evokes an essentialist view of sexuality, uncontrollable and potentially destructive. The social setting provides inadequate constraints on such potential, and in consequence the professionals are confronted with a dilemma. Changes in sexual mores have an intrusive impact on their practice, because they pose a challenge to the ordered qualities of 'family planning'. The notion of contraception encouraging girls to have sex is underwritten by a further element in the construction of the potentially chaotic nature of young women's behaviour, which, almost independently of their will, predisposes them to irresponsibility. The 'floodgate' image of sexuality, in which sexual drives are, in essence, uncontrollable, is given free rein by the mores of a 'permissive society'. Each is presented as responsible for the turbulence of young women's sexuality:

> *Nurse #4 (40 years):* Unfortunately, once they've had a partner and have been sexually active, it is taken for granted when they've finished that relationship . . . as soon as they've gone out a few times they think 'this is the boy' and they will restart. And I don't think putting them on the pill makes that. They've already cast the die when they have been sexually active.

Once the 'die has been cast', girls are now subject to pressures of culture as well as of nature:

> *Nurse #2 (40 years):* They're always looking for a better sex life. I mean, every magazine you pick up, they've got all these poor women who can't have an orgasm. I mean, you get sixteen year olds coming in and saying, 'I haven't had an orgasm'. When you find out it's a quick five minutes in the back of a car . . . they're never going to have an orgasm, but they're still searching for it because it's their right to have it. Well, the idea of a sixteen year old in the back of a Mini trying to get an orgasm! . . . But I think they're all looking for it.

What, then, constitutes 'being sexually irresponsible' in family planning discourse? First, there is the perceived nature of sexuality itself. Constructed as a 'natural drive', sex is not easily subject to individual control. Yet there is also the recognition of societal influence. In either case, we get a sense of young women helpless in the face of both 'nature' and 'culture'. This potentially chaotic situation sits uneasily with the ordered, rational ethos of family planning. 'Family planning' in its accepted late twentieth-century form, is about planned contraceptive practice, where arguably not just pro-creative but erotic practices require the containment that the notion of 'planning' suggests. Young women, with their imputed characteristics, pose a threat to this endeavour. Their ability to behave in a rational and planned manner is severely compromised by their potentially chaotic sexuality en-couraged by the permissive society in which they live. Behind the unease about the idea of a 'permissive society' lies the recognition of the tensions between liberal notions of individual freedom implied in the notion of re-sponsibility, and the socially undesirable consequences of *some* individuals exercising this freedom. Planning a family, under the umbrella of state pro-vision of contraception, is acceptable. But the dark side of the freedom of choice permitted by state intervention is the possibility that unacceptable consequences will follow. Choosing to 'go away and have sex with everyone' is one such undesirable outcome. However, state directives do not allow for the exclusion of such disruptive elements in the family planning environ-ment. DHSS Health Circular (IS)32 (1974) emphasized the 'need for contra-ceptive services to be available for and accessible to young people at risk of pregnancy, irrespective of age'. This directive was subsequently reinforced in 1980, and by the Law Lords' judgement on the Gillick Ruling in 1985. It is left to the discretion of health professionals to balance out these tensions in the provision of contraception for all who need it. The disquiet engendered by this tension is articulated through notions of the irresponsibility of youth and youthful sexual behaviour, through which young women are marginalized as responsible family planners.

## Conclusion

The gradual reversal of the negative signification of sex in the twentieth century carried within it a reinforcement of the primacy of heterosexuality, but it was a conditional promotion in which can be understood both a limited extension of sexual freedoms and the retention of strategies for regu-lation. The legitimation of heterosexuality as productive sex has a long his-tory. But one aspect of this relationship was constraint, which fecundity placed upon coital sexual pleasure. Methods of birth control have likewise been deployed for many centuries, but the nineteenth century saw a con-junction of exogenous factors which added impetus to contraceptive use, in a historical context characterized by increased surveillance of sexual desires. The increased 'democratization' of birth control had the potential for frag-menting the frameworks in place for regulating sexuality in the context of bourgeois priorities, and of promoting pleasurable sex over procreative sex. The early blanket opposition to birth control indicates the reality of such possibilities. The opposition continued until, once more, exogenous factors – arise in abortions, maternal mortality and illegitimate births – began to indicate that the negative consequences of continued antagonism to birth control outweighed those of its conditional approval (Davies 1980).

   Family planning was the rubric under which the disorderly potentials of both non-reproductive (and pleasurable) sex and the democratization of contraception could be contained. Planned sex might or might not be reproductive, but it was a mode of expression of sexual desire that was motivated and ordered by a rational model. Planned sex was also heterosexual sex, its twinning with family planning retaining as primary a context of at least stable monogamy if not marriage. This deployment of the notion of planned sex was not, it has been suggested, entirely successful in circumscribing undesirable consequences of the valorization of heterosexuality. In the contexts of family planning clinics, whose rationale was the promotion of planned sex, the activities of putative 'family planners', whose sexual lifestyles are deemed inimical to planning, strikes a jarring note. The responses to these 'unwanted guests' suggest that the promotion of planned sex has left untouched pockets of anxiety about the characteristics of sex that have a much longer history.

# 6 Pleasurable sex

In the wake of increasing anxieties about the implication that small families and rising divorce rates were having for the stability of the family, more attention was being paid to ways of achieving greater companionship between husbands and wives, and, in particular, to sexual compatibility.

(Lewis 1984: 134)

A striking feature of the sexual discourses by the mid-twentieth century was the shift from the individual to the social. Emphasis was increasingly placed on the advantages of properly ordered expressions of desire for a healthy integration into both the domestic and wider social world. While the distinction between 'normal' and 'abnormal' expressions was retained, the causes and consequences of these categories were increasingly discussed in social rather than individual terms. 'Sexual anomalies' – functional impotence, adult masturbation, sexual incontinence and transvestism – were not indications of dysfunctional individuals but of 'emotional stress which is cultural or economic in origin' (Fletcher and Walker 1955: 152). The focus on the environment as the causative factor in immature or aberrant sexual behaviour produced a small but widely available literature on 'sexual sociology' (Comfort 1950). The leading writers in this field – Walker, Fletcher and Comfort – were all medically trained, and used the term 'sociological' in a descriptive rather than an analytical sense. Sexual sociology comprised not critical analyses but descriptions of the connections between individual manifestations of sexual behaviour and the social environments that were deemed to produce them. In what was essentially a conservative position, the overall themes of this 'sexual sociology' were concerned with the coordination of the more progressive sexual attitudes with the post-war shifts in structure and expectations of marriage and emotional relationships. Concerns were being expressed towards the mid-century about the negative influences on sexual behaviour of industrial urban societies, and of the increasingly evident contradictory influences of advertising, cinema and literature, which by now were reaching mass audiences. The tensions set up by on the one hand promotions of more traditional forms of sexual behaviour, and on the other the primacy of romantic love in the context of unprecedented economic and physical freedom of young unattached men and women, led to 'unsatisfied sexual needs and sexual maladjustment' (Comfort 1950: 47). The task of sexual sociology was to investigate the causal connections between individual sexual behaviour and the social environment. The aim was not to regulate the individuals concerned directly, but to provide them with dispassionate information about choices and consequences:

> The objective of sexual studies is therefore fairly clear-cut – to determine on a basis of factual research the types of conduct best suited to the realisation of mental and spiritual health and to inform the public accordingly, both by ascertaining the facts and presenting them, and by a cooperative effort with education and psychiatry to end a long-standing association between sexuality and guilt.
>
> (Comfort 1950: 79)

While widely circulated, and written for an informed lay audience, these texts were only part of a wider integrative process. In women's magazines and in advertising, the usefulness of sexual harmony was promoted as a vital component of social as well as individual health. Yet, as before, this promotion was conditional. Sexual pleasure was not an uncharted territory in which individuals were encouraged to wander at will. The work of the scientists of sex had implanted the importance of benign but expert guidance in its proper direction.

## 6.1   Challenges to the orthodoxy

The promotion of conjugal pleasures in the printed word is not a twentieth-century phenomenon. Nicholas Venette's *Conjugal Love*, first published in the early eighteenth century, was widely circulated and reprinted. The promotion of sexual pleasure in marriage was a central element in Puritan teachings. The curious distinction made in the nineteenth century between the erotic awareness of 'pure' and 'fallen' women halted all talk about sexual pleasure in marriage, whatever the realities of the matter (Harrison 1967; Degler 1974). At least within the orthodoxy, pleasurable sex was something that distinguished extra-marital from marital sex. This was implied in the much promoted characterizations of women's sexuality and, in particular, their severely impaired capacity for sexual pleasure. The effectiveness of the promotion of these ideas, and their lack of grounding in the reality of women's experience, is clearly evident in the anxieties, confusions and personal pain expressed in the letters from married women of all ages and social backgrounds to Marie Stopes following the publication of her elegiac tract, *Married Love*, in 1918 (Hall 1978). These correspondents expressed anxieties about their 'unnatural' feelings of sexual desire, or about their lack of pleasure in the physical side of marriage; their confusion over whether they should listen to their bodies or to what they had been taught about 'respectable women'; their personal pain in reconciling these contradictions in their expressions of love for their partners, and the notion of being a failure if unable to unravel these contradictory messages. The evidence suggests that in relation to any realistic expression of sensual pleasure, women were 'damned if they did and damned if they didn't'. Caught in the cleft stick of male-defined confusion, it is little surprise that many married women took refuge in a tolerant silence in the bedroom.

Stopes's book was a voice in the wilderness in the first years of the twentieth century. The impact of this small book was increased by the unique combination of romance and science in style and content. Her spotlight on married sexual relations shook the establishment and challenged assumptions about the 'naturalness' of the experiences of heterosexual coitus. Most shockingly, she uncompromisingly promoted the reality of women's active and pleasurable sexuality. Coming from the pen of an entrenched middle-class (if somewhat atypical) woman, and despite reluctance of publishers initially to publish, the runaway success of the book made it more difficult to maintain the fiction of 'respectable' women's sexual anaesthesia. The sensual supremacy of men, so necessary to the maintenance of the sexual double standard and the idealization of the domestic sphere, was promoted as being the dictate of nature.

The predominant theme in *Married Love*, given added weight by the author's personal experience, was the equal sensual capacity of women and men. While this may have well resonated with the experience of many in the privacy of their homes, it was, in many ways, an ideological bombshell, challenging as it did the central tenets of bourgeois sexual ideology. The works of Ellis, Bloch and Freud, which similarly posed a (more measured) challenge to some of the more rigid characterizations of female sexual anaesthesia, were confined, for the most part, to academic and scientific circles. Despite the fact that Stopes had to finance the publication of the first edition herself, *Married Love* sold 2000 copies in the first fortnight and more than half a million in the next four years. As Margaret Jackson (1994: 129) comments, 'it was listed in 1935 as sixteenth of the twenty-five most influential books of the previous fifty years'.

There was, behind Stopes's work and within even the more enlightened contemporary ideas about women's sexuality, an assumption that 'nature' was an insufficient teacher of sexual techniques, *especially* in the case of women. One of the principle legitimating ideas about heterosexuality, promoted for centuries, was that it was mandated by nature and was thus beyond the remit of conscious volition. Even the acknowledgement of women's lesser sexual capacity stressed the latent 'presence' of the bud of desire, which would flower in maturity under the guiding influence of the active and activating male sexual presence. Active or passive, the potential was there – waiting, as it were, behind the barriers for the starting signal.

In this ideology of natural sexuality, whether positively or negatively weighted, there was no suggestion of the need for instruction, for a natural propensity requires no education. Jane Lewis (1984) and Anna Davin (1978) have discussed similar ideas in relation to motherhood and the anxieties about the wisdom of leaving to nature the upbringing of the nation's children. There was a rapid development of techniques of mothering in the decades before the First World War, with their accompanying experts – the mothercraft instructors, the mothercraft manuals and the associated rework-ing of the ideology of natural motherhood with the notion of the need for expert instruction. Nature was supplanted by 'the experts', who could pro-duce a more predictable outcome by the more detailed breakdown of the stages of the production of the child, and hence could both intervene in and regulate the process. The anxieties that promoted this attention and the creation of a new specialism as well as sphere of surveillance concerned the condition of the work and defence force, indicated not just by adult infir-mity but, crucially, infant mortality. There was a growing recognition that nature provided few certainties in a world that was becoming increasingly distrustful of unpredictability of outcome.

The inter-war challenges to the bourgeois heterosexual norms came from a number of directions. Women had almost attained political parity, and the experience of wartime had begun to fragment traditional patterns of their economic and social marginality. Moreover, the increasing though still conditional availability of contraception offered the possibility of more per-manent uncoupling of procreation from sex. Anxieties about the consequences of these changes for an expansion in women's sexual freedom were evident in the concerns about, and strategies for, the containment of wartime sexual behaviour. Although these strategies were developed in relation to fears about an increasing incidence of venereal disease, there were, as Lucy Bland has argued, differences as well as similarities with the Contagious Disease Acts of the previous century. The differences related to the new focus on 'amateurs': women who were sexually active outside the confines of marriage, but who were not motivated by economic factors:

> The term 'amateur prostitute' or simply 'amateur' entered the debate almost overnight. Despite the ambiguities of the term there was gen-eral agreement that it applied to a young woman engaging in promis-cuous sexual activity for 'free' . . . The 'amateur' engaged in gratuitous sex and was believed to be drawn from all classes (unlike the working class professional) and to be younger than most professionals.
>
> (Bland 1985: 202)

Although these concerns were at least ostensibly limited to the impli-cations for the spread of disease, they pointed to changes in mores of sexual behaviour outside marriage. The incidence of women who engaged in pre-marital sex showed a steady increase in the inter-war years, rising from 19 per cent of those born before 1904 to 36 per cent of those born between 1904 and 1914 (Weeks 1989: 209). The permanence of marriage was also being questioned by the increase in divorce figures, first evident during the First World War but continuing to increase in the inter-war years. Caution must be exercised, as Weeks points out, in the interpretation of both these trends, for although the increases were evident, individuals who engaged in pre-marital sex or who filed for divorce remained firmly in the minority, both in quantitative and in moral terms.

These external shifts in the behavioural patterns of sex and marriage were matched by shifts in behaviour and expectations within the domestic sphere. Family size continued to decrease across all classes, infant mortality was declining, and the increased provision of both public and private housing in the 1920s and 1930s, all provided a new locus as well as appearance of the nuclear family. While the smaller, more self-contained family signalled a further 'privatization', activities in the domestic realm attracted attention from a number of directions. First, the home became a primary location of consumption of the proliferation of products from the 'new industries'. Second, with the erosion of more traditional family networks as a consequence of housing policies and a demand for a more mobile labour force, the management of a self-contained home was increasingly presented as a science – the birth of 'domestic science', which some of us were still forced to study in the 1960s! (Reiger 1985). This was both reflected and encouraged by the proliferation of magazines specifically directed towards the housewife, between whose covers 'housewifery' was elevated into a profession, if not a calling (White 1970).

## 6.2  Housewifely duties and marital pleasures

The structuring and organization of all the duties of the housewife in many ways mirrored those of the organization of work on the factory floor:

> *Good Housekeeping* proudly christened housewives 'The craft workers of today', and in advocating the application of craftsmanship to home management praised it as a 'form of service appreciated by everyone', bringing 'instant material and spiritual rewards'. It even urged women to take up a scientific training so that they could use scientific principles to help them solve their domestic difficulties.
>
> (White 1970: 103)

The pages of these weekly or monthly journals were filled with articles by expert advisors on diet, child-care, health and hygiene, even flower arranging. Although these areas of expertise were concerned with the service of others, the reader herself came under equal scrutiny. In the construction of the new 'angel in the home', attention was paid not so much to her moral function but her physical expertise in all matters pertaining to her life as wife, mother and home-maker. The relaxation of extra-marital sexual mores was paralleled behind the curtains of these domestic domains. The journals of the inter-war years were cataloguing as well as reflecting these developments. Articles regarding the changes in sex relations, as they were termed, and letters to problem pages revealed the persistence of sexual problems and highlighted the negative aspects of the sex lives of their readers. At the same time, these journals were also engaged in actively promoting a new marital sexuality:

> Freud, whether right or wrong, did succeed in convincing women that their sex desires were not wicked; that to repress them was as difficult and dangerous to women as to men, and that they need no longer pretend that *all they wanted was at most motherhood, when it was quite natural for them to want loverhood* [my italics] ... It was perhaps an

inevitable reaction from the false belief that the physical side of marriage meant nothing to a woman, to the obsession with sex which has prevailed now for some years.

(*Good Housekeeping* 1938, quoted in White 1970: 108)

This last echoes the tone of the rapidly expanding literature on sex in marriage between the wars. On the one hand, there was a stout assertion of the positive nature of women's sexuality and a break in the damaging old prudery of previous generations, the source of unhappiness and confusion that was felt to be reflected in the increasing divorce rates and the problem pages. On the other, there was evidence of a tension between the promotion of more relaxed and pleasure-centred sexual ethics with the possible negative consequences of the release of traditional strictures on women's sexual autonomy. The question therefore arises, 'how are the girls of the period prepared for a state of society wherein sex relations are in this transition stage and difficult to define?' (*My Weekly* 1920, quoted in White 1970: 107).

The answer to this rhetorical question might in retrospect be the wholesale promotion of marital sex and the marginalization of the life of the single woman. In the moulding process of the eroticized angel in the home, women who chose to remain single were told, in no uncertain terms, that they had a problem. For the rejection of marriage entailed not just the rejection of their natural roles as housekeepers and mothers, but increasingly with the promotion of marital sex, a rejection of their sexual potential as well. 'Old maids' and 'bachelors', individuals who had publicly eschewed the only sphere for legitimately pleasurable sex, had become pitiable figures whose sexual credentials were, to say the least, suspect. However, as White points out, despite the persistent presence of references to 'changing sexual relations', these journals stopped short of explicit advice, even if directly approached. 'Correspondents . . . often got no help at all, such as the *Home Chat* reader who was told by Mrs Jim: "I am sorry I cannot handle so intimate a question in these columns, and I am rather amazed at your ignorance about the facts of life. Ask an older friend to tell you"' (quoted in White 1970: 111).

Initially at least in this new cautious celebration of sex, the lead was taken by trained experts, usually medical practitioners. The terms in which sex was promoted showed subtle changes over the first half of the century. Despite their clear and conscious reversal of the former negative constructions which emphasized the physical and psychological dangers of sex, these writings now appear to the reader as comically formal and stiffly traditional:

In the old days, silence drove one of the necessary instincts within . . . We want to liberate the sex impulse from the impression that it is always to be surrounded by negative warnings and restraints, and place it in its rightful place among the great creative and formative things.

(quoted in Wright 1935: 8)

In the new discourse of positive sex, there was a conscious recognition of the costs of the silence and prudery of previous generations. It was these old denials of sex that lay at the heart of the marital misery, which became the legitimating basis for the promotion of sexual pleasures in marriage. The silence had two consequences. First, it had fostered ignorance and shame about sex. Of the two, ignorance was the more significant. People simply could not be left to their own devices to 'learn' about sex. Neither nature nor experience was to be trusted to deliver the desired outcome. Second, hiding behind silence and denial in effect left the sexual 'impulse' in charge – rational ordered sex was not possible without knowledge and education, and both required the fostering of positive attitudes. The exponents of sexual hygiene and marital education were clear about the social significance of sexual promotion, which went beyond the reversal of internal marital un-happiness. 'Each of us belongs to a community of the world, and will be a nuisance to other members of that community if we don't learn how to keep our bodies healthy, beautiful and in perfect working order . . . for the sake of the community it is up to you to manage your body properly' (Eyles 1933: 40–41).

Whereas nineteenth-century sexology operated largely within the re-mit of the individual – of individual behaviour and pathologies – twentieth-century sexual commentators actively promoted the normal. This strategy was consistent with the decline of the notion that all aberrant behaviour was evidence of congenital and inherent pathologies. This nineteenth-century pessimism was beginning to be replaced by a more optimistic faith in the efficacy of education as a reformative measure. The promotion of guilt-free informed and *appropriate* sexual behaviour was to be accomplished through two strategies: first, through an emphasis on techniques and, second, a form of moral hygiene in which the successful accomplishment of marital sexual arts was a necessary aspect of womanhood and her contribution to the moral and physical health of the marriage.

## 6.3 Enskilling sex

'There are techniques of marriage that husbands and wives need to know just as surely as the painter needs to know the techniques of his art' (Wright 1935: 12). Knowledge of sexual techniques were the antidote to the mentally and physically debilitating effects of sexual ignorance and misplaced shame. Lack of attention to the correct direction of the sexual impulse resulted in nervous ill-health, sexual starvation, infidelity and a lifetime of 'that ugly thing called mutual toleration' (ibid., p. 11). The techniques focused on the importance of mutual pleasure in marital coitus and the direction of the sexual impulse towards the ultimate goal – mutual orgasm.

> . . . for a marriage to be healthy, stable and happy it is necessary for their to be love, unselfishness and sexual happiness on both sides. With the women, the latter may be less apparent at first, but it should develop through courtship and marriage.
>
> (Hutton 1926/1953: 19)

In one sense, this promotion of mutual orgasm directly confronted the previously orthodox emphasis on women's orgasmic inferiority to men. Yet although it challenged one aspect of old orthodoxies, there was a continuation of gender distinctions along the pathway to this goal. First, despite the increase in pre-marital sexual experience (in 1938, 40 per cent of girls married before the age of twenty were pregnant, 30 per cent married at twenty and 20 per cent at twenty-one (Comfort 1950: 90), women's virginity, or at least technical virginity, and sexual inexperience were still expected. Women's sexual inexperience was, in terms of successful education, further complicated by their more passive sexuality, which presented a difficulty for, if not an obstacle to, the attainment of mutual orgasm. It was assumed that men would be sexually experienced and this, exacerbated by their 'active' sexuality, which required no 'fanning into life', instilled an urgency into the sexual education of married women. This entailed the sometimes quite tortuous manipulation of the gendered ordering of sexuality, and one in which the attention was focused on the ability of the woman to learn the skills. The promotion of the orgasm was the resolution of the still maintained mismatch between men's and women's sexuality and, to a great extent, their sexual 'motives'. For women's sexuality was not just passive and latent, but integrally associated with their maternal and caring instincts. If men and women, as it was believed – or at least promoted – had profoundly different motives for sexual attraction and congress, this would constitute an inherent fault line in the continuity of marriage – one which, in the climate of changing sexual mores, might be fatal to the maintenance of its traditional format. This difference must therefore be carefully managed and directed to ensure a shared aim and outcome. The promotion of technically correct sexual pleasure, measured by the orgasm, provided such a focus:

> Sex relationships in marriage must be prepared for carefully, must never be hurried or disturbed; must be mutually desired and technically correct, and of sufficient length to provide an orgasm. A clitoral 'sensation' is not the same thing as a real orgasm which includes the whole being.
>
> (Griffith 1948: 78)

Technically, skilled sex is promoted independently of reproduction. To use a metaphor of production, this is a division of labour for a different product. A division of labour is necessary for the production of technically correct sexual pleasure (the orgasm). This monitoring of marital sex begins before the marriage, with machine checks on the equipment. These, of course, are not necessary in the case of men beyond a cursory check that the required organs are in existence. For women, it is an all together more complicated procedure:

> A preliminary examination to assess the nature of the vaginal orifice is essential, for not only may the hymen itself be rigid, but the passage may be small and the muscles tight. All this must be attended to before coitus takes place. The proper person to do this is the patient herself, with the assistance of the doctor.
>
> (Griffith 1948: 208)

In a number of manuals of the period, the hymen – the proof of women's virginity – posed a problem to the smooth running of the production of marital pleasure. While some, like van de Velde, openly acknowledged the pain associated with first coitus for women, others went to lengths to avoid this, with detailed instructions for women soon to be married about prepara-tory dilatation procedures. This surveillance continues to the connubial bed-side, with equally detailed instructions about pre-coital entertainment, the distance of the honeymoon location from the wedding and the need to avoid excess excitement. Even the bed itself does not escape attention:

> Double or single beds are a matter of personal choice and the best of both is obtained . . . where twin beds keep their undersheets but are covered by one gigantic size covering. This gives both husband and wife the chance of close proximity without the overwhelming continu-ous intimate physical contact which can be mildly distracting for both at this time.

> (Hutton 1926/1953: 28)

The most widely circulated and enduringly popular of the manuals of sexual techniques was *Ideal Marriage*, written by a Dutch gynaecologist, Theodoor van de Velde, in 1928. This work epitomizes the male-centred features of the enskilling process, for although the initial instruction came from the experts, it was the husband who was to accomplish the sexual maturity (defined as attainment of orgasm) of his wife: 'Woman is a harp who only yields her secrets of melody to the master who knows how to handle her . . . his reward comes when the harp itself is transformed into an artist in melody, entrancing the initiator'(quoted in Jackson 1994: 164).

In addition to retaining the traditional sexual power relations between men and women, van de Velde's advice retains also the coital imperative, the ordering of sexual pleasure with the coital orgasm at the pinnacle. In keeping with his medical background, and in the tradition of the science of sex, *Ideal Marriage* deals in detail with techniques of physical stimulation of both partners, but particularly of the woman. In this text, great emphasis is placed on the techniques of foreplay, which include the erotic kiss, the genital caress and the genital kiss. The latter is recommended as effective foreplay for both partners, but particularly so for the woman whose orgasmic readiness may be lacking: 'The genital kiss is particularly calculated to over-come frigidity and fear in previously inexperienced women who have had no erotic practice, and are as yet scarcely capable of specific sexual desire' (quoted in Brecher 1970: 93).

This emphasis on non-coital sex may seem surprising in the context of the promotion of coitus as the primary aim. In this regard, van de Velde makes a critical distinction: whereas he finds cunnilingus and fellatio entirely acceptable forms of foreplay, '*absolutely unobjectionable and legitimate*, ethic-ally, aesthetically and hygienically' (ibid., p. 98), attaining orgasm by these methods, on the other hand, is abnormal, pathological and perverse.

Technical enskilling of the marriage partners by medical experts steered these explicit promotions of orgasmic marital sex through the troubled waters of sexual morality, which had been so evident in earlier anxieties about speak-ing about sex. Against the background of the new social significance of sexual union in marriage, and retaining the gendered sexuality that continued to emphasize the naturally ordained differences between male and female sexuality, the containment of this ordered celebration of sex in marital power relations seemed to have defused past anxieties about the negative consequences of ending the silence. Yet there was another element in the promotion of marital sex, which was directed specifically towards women and their role in this new marital sexual order.

## 6.4  Sexual hygiene and women's sexuality

Hygiene has to do with the maintenance of health, and hygienic practices are those by which freedom from disease is sought. But at another level, the maintenance of health has taken on a social as well as individual significance. 'Hygiene' in this context came to mean more than, for example, antiseptic practices. The social dimension to hygiene introduced a moral content – where healthy behaviour carried with it an imperative element. The deployment of hygienic practices was indicative of 'goodness', of a policing of self that went beyond the practices themselves. Much of this internalized morality involved the domestic practices of women. Thus, a good mother kept a clean home. Whiter whites were a sign of superiority. Hygiene moved beyond the domains of preventative practices, where it was a means to an end. Hygiene had become, in this moral sense, an end it itself. In the title of one source text, 'Hygiene in Marriage' was not about prevention of disease, or at least not about prevention of *physical* disease. Sexual hygiene was not concerned with the avoidance of sexual diseases, but with the promotion of what were considered healthy practices. These were practices that were healthy in relation to the individual and to society. In many senses, sex offered a bridge between wider social necessities and the increasingly privatized domestic arrangements that accompanied the rise of the nuclear suburban home. In the post-Freudian world of sexual psychology, sex was necessary to the health of the individual. But not, crucially, any sex. It was the attainment of correctly directed sexual adulthood that was the sought-for end in individual psycho-sexual development. Marriage offered both the goal and the location for this coming of age. It was this sense of the centrality of sexual health – indicated by correct expression of adult sexuality (mutually pleasurable heterosexual coitus) – which contributed to the view that the apparent failure of the institution of marriage, indicated by the increasing divorce rate, and the evident misery of many for whom divorce was unattainable, was due to a failure to attain sexual health.

The failure involved two factors. First, in the new positive construction of sex, the experience of (hetero)sexual pleasure was considered to be natural and desirable for bodily health. Yet this naturally ordained equation was complicated by the promotion of women's sexuality: passive and awaiting sexual awakening by the male. Much of what was said in the marriage manuals, as Jackson has pointed out, was directed towards educating the male in the techniques of performing this task. To this extent, failure of the man to heed advice would produce sexual unhappiness in the marriage, as the letters to Marie Stopes so eloquently testify. Yet there was a second and

more subtly promoted element of sexual hygiene, which was equally necessary for sexual health. This was specifically the woman's responsibility and
followed similar patterns to other discourses of domestic hygiene in relation
to, for example, motherhood. Having been told for generations that evidence
of sexual pleasure was a mark of the fallen woman, it was now the woman's
responsibility to overcome her resistance to a new shaping of her sexuality,
in which she must not only be the provider of food and home comforts but
of sexual pleasure as well. Failure to do this meant at least tacit encouragement for extra-marital infidelity by the man. For despite the sanctification of
the married monogamous state, the grounds for filing for divorce were being
expanded to include, among others, adultery on both sides in the Matrimo-
nial Causes Act of 1923 and 1937.

The sexual education of women was thus imperative for the maintenance of a monogamous and stable marriage. To some extent, this was the
inevitable consequence of retaining the gendered differences in sexuality,
and with these the centrality of the active male sexual appetite. Feeding the
husband the right food was not very far from feeding him the right sex in
the scripts of sexual hygiene. Women were warned of the consequences of
letting their 'natural' sexual reticence interfere with these essential domestic
tasks:

> If you do, you will certainly spoil your marriage. Do think things out
> a little further! You have in your capacity a responsive passion . . . If
> and when you attain to that experience your full womanhood will for
> the first time have come to birth. You will actually look more alive.
> The idea that by taking wholehearted delight in love's embrace you
> will become a less spiritual person is entirely untrue . . . You will find
> yourself more highly vitalised and therefore more able to appreciate
> every lovely thing through which the beauty of God is revealed to us.
>
> (Wright 1935: 15)

But although there was an ethos of equality in this promotion of
marital sex, this was more of a gloss than a reality. On the one hand, women
were expected to overcome the damaging prudery of the past. There was
almost an equation of modesty and prudery in which the latter's negative
connotations applied to both. On the other hand, there were definite traces
of the past in the sex manuals of the 1940s and 1950s. Possibly as a result
of the escalation of challenges in sexual mores during the Second World
War, there were now clear indications of anxieties about the consequences
of an over-emphasis on the physicality and the consequent downgrading of
the spiritual side of women's sexuality. There were, as well, less clearly ar-
ticulate anxieties about the consequences of an over-promotion of women's
orgasmic capacity, its relation to the clitoris and the more discomforting
associations with masturbation. Finally, in an apparently contradictory sense,
anxieties were also expressed about women who apparently refused to be
educated in this way – the sexual recalcitrants. Yet there was a common
theme in these anxieties despite their apparent lack of direction – the
monitoring of women's sexuality.

The emphasis on the physicality of marital sex risked encouraging women to relinquish other vital elements in their domestic roles, which were underwritten by nature. Eustace Chesser, a leading writer of sexual and marital manuals throughout the inter-war years and after, expressed the misgivings about the dangers of over-equation of women's sexuality with that of men:

> The emancipation from the thraldom of man will bring women face to face with a much more dangerous enemy that man is or ever could be – Nature herself. The rejection of the maternal role is not included in the familiar list of perversions which appear in text books – yet *it is the greatest perversion of all.*
>
> (Chesser 1949: ix)

Chesser was critical of sexology, which, he said, neglected the emotional and psychological aspects of sex. Encouraging a form of sexual anarchy in marriage, where physical pleasure was the single aim in sexual intercourse, would have had disastrous results, particularly for the woman. This anxiety must be read against the background of a still falling birth rate, and the sense of seige about the state of pre-war moral values. Encouraging physical sex had negative consequences not just for individual couples but for the nation itself. For in its mistaken promotion, women were being encouraged to deny their natural instincts as mothers, 'ignoring to their bitter cost the fundamental difference between the sexes – the maternal instinct which is woman's and woman's alone' (ibid., p. 73). Women who pursued the pleasures of sex for selfish reasons were 'killing the mother in themselves', Chesser warned darkly. For full marital satisfaction, women needed more than physical release. In ways that reflected the persistence of many features of former constructions of women's sexuality, women's fulfilment was integrally related to her role as mother and to her lovingly subordinate position as a wife. 'If women's experience of men and of marriage is happy, there will be fewer who will turn away from that happy spontaneous surrender to husband and later to children, in which the woman finds her real self and secures her highest satisfaction' (ibid., p. 174).

The emulation of the patterns of male sexuality, in which physical satisfaction was the indicator of success, were never fully embraced, nor promoted unproblematically. Wholesale promotion of female sexuality threatened masculine superiority. Ehrenreich and English (1979) suggest that in the United States marital sex was promoted as therapy for the whole family. And the provider of this universal panacea was the husband. As a 1947 sex manual put it:

> A man who is a good lover to his wife is his children's best friend . . . Child care is play to a woman who is happy. And only a man can make a woman happy. In deepest truth, a father's first duty to his children is to make their mother feel fulfilled as a woman.
>
> (quoted in Ehrenreich and English 1979: 219)

This enthusiastic marital pairing had the added benefit of ensuring appropriate gendered sexual learning of the children in the family. Yet sexual hygiene involved more than physical expertise; it entailed the monitoring and definition of motives, attitudes and priorities. Sexual re-education entailed not just training manuals, like those one is given with a car or appliance. The negative consequences of encouraging sex were to be offset by fostering the correct attitudes, motives and priorities, particularly in women. For this task, another set of experts was recommended: marriage guidance counsellors, whose brief involved counselling on a 'physical, mental, emotional and spiritual level' (ibid., p. 211).

That there was a need for this further fine-tuning of sexual hygiene is illustrated in a later volume by the other leading commentator and writer on sexual hygiene, Helena Wright. Her *Sexual Fulfilment in Married Women* (1947) focused on those women who failed, for some reason, to follow instructions and experience sexual pleasure in marriage. For Wright, it was the job of sexual science to discover why certain women have remained impervious to the blandishments:

> Dr Katherine Davis's enquiry conducted in 1929 may serve as a striking example of how the general public reacts when confronted by a question of this kind. Of the 1200 women who were asked whether they thought intercourse essential for their mental and physical health, 62 per cent answered NO!
>
> (Wright 1947: 31)

The evidence that women were refusing, despite the efforts of the sexual scientists, to take the importance of sexual intercourse in their lives sufficiently seriously, produced a deeper level of scrutiny into their sexual 'workings'. There was a new name for such women in the annals of sexual science: women who were in complete or partially complete 'sexual failure'. There was clearly something missing in the script of sexual enthusiasm that would account for this otherwise inexplicable phenomenon, and what was missing was an incomplete comprehension, on behalf of women, of the brave new analyses of their sexuality:

> There seem to be three misunderstandings which occur most frequently and these are: failure to grasp the difference between sexual response in the erogenous zones and an orgasm; lack of understanding of the unique role played by the clitoris; and the more or less unconscious adherence to a pre-conceived mental picture of what women *ought* to feel during sexual intercourse, which turns out to be based on the male instead of the female pattern.
>
> (Wright 1947: 46)

At one level, this represents an advance on the erstwhile male-centred and defined themes of sexology; namely, the acknowledgement that patterns of sexual responses may differ between males and females. There is now the recognition of the role of the clitoris in women's sexual pleasure. The sexual recalcitrance of many women who stubbornly refused to experience sexual pleasure in heterosexual coitus was simply a matter of inappropriate understanding of their sexual machinery. The solution was further mechanical training:

What does the clitoris need? The answer is *rhythmic friction*. These two
words are at the heart of the matter. Without rhythmic friction no
sexual sensations are possible either for a man or for a women. It is just
at this point that the general lack of sexual success among wives can
be observed and accounted for . . . Orgasm failure at the outset of sexual
experience is unavoidable if the clitoris is not discovered and correctly
stimulated.

(Wright 1947: 63)

Men know 'by instinct' how to deploy rhythmic friction, but women
have to be taught. In this updated version of biological determinism, it is
society not nature that is the source of this discrimination in self-knowledge.
In order to overcome this sexual failure and the social education that produced it, women must be trained in the usefulness of their clitoris. Now the
clitoris had been located as the source of women's sexuality. But this posed
problems for the primacy of heterosexual coitus. If the seat of pleasure was
the clitoris, what were the implications for the naturally ordained 'fit' between
the penis and the vagina? 'It must be frankly admitted that the vagina is a
rather mysterious organ from the point of view of sensation potentialities'
(ibid., p. 70), conceded Dr Wright. This problem was overcome in ways that
were to become characteristic of almost all sex advice texts, past and present
– a curious combination of detailed physiology and erotica. The complication for a straightforward promotion of heterosexual coitus introduced by
the acknowledgement of the clitoris as the *real* source of women's sexual
pleasure was resolved by the process of training the vagina. The reason for
the excitability of the clitoris was its possession of a generous nerve supply.
The vagina, on the other hand, had a sparse nerve supply but was a highly
muscular organ and, argued Dr Wright, like other muscles, required training
to reach its full potential: 'When a new physical action, such as playing
tennis or swimming is being learnt, it always takes time for the muscles
concerned to acquire facility in the new movements asked of them' (ibid.,
p. 71).

The problem posed by the vagina's lack of sensitivity is solved. Women's
failure to experience sexual pleasure is due to an untrained vagina – and the
role of the hypersensitive clitoris is to train the vagina's musculature to react
in the appropriate way. 'The clitoris can therefore be regarded as a kind of
teacher for the vagina' (ibid., p. 72). The vagina has to undergo a kind of
training programme where the theory of the manuals is complemented by
the practice in which the clitoris is the trainer. The hypersensitivity of the
clitoris and its consequent easy path to orgasm has another function:

Success in attaining clitoral orgasm is the essential feminine experience
which demonstrates sexual capacity, and that success automatically
removes the haunting sense of inferiority and failure which is otherwise unavoidable. Every wife who has learnt the behaviour of her
clitoris is reliable finds it easier to believe that one day her vagina
might also come alive.

(Wright 1947: 74)

Even in the face of what otherwise might be seen as a promotion of women's sexual autonomy from within a dispassionate and rationally ordered medical project (note Alex Comfort's description of the role of sexual sociology, to identify the most straightforward means to untroubled sexual pleasure), there persist many old ideas and anxieties about the consequences of a female sexuality that exists, sensually and ideologically, independently of male stimulus and involvement. This anxiety arguably has less to do with straightforward sexual and physical spheres but emanates from and reflects a more deeply seated and long-standing relationship with political domination. The indivisibility of the social relations in 'sexual production' from those of the often amorphous net of patriarchal domination is illuminated in the convolutions evident in the structuring and re-structuring of women's sexuality. In the context of the nineteenth-century bourgeois denial of women's sexual capacity, the connections were clear and unproblematic. But the climate of the mid-twentieth century, which had been influenced deeply and irreversibly by the lived experience of two world wars, and by the political gains made by women and the working class in a startlingly short period of time, placed a strain on pre-existing supports for patriarchal sexual relations. For any form of domination to continue to operate successfully, it must retain a degree of flexibility. The relationship between the promotion of heterosexual coitus and the viability of patriarchal domination may have been clearer within what Foucault called the 'repressive thesis'. But it is arguably more effectively operated in a climate that on the one hand values women's sexuality positively, but on the other denies them any real autonomy in its exercise.

## Conclusion

There are a number of ways in which the foregoing informs an understanding of the construction and reconstruction of ways of thinking about sex and sexuality. The striking feature of the discovery of 'acceptable sex' was its rapidity of appearance. In the space of no more than three decades, it had become acceptable, even required, to speak about sex, about penises, vaginas, orgasms, clitorises, with a directness only previously to be found in the annals of pornography and erotica. How was this to be explained? It was not as if there had been a wholesale sexual revolution in this period; as we have seen, the major planks of orthodoxy – virginity, gendered sexuality and marriage – remained intact throughout the first half of the century, with only virginity toppling from the pedestal in the decades that followed. What had changed was who was doing the speaking, and in what terms.

The science of sex did not stop with the cataloguing of sexual perversions in the late nineteenth century, nor the clinical electronic measurements of orgasms in the laboratories of Masters and Johnson. Sexology was not just a practice but an ideology, which, like all ideologies, operated on more than one level. A central feature of twentieth-century sexology and one which conferred on it enduring legitimacy was its commitment to the provision of factually based choices in sexual behaviour and its self-conscious denial of the existence, or even relevance, of moral content. The notion of informed choice was integral to the equally prominent legitimating idea of rational action – the informed (free) choice of means to a desired end. Neither the means nor the end were subject to moral scrutiny. Indeed, as Zygmunt Bauman (1989a: 28) has argued in another more chilling context, 'The civil-ising process is, among other things, a process . . . of emancipating the de-siderata of rationality from interference of ethical norms or moral inhibitions'. The dissolution of the irrational elements of morality in rational action allowed the scientists of sex to speak with impunity about sexual pleasure. For the consideration of rational action was the organization of the means in order to achieve, in the most direct and *reproducible* manner, the desired outcome. Bauman's book presents powerful evidence that a single–minded belief in the efficacy and legitimacy of rational action, and the silencing of the irrational and affective, encourages a condition of amorality in which the Holocaust was an explainable and predictable outcome. In relation to the rationalization of sex, the role of the experts and in particular of the medical experts was central and crucial for its popular acceptance. We have seen how, under the guise of medical expertise, not only advice but practices that might in other contexts be unthinkable barbarism were unremarkable; for example, the pre-marital stretching of the hymen to avoid the pain associated with virgin intercourse. Behind the veil of professionalism, experts invaded the intimate spaces of couples through detailed description of their sexual relations. The scientists of sex actively encouraged their pupils to cast off their outmoded and inefficient prudery with the same commitment as they themselves approached their task. The promotion of pleasurable sex in the context of marriage and monogamy was not automatically acceptable *because* it was presented as part of the model of rationality. This would be too deterministic a proposal. The suggestion is, rather, that the ways in which pleasurable sex were presented exemplified the effectiveness of a model of rational action in disqualifying moral considerations beneath the label of irrationality. The rules of this discourse make possible the discussion of other-wise undiscussable things, crediting the discreditable.

There is a further point to be made in conclusion, one which concerns both the issues of pleasurable sex and planned sex. Throughout this text, historical contexts are integrally related to the formation of ideas about sex and sexuality. The relationships have not always been direct, one-way or singular in their connections. At certain times, certain considerations and values take precedent over others. In the first half of the twentieth century, the dominant framework for the formation of ideas about, to use the broad-est possible term, social action, was that of efficiency of organization of its execution and outcome. This was the case whether the action in question was the making of motor cars or of healthy children. The primacy of rational action found its apotheosis in the organization of modern industrial produc-tion, itself epitomized in the form of organization that came to be known as Fordism. But just as the science of sex was an ideology in addition to a practice, so were the ideas that underpinned the organization of production. The motif of production was planning, a structuring of action that was intended to ensure a predictable outcome. The almost religious faith in the efficacy of rational planning went beyond its immediate instrumental advantages. The attraction lay also in older human preoccupations which concerned, as has been suggested in an earlier argument, the mastery of the more fearful aspects of the forces of nature, which have been equated, over time, with 'the irrational'. These unpredictable and irrational elements in human existence have been an unavoidable element in considerations of sex and of the constructions of sexuality. The pre-eminence of rational action in the ordering of human existence in the context of modernity, or of the civilizing process, offered an ideological context in which long-standing anxieties about the 'disorderliness' of sex could at last be overcome. There was nothing magical in this process. The application of rational considerations in the production of orderly sex depended on the presence of a body of expert knowledge, and of experts who would educate and direct human sexuality along paths shaped by informed choice towards a desired outcome – the production of children or of a stable and permanent marriage.

# 7  Liberalizing heterosexuality?

From the mid-twentieth century onwards, distinctive features became evident in sexual mores and sexual behaviour, the essence of which is the now familiar epitaph, 'the swinging sixties'. In popular imagination, the decade of the 1960s in modern industrial societies is specifically associated with sexual liberation. The decade has its own iconography – the mini-skirt, flowers, long hair, public nudity, hallucinogenic drugs. All were the domain of the young and all directly or indirectly involved or entailed open confrontation of the sexual mores of the previous generation. Young people of this period adopted sex just as their own children were to adopt recreational drugs as a marker of the boundary between their world and that of their parents. There was both truth and oversimplification in this popular understanding. The 'truth' was that there was something distinctively different in the construction of heterosexuality in the second half of the twentieth century; the oversimplification lay in the assumption that, qualitatively, different equalled better.

The most obvious feature of the liberalization of heterosexuality in retrospect was the uncoupling of sex from marriage and reproduction. While the availability of the contraceptive pill was one principal factor in this shift, it will be suggested that the disengaging of sex from marital monogamy entailed more complex processes, of which the development of the contraceptive pill was one crucial element. The second distinctive feature of the liberalization of heterosexuality was its relationship with the commodification of desire. It has already been suggested that legitimate sexual acts and sexual pleasures were those which corresponded to the Fordist production process – repetitive and reproducible detailed tasks with a single endpoint in mind, mutual orgasm. In this sense, sex might be understood as a product, an outcome of a preordained labour process. Planned, pleasurable, ordered sex was thus the reflection of a wider socio-economic ethos of planning, and one which reflected the prevailing ideological organization of the work process.

This chapter suggests that the liberalization of heterosexuality reflected many of the features of 'flexible accumulation' – an organization of the work process that was dependent on rapidly manufactured and short-lived consumption patterns for its viability. In order to fan flagging demand in a market saturated with 'consumer durables', products and, increasingly, ideas were promoted not for their utilitarian characteristics, but for more esoteric and fleeting, even at first sight irrelevant, associations. The common feature in the promotion of the qualities of the products on offer was the emphasis placed on 'choice' and the implication that making such a choice was a vital element in shaping, even creating, the self. 'Choice' became the lifeblood of late capitalism, a motif that was as dynamic and all-pervasive as its predecessor – 'rationality'.

The third distinguishing feature of liberalizing heterosexuality was the sometimes complex role played by women in challenging – both theoretically and in practice – the long-established and insidiously effective construction of sexual pleasure, which was, they argued, male-defined, male-centred and, quite simply, wrong. The final feature is the implication that heterosexuality has ceased to be a fixed terrain, interlocking gendered desire and institutions of lifetime marriage or long-standing monogamy. The work of Anthony Giddens will be reviewed and examined in this regard, particularly the potential of his reflexive selves and plastic sexuality to offer a truly liberalized heterosexuality.

## 7.1  Uncoupling sex

> The permissive era's object was to recruit women into active engagement in heterosexuality.
>
> (Campbell 1982: 136)

The 1960s and 1970s put sex on the market as an element of human life, which was not necessarily, nor even desirably, to be spoken about in the same breath as marriage, reproduction and monogamy. Yet at the same time, this 'uncoupling' of sex entailed more conservative elements, which continued to bind women, and their sexuality, to revamped but recognizably male-orientated heterosexuality.

Uncoupled sex at first sight was the antithesis of the previously promoted marital sex. Marital sex implicitly supported the stereotype of the supportive yet passive sexual hygienist, the wife whose responsibility was the sexual housekeeping of her husband. Marital sex was at least potentially reproductive sex and, despite the enthusiastic promotion of suitably contained sexual pleasure, essentially *respectable* sex. The respectability lay largely in the fact that however much emphasis was placed on sexual pleasure, the pleasure was contained within the fixed framework of a monogamous partnership, and reinforced by the ideology of 'the family' as the only legitimate site of reproduction.

But the security of this framework was beginning to fracture in the post-war years. The challenges came from a number of directions. First, there was a slow yet steady escalation of the economy, with an accompanying increased demand for labour to full employment. With the economic independence that this offered, women were less likely to see marriage as the only reliable source of economic security for the future as well as the present. Second, and relatedly, full employment offered the young unprecedented and early independence from their parents and the constraints of the parental home. The moral distance between parent and offspring made possible by both full employment and the 1947 Education Act's recruits to higher education, opened up a space in which an alternative teenage culture flourished.

In the 1960s, and in contrast to its former reluctance to involve itself in moral issues, the state enacted a series of statutes that were specifically moral in their subject matter if not their intent. Divorce, contraception, pornography, homosexuality and abortion were all the focus of legislation designed to confront uncomfortable yet unavoidable social issues. The unprecedented involvement of the state in the apparent promotion rather than restriction of sexual freedom was consistent with the post-war ethos of the benevolent pluralist state whose task was to balance and mediate between opposing factions in the interests of the 'greater good'. Christie Davies (1980) has argued that in regard to the Acts relating directly or indirectly to sexual morality, rather than actively promoting more relaxed sexual mores, the state was concerned to avoid the worst consequences of continued non-intervention on these issues: illegal abortions, unwanted pregnancies, fragmented families. The legislation was driven by pre-existing and increasingly evident problems relating to these aspects of sexual behaviour, rather than seeking actively to swing public actions or opinions. The 'negative utilitarianism' that Davies outlines sought to provide a limited legal framework in which the troubling consequences of illegality of abortion, contraception and homosexuality could be avoided.

Notwithstanding these changes, the central moral frameworks remained largely intact. Homosexuality continued to be marginalized as a sexual choice by the caveat of 'consenting adults in private'. Public displays of same-sex love were still illegal. Abortion and contraception were permissible in specific and straightened circumstances and remained under the jurisdiction of the medical profession.

Yet this legislation reflected and implicitly condoned the uncoupling of 'acceptable sex' from marriage and the heterosexual reproductive couple. In a context of full employment and the increasing economic and political profile of young people, attention shifted to a more serious scrutiny of their sexuality. Once denied or ignored, young people's sexuality had become a 'social problem'. In 1964, the British Medical Association published a report on the connection between venereal disease and sexual promiscuity among the young. This was the impetus for the commissioning of the first study of sexual behaviour in young people by Michael Schofield, published in 1965. Schofield found that at the age of eighteen, 34 per cent of boys and 17 per cent of girls were sexually experienced (Schofield 1965: 223). His findings suggested that the changes in sexual behaviour reflected an autonomous teenage subculture whose basis was the cinema and a 'media-created image' of how young people ought to behave (ibid., pp. 234–5).

Though the availability of contraception was initially restricted to married women, by 1975 the DHSS drafted a circular to local health authorities encouraging them to provide contraception advice and treatment to all women regardless of marital status or age. The impetus behind this quietly radical departure from traditional anxieties was not a commitment to sexual freedom, but concerns about escalating abortion and pre-marital pregnancy figures, particularly among young women. The circular was also a tacit acknowledgement of a slow but persistent trend in extra-marital sexual experience that had been evident since the inter-war years, but which had fed by the flowering of a sub-culture of economically independent young people.

The state-sanctioned relaxation of sexual mores, and in particular the availability of reliable contraception that women themselves could choose, suggested a full frontal attack on the traditional parameters of the formerly impervious heterosexual hegemony. Wider sexual experience was at least condoned, at most positively encouraged. Even firmly mainstream sexologists like Alex Comfort and Helena Wright were, by the 1960s, extolling the advantages of pre-marital sex with more than one partner. In the wake of the work of Kinsey *et al.* (1948, 1953) and Masters and Johnson (1966, 1970), the 'scientific truth' of women's active sexuality could no longer be denied. The clitoris had been let out of the closet and would not be returned. The 'discovery' and then celebration of women's sexual prowess was, from the beginning, a double-edged sword. On the one hand, it finally dispelled the myth of sexual anaesthesia promoted so vigorously in the previous century. Women no longer had to deny their desires and feelings. On the other, this discovery of the scientists of sex (no doubt not so much of a discovery for many women) was immediately expropriated as the principal component of a new construction of women's sexuality by men.

The theme of this new discourse was, if women were blessed with this magical path to multiple orgasm it was their duty to use it. The attainment of sexual pleasure became the new marker of liberated femininity. What might have offered the key to sexual autonomy for women was subordinated in the service of promoting, even rejuvenating, the heterosexual coital imperative. The enthusiasm with which this discovery was received was fuelled by the incorporation of the pursuits of sexual pleasure into the radical programmes of what might be called the new Utopian socialists. The work of Reich and Marcuse promoted the central role of active engagement in sexual and orgasmic freedom in the confrontation of the disenchanted and dehumanized consequences of twentieth-century capitalism (Robinson 1972; Weeks 1985: 157–77). This revolutionary potential of sexual pleasure became the popular motif of challenges to the Establishment, expressed through the media of theatre, novels, music and fashion.

As Lynne Segal (1987) has pointed out, this about-face in sexual mores was experienced as 'liberating' for those who came to adulthood in this period. Yet its siren call enticed many for too long to remain uncritical of the hidden agenda. But the enthusiastic promotion of women's sexual freedom within a male-defined paradigm had a number of unforeseen consequences; within less than a decade, women began to question the reality of the much vaunted 'freedom to fuck'. And they did so from a variety of political positions and experiences.

Perhaps the first consequence was that there was a specific separation of experiential spheres for women. The degree to which women could explore the possibilities of sexual autonomy was dependent on whether or not they were married and, in particular, whether they were mothers. In one sphere, there was 'the single girl', free, swinging, sexually uncomplicated and protected by the pill. This woman occupied a sphere of economic inde-pendence, though not one which equalled male counterparts. Her social independence was marked by living arrangements, by disposable income not drained by responsibility to parents or children – a world that was increasingly commodified, packaged and sold as desirable and a statement of personal freedom. The promoted figure in this sphere was a 'new woman' whose sexuality was not draped in the respectable garb of motherhood or modest femininity. This new woman was promoted as an unashamed and enthusi-astic 'sexual consumer'.

In 1962, a book was published that was to become the bible for many women (much as they might want to forget it now!) who had embraced the lifestyle of the 'working girl'. *Sex and the Single Girl*, written by Helen Gurley Brown, later to become the American editor of *Cosmopolitan*, unashamedly offered sex as an essential element in the lifestyle choice of single women. For Gurley Brown (1962: 75), premarital chastity was 'a cultural blight', the suppression of women's 'natural predilection to be sexy'. 'Being sexy' was what this book and a generation of its progenitors was to sell women:

> Liking men is sexy. It is, by and large, the sexiest thing you can do. But I mean really liking, not pretending. And there is a lot more to it than simply wagging your tail every time a man pats you on the head. You must wag your tail, or course – his collie dog does *that* much – but there are about five thousand more aggressive ways to demonstrate liking, none of which is dashing along to the nearest motel. You must spend time plotting how to make him happier. Not just him . . . *them*!
> (Gurley Brown 1962: 90)

Being sexy often had little to do, directly, with 'having sex'. In the hiatus of the 1960s, between the dismantling of traditional constraints and the emergence of second-wave feminism, being sexy was, as Linda Grant (1993: 119) put it, 'smart, not sluttish'. Being sexy entailed fine-tuning and monitoring of make-up, dress, entertainment patterns, living arrangements, even what car one drove.

In retrospect, the logic of this promoting of independent sexiness for women was contradictory. Ostensibly aimed to confront Gurley Brown's suburban married 'mouseburger' with the single independent mistress of her own life, this bible of lifestyle imposed a new set of imperatives which sexualized *every* aspect of women's existence. The single working girl had become another figure in the landscape of a manufactured market, this time not for efficient domestic appliances but for an endless variety of accoutre-ments with which to ensure 'sexiness' – the signifiers of which were as traditional and male-orientated as those which accompanied the figure of the erotic housewife.

However, this upfront, dynamic, commercialized sphere had a more shadowy and more distressing counterpart, epitomized in the contexts of the newly built, out-of-town suburbs. The homogeneous and untroubled appearance of the neat house hid the unhappiness and frustration of the women for whom this was life. The figure in this sphere is one who received less attention unless it was ridicule and disbelief. For these women epitomized femininity, motherhood and the perpetuation of the traditional gendered roles. Why, then, would they not be happy? In the post-Freudian world, these were the winners in the biological and cultural race, those who were able to realize their full feminine potentials. These women were also targets for the image-makers, who romanticized the chintz-walled prison until the inhabitants began to believe that their lack of enthusiasm for this nirvana was an indication of physical or mental disorders (Friedan 1965).

Mature Western capitalism drove the commodification of sex in this hard-sell of individual freedom, which was an integral part of the production not just of goods and services, but also of needs, wants and moralities. A central element in this production was the manipulation of women and their sexuality. As Juliet Mitchell (1971: 42) has argued, 'women were used, sexually and aesthetically to sell themselves to themselves'.

For what it promoted was, as the Gurley Brown extracts show (which typify the tone of her book, and to a great extent the age), was that sexual freedom, defined simplistically as more sex, opened the door for women to enjoy equal participation in sexual citizenship. The structural obstacles that had been the pillars supporting patriarchal domination for centuries had been draped in new cloth, but their presence and to a large extent their function remained. While these were more easily disguised in the hard-sell of swinging sexiness directed towards the newly economically independent single girl, they remained in high profile in the experience of women who followed the still well-cleared path to marriage and maternity.

In many ways, the housewife and mother was redundant in late capitalism. Much of the traditional domestic labour was dismantled by technological advances, although this proceeded more rapidly in the USA than in Britain (Mitchell 1971: 138). If the late capitalist family had left any role for women unrelieved by technology, it was motherhood. If one doubts that, still in the late twentieth century, a full-time mother is not encouraged to rank sexual desire high in her life profile; one should consult the monthly journals whose titles – *Good Housekeeping, Parent* – suggest their readers exemplify this category. The separation of spheres, evident in the ideological sell as much as in the experience, desexualized motherhood.

The dark side of this reconstruction of women's experience and context are graphically depicted in the work of Betty Friedan in the USA and Hannah Gavron in Britain (Friedan 1965; Gavron 1966). While there were some distinctions between the details of the lives lived by women who were 'captive wives and housebound mothers' (Gavron 1966), there were striking and disturbing commonalities. Women were disproportionately suffering from depression, tranquillizer and alcohol dependency, as well as other less specified mental disorders. For the still male-dominated medical profession, this was evidence of women rejecting their biologically determined female roles. However, the unthinking acceptance of the rhetoric of sexual freedom blighted the lives of a significant proportion of a generation of women.

In the celebrations that accompanied the decline of traditional constraints, these women were forgotten, or viewed as objects of pity – even
sometimes by their sisters. But the 'natural homemaker' and the 'sexual
hygienist' were to produce their own 'sites of resistance'. As Friedan (1965:
9) put it, 'there was a strange discrepancy between the reality of our lives as
women and the image to which we were trying to conform'. In addition to
Friedan's work, *The Female Eunuch* (Greer 1970) and *The Second Sex* (De
Beauvoir 1972: 72) spoke passionately to women's experience across the
boundaries of nation and class.

Though not solely or even predominantly concerned with *sexual* liberation, these hugely influential books and the equally influential grassroots
responses they engendered, collectively and individually cleared the ground
for the airing of women's experiences *by women*, not by men or male experts.
By opening the floodgates to women who spoke the language of sexual
autonomy, they confronted the male-defined and male-centred sexuality
integral to the system that had produced the 'problem which had no
name'.

The unintended consequence of liberalizing heterosexuality was that
the process produced its own central contradiction (or antithesis), embodied
in the feminist challenge and critique of liberalized sex. Second-wave feminism
challenged assumptions about women's sexual, social and political roles in
the public and private spheres. The centrality of patriarchy as the form of
domination central to women's oppression led directly to a challenge to
patriarchal sexual relations. The issue of abortion as a woman's choice, and
the campaigns against pornography and sexual violence against women, all
had as their centre the predominance of the assumptions about male sexuality and its expression, whether this took place in the privacy of the bedroom
or on cinema screens. These assumptions, which gave male sexuality primacy,
had not, feminists argued, been eroded with the apparent dismantling of old
prudish and repressive views about sex. The availability of contraception and
the relaxation of sexual mores likewise did not free women to a world of
sexual autonomy. The changes simply made women more sexually available
and more vulnerable to exploitation in the name of (male-defined) sexual freedom. Feminism sought to reclaim women's bodies from the male-orientated
medical spheres, which continued to monitor women's reproductive capacities. Women were also reclaiming their *sexual* bodies by gaining dominion
over their erotic potentials. Just as sexual politics were central to patriarchy,
so sexual politics were mobilized to confront it. Women were encouraged to
explore and celebrate their sexual autonomy, independently of men.

The trajectory this took was complicated, and at times contradictory.
The work of Masters and Johnson has been suggested to have been of central
importance in the promotion of a *women's* sexuality, as defined by, and in
relation to, women (Robinson 1976: 158). Yet their promotion of sexual and
more importantly orgasmic equality with men never really escaped from the
directive quality of earlier sex manuals (Segal 1993: 98ff.). For Masters and
Johnson, there remained in the celebration of women's sexuality, the strong
suggestion of a duty in the pursuit of the holy grail of the orgasm – a sort
of sexual housekeeping that implicitly retained the primacy of male-defined

sexuality. Yet Segal also argues that, following Masters and Johnson, there appeared a body of 'feminist sex research' that called on the language of bodily sovereignty: 'Over and over again, women were told by one expert after another "it's *your* choice, *your* body, *your* responsibility" . . . These women experts were also confident that women's sexual independence and fulfilment, seen as a type of learned competence would spread to other areas of a woman's life' (Segal 1993: 103).

Despite the fact that the much vaunted sexual freedom of women was circumscribed by, and retained deference to, a male-defined coital imperative, the active promotion of this 'freedom' provided a space within which women could speak to women about sex. The pioneers of this trend were Shere Hite and Nancy Friday, whose books charted in respondents' own words the sexual landscapes in reality and fantasy of thousands of women. However, evaluation of the content and effectiveness of these books is complicated. In one respect, they were ground-breaking in that the voices of the experts (for the most part male) appeared to have been, at least temporarily, silenced. While meticulously researched and presented, *The Hite Report* (Hite 1976) and *My Secret Garden* (Friday 1976) offered many women a sexual sphere of their own, through which, possibly for the first time, they could explore their sexual bodies. Yet, at the same time, as Segal has pointed out, women's sexual responsiveness remained closely associated with the behavioural models of mainstream sexology. Moreover, though opening up a sexual sphere for women, their enthusiastic exhortations to explore and achieve self-attained sexual pleasure fed the commercialization of women's sexuality by retaining the sexual, if not coital, imperative as an almost compulsory central element in their sexual citizenship. Finally, there was, despite some inclusion of same-sex desire, an implicit prioritization of heterosexual sexual choice, an aspect of the liberalization of heterosexuality that was the focus of radical feminist challenges.

The apparent creation of an autonomous sexual sphere for women had duped women into seeing as freedom what was in fact a more sophisticated form of sexual slavery. The situation called for radical measures to be taken and, given the analysis, the logical response was the sexual rejection of men. Women who emulated male heterosexual freedoms were colluding in their own repression and in that of their sisters. For women, liberalized heterosexuality was 'sleeping with the enemy', and a real challenge to patriarchal domination required the rejection of heterosexuality as its most effective script for sexual regulation (Onlywoman Press 1981; Coveney *et al.* 1984). The processes involved in the uncoupling of sex indirectly opened up a space for the affirmation of fully autonomous sexuality that consciously rejected heterosexuality itself. This development will be discussed as an element in a movement of sexual resistance in the following chapter.

The uncoupling of sex thus had both operated to reinforce and to provide the basis for a challenge to the heterosexual hegemony. But it was also a crucial element in the shaping of late twentieth-century discourses around sex: one which was directly related to the emerging centrality of individual choice in the context of flexible accumulation and the accompanying manipulation of consumption.

## 7.2 From sex as production to sex as consumption

A second element in the conditional liberalization of heterosexuality was the promotion of individual choice as an almost moral imperative. In the logic of Fordist mass production, the issue of choice was secondary to that of availability and usefulness. The famous maxim, 'Any colour provided it is black', testifies to this. The manipulation of demand for manufactured goods entailed the promotion of the use value of the products. People were encouraged to buy washing machines, cookers, toasters and vacuum cleaners because they made domestic labour less physically onerous. Other goods were promoted for their contribution to the quality of life or the maximization of pleasure. There was, in promotional advertising, a direct relationship made between the product and the outcome of its purchase. Fordist mass production demanded 'appropriate consistencies of individual behaviours with the schema of reproduction . . . a *mode of regulation*' (Harvey 1989: 122). This mode of regulation extended to spheres beyond the immediate site of production. Gramsci suggested that the regulation of sexuality and of sexual behaviour in specific ways was a necessary element in the sustenance of the mass production techniques of Fordism. Specifically, he argued that the sexual lives of workers cannot be left to the vagaries of whim or desire. Just as the activities of the worker in the work process must be carefully shaped towards the given end, so their appetites outside the workplace must reflect the prevailing ideology of ordered rational action.

> It is worth drawing attention to the way in which industrialists (and Ford in particular) have been concerned with the sexual affairs of their employees and with their family arrangements in general. One should not be misled, any more than in the case of prohibition, by the 'puritanical' appearance assumed by this concern. The truth is that a new type of man demanded by the rationalisation of production and work cannot be developed until the sexual instinct has been suitably regulated and until it too has been rationalised.
>
> (Gramsci 1971: 297)

Changes in the organization of production, from mass production to flexible accumulation, brought with it a new organization of the work process and an accompanying new mode of regulation. Just-in-time delivery systems, small-batch production, intensification of the labour process and the re-skilling and re-structuring of the workforce process to adapt to both new technologies and the requirements of the rapidly changing consumption demands, marked the distinctiveness of flexible work processes.

Gramsci's essay, *Americanism and Fordism*, draws attention to the symbiotic relationship between the economic political and social processes in the capitalist mode of production, and to the myriad of threads, often unseen, which connect them. A world dominated by the requirements of flexible accumulation demands another 'new type of person', achieved through the ideological shaping of expectations and motives in the life spheres beyond the workplace. Harvey has argued that in relation to the consumption patterns of goods and services, the distinctive feature is one of short-lived and ephemeral demands:

> The dynamics of 'throwaway society', as writers like Alvin Toffler (1970) dubbed it, began to be evident during the 1960s. It meant more than just throwing away produced goods ... but also being able to throw away values, lifestyles, stable relationships and attachments to things, buildings, places, people, and received ways of doing and being.
>
> (Harvey 1989: 286)

The significance of the product in relation to the individual self-identity is the central dynamic of the rapid changes in demands. At the centre of a 'culture of imagery' lies the advertising industry, whose effectiveness is dependent on the communicability of images and what they signify. 'Given the ability to produce images as commodities more or less at will, it becomes feasible for accumulation to proceed at least in part on the basis of pure image production and marketing' (ibid., p. 289). Harvey argues that the distance of the images from the 'reality' of the product from which they are derived, gives the consumer the illusion that purchase of the goods is, in fact, an indication of free choice and individual distinctiveness.

Bauman (1989b) points out there is a more depressing dimension to this marketing of delusion. Consumers have become dependent on the very endlessness of choices in the purveyance of imagery. The selling of products as a panacea for sexual insecurity, anxieties about parenthood, even the effectiveness of our ability to communicate socially, bind us to the values of the system in more insidious ways. The very failure of the goods to deliver these promises keeps alive, Bauman argues, the hope that the next 'improved version' will:

> The role of new products consists mainly in outdating the products of yesterday; together with the 'old' goods disappears the memory of their unfulfilled promises ... Jean Baudrillard said of fashion that it 'embodies the compromise between the need to innovate and the other need to change nothing in the fundamental order'. We would rather shift the emphasis: fashion seems to be the mechanism through which the 'fundamental order' (market dependency) is maintained by a never ending chain of innovations; the very perpetuity of innovation renders their individual (and inevitable) failures irrelevant and harmless to the order.
>
> (Bauman 1989b: 165)

For Bauman, market dependency occurs at three different levels. First, 'new commodities create their own necessities' (ibid., p. 164). Second, market dependence is created by the 'progressive destruction of social skills ... the ability and willingness of men and women to enter social relations, maintain them and repair them in case of conflicts'. In place of stable long-standing social relationships, which may run the gamut from friend to lover or life-partner, this element of market dependency leads us to seek fulfilment, distraction and self-discovery in products of the market, be they sound production systems, therapy or exotic holidays. In this bleak landscape, our relationships with people are increasingly restricted to their 'bit-player' roles in this highly 'individualized' market led process. Finally, the dependence on goods and services deepens to a dependence on the market itself, a belief that:

> ... for every human problem there is a solution waiting somewhere in the shop, and that the one skill men and women need more than anything else is the ability to find it. This conviction makes consumers still more attentive to the goods and their promises, so that dependency may perpetuate and deepen.
>
> (Bauman 1989b: 165)

With these insights in mind, re-examining the liberalization 'thesis' suggests its equation with what amounts to a market of heterosexual sex. Products, imagery, how-to-do-it directives, expert advice in magazines, newspapers or on television, 'special-interest' sex guide videos and books have all proliferated since the mid-twentieth century. The outstanding feature of all of these is the simultaneous emphasis on individual choice and the advantages of conformity to the 'latest fashion' in sexual expression. It might be argued that this market in sex, with its increasing promotion of disembodied eroticism evident in the short-lived almost vicarious nature of the discourses, has replaced that of sex in stable, fixed, more socially embedded relationships. The market in sex presents an ever-changing panorama of choices in which the individual is encouraged to construct their own identity through a form of erotic 'window-shopping'. One possible consequence of a market dependency in relation to sexuality would be that involvement in the choice of, and identity with, sexual imagery would become more significant than what is *done* sexually.

The liberalization of heterosexuality in the context of the transition from 'sex as production' to 'sex as consumption' is more illusion than reality. The choices that are for some the indicators of freedom are in fact a more subtle form of regulation through the myth of individual autonomy inherent in consumer choice. Belief in the disentanglement of individual sexual expression from the constraining contexts of permanency or monogamy, as erotica is increasingly expropriated by the directors of the 'image culture', is central to the effectiveness, both economic and cultural, of 'choice'.

## 7.3 Lifestyle sex and 'the reflexive project of the self'

In the introduction to his *Modernity and Self-Identity*, Giddens (1991) tells us that late modernity offers us, and perhaps can even be defined by, a proliferation of 'lifestyle choices', through which we reflexively constitute our self-identity:

> The reflexive project of the self, which consists in the sustaining of coherent, yet continuously revised, biographical narratives, takes place in the context of multiple choice as filtered through abstract systems. In modern social life the notion of lifestyle takes on a particular significance.
>
> (Giddens 1991: 5)

The crucial characteristic of the dynamics of the project of self and lifestyle choice lies not just in its reflexivity, but in the degree to which we are conscious agents of those choices. 'All human beings continuously monitor the circumstances of their activities as a feature of doing what they do and such monitoring always has discursive features' (ibid., p. 35). While Giddens concedes that such activities and perceptions take place within, and are in part reflective of, the material conditions of late capitalism, he suggests that the outcome of the choices and discursive practices are not structured by these in orthodox ways:

> In some circumstances of poverty, the hold of tradition has perhaps been more thoroughly disintegrated than elsewhere . . . Lifestyle habits are constructed through the resistance of ghetto life as well as through the direct elaboration of distinctive cultural styles and modes of activities.
> (Giddens 1991: 86)

For Giddens, one distinguishing feature of high modernity is the dissolution of the hierarchically ordered distinction between experts and lay audience. In this former arrangement, there was a one-way channel of knowledge and experience from the active 'educators' to the passive 'educatees'. In high modernity, the relationship becomes reflexive, a two-way process. This reflexivity lies in the proliferation of expertise associated with all aspects of daily life on the one hand, and the active participation of the agent engaged in the project of the 'self' on the other.

The second particularity of late modernity is that while the individual is confronted with a 'complex diversity of choices' (ibid., p. 80), these exist independently of a more traditional context that might shape or influence the choices along more traditional lines (e.g. class trajectories). In one sense, then, the 'choice' is not a choice in that one cannot choose between inaction (leaving things 'as they are') and the alternative(s) on offer. For there is no meaningful state of 'things as they are'. Late modernity lacks the traditional frameworks that allow for the inheritance of lifestyle. In these conditions, lifestyles *must* be adopted through choice (ibid., p. 81). In a commonsense understanding, 'lifestyle' is defined by consumer choices. In Giddens' work, lifestyle is not an end-point but a process, one which entails the *creation* of self in the context of a multiplicity of choices. It is not just the act of choice but the process of getting there that lies at the core of self-identity.

Lifestyle choices are constituted, first, by the existence of the context in which they are to be made. For example, to choose to smoke cigarettes in the context of evidence relating to ill-health is a 'lifestyle choice'. Second, they are constituted through our existence in a multiplicity of parallel worlds: workplace, family, friendships, sexual relationships. The domains of the public and private are no longer recognizably distinct but, to a greater or lesser degree depending on the context, overlap. Third, post-Enlightenment certainties about the permanency of scientifically legitimated knowledge have been replaced with a much less secure notion of 'until further notice' contingencies. Finally, choice takes place against a background of 'mediated experience', an increasingly virtual reality made possible by globalization of images and information. These conditions apply to the phenomenon of lifestyle choice irrespective of the individual capacity to participate.

The universality of these conditions which Giddens emphasizes, constitute the structural conditions under which choice in late modernity is constituted. The absence of the more fixed, traditional frameworks within which we *experienced* rather than *created* our identity, has conferred upon the body a new role and meaning. In a context in which our identity, sexual or in other contexts, is not a given:

> Body regimes and the organization of sensuality in high modernity become open to continuous referential attention against the backdrop of a plurality of choice. Both life-planning and the adoption of lifestyle become (in principle) interpreted within bodily regimes.
>
> (Giddens 1991: 102)

In what has been said so far, the body has been a constant presence. Sometimes eroticized, sometimes dissected, ignored or celebrated, hidden or exposed, the body in modernity has been, to use Foucault's terminology, both the 'object of knowledge' and the 'subject of power'. In high modernity, Giddens argues, the body itself has been disengaged from the fixities and certainties of the 'categories of givens'. It has become an integral and flexible element in the process of the self, both in the way we experience living in it and the ways in which we deploy it as identity in material form. This potential for active use of the body in the shaping of self can be seen in the management of appearance, of dress and adornment, and of how and in what ways we choose to experience pleasure (or pain). This experience and presentation of self draws from, and feeds back into, the proliferation of regimes – the ever-present guides for the proper management of self. What is distinctive about these regimes, Giddens' work suggests, is that they no longer operate as regulatory blueprints, underpinned by fixed notions of either/or, right or wrong, pathological and normal.

## 7.4 Illustrating consumer sex

The lifestyle journals that line the walls of newsagents might be seen as evidence of the ever-widening choices made available by the march of technological advance. In these 'bibles' of ever-increasing range, the distinction between advertisement and feature articles becomes increasingly blurred.

The tone in which the 'advice and guidance' is communicated lays stress, explicitly or implicitly, on choice – a curious mixture of the unique individual, released from gender-, class- or age-based constraints in a carnival of consumption, and the dedicated follower of fashion. One striking feature is the way in which 'the body' has emerged as a central focus for this making of self through choice. Whether through fashion, diet, make-up, cosmetic surgery, reflexology, aromatherapy, detailed and obsessive shaping of the body in gymnasia, potions for internal and external application to nourish, shape and defoliate, the body has become the most fertile ground for the cultivation of self. But the extent to which 'choice' in late modernity offers a mode of self-expression that is significantly independent from the linchpin values of social order is problematic.

The symbiotic relationship between discourses of self-expression and the maintenance of dominant ideologies can be seen in the seemingly inexhaustible fascination with sex in women's monthly magazines. To exemplify this connection, a sample of leading women's magazines on the shelves of British newsagents between 1992 and 1994 was taken. All those randomly selected featured prominent articles on sex. In one respect, these often highly explicit and detailed discussions are evidence of the 'every-dayness' of sex in late modernity:

> Wednesday night we tried alfresco nookie just west of the barbecue. Thursday we tried a vertical perspective, I wore high heels. Friday we were shagged out . . . Saturday massaged each other followed by a vigorous workout in the cutlery position, Sunday was exclusively oral.
>
> (*Cosmopolitan* 1994)

Giddens (1992: 2) has suggested that in late modernity, sexuality has been freed from 'the rule of the phallus, from the overweening importance of the male sexual experience'. Yet the tone of the articles surveyed continues to prioritize male-centred erotic practice. The following is from a feature entitled 'How to handle a manhood', subtitled 'The user's guide to manual sex' (*Cosmopolitan* 1994). The general tone is typical 'Cosmo', a series of cartoon 'willies' manipulated by determined looking cartoon women, with the only real visual image that of a half-peeled upward curving banana. There follows twenty increasingly explicit descriptions of how to handle the penis, for the pleasuring of the *man*, and of course to ensure that the reader increases her sexual proficiency. One example will suffice:

> After your man has been tied up for a while, sit astride his chest with your back to his face. Firmly grasp the root of his penis with the one hand and with the other, stroke upwards very rapidly and sharply. Wait for the space of one heartbeat and repeat. Do this 10 times. Then give him ten more strokes, but this time perform them in rapid succession, allowing yourself no time to pause in between. Alternate these two stroking groups for five to eight minutes until he screams for mercy. Finally, give him a spectacular orgasm by way of your hand, mouth or vagina. Be sure to untie him quickly . . . then just let him lie there basking in the glory of you.
>
> (*Cosmopolitan* 1994)

Despite the frivolous and humorous imagery (the article ends with the erect cartoon penis saying 'Got that? Now put down the magazine and come here'), the distinctions between this copy and that of what is marketed as 'pornography' are blurred.

Given the emphasis on flexibility in late modernity, one might expect a low profile or even absence of fixities like normal/abnormal, and of a sense of anxiety about correct performance, in which the performance of the woman in heterosexual relationships is the focus of expert attention. Dr Ruth Westheimer, an American media sexologist, gives the following advice to women:

The secret is to encourage desire. Functional sex can be technically satisfying but it's boring. Every relationship needs an erotic atmosphere between you even when sex is the last thing on your mind. When you phone from work, slip in a comment on what you'd like to do to him. Brush up against him. Undressing can be solitary and forgettable, or you can ask him to undress you, bath times can be private and sexless, or shared and arousing.

(Westheimer quoted in *She* 1994)

The implication is that _all_ aspects of the woman's day could (and should) be sexualized in order to avoid the dreaded sexual boredom. A sense of autonomy of self, particularly for women, is negated in the exhortations to stoke the fires of desire. One can never let up sexually. Similarly, in an article apparently devoted to exploring alternative sexual practices in the same issue of *Cosmopolitan*, a number of women interviewees indicated their unease about partner's requests for oral or anal sex, dressing-up, domination, or role-playing. The editorial response to these misgivings illustrates the tensions in the notion of women's sexual self-determination. On the one hand, their reluctance is validated: 'Our likes and dislikes in bed are just as legitimate as our likes and dislikes out of bed ... everyone's been made to feel as if she has a moral obligation to fulfil every one of her and her partner's fantasies'. On the other, saying no – *choice* – has troubling consequences: 'So if your partner asks should you just say no? Obviously you have the right to refuse anything that you find unappealing, stupid or offensive, but bear in mind that "no" is a harsh word to hear in bed from someone you love'.

The principle of the right to say 'no' is now qualified by engendering anxiety about *how* you say no. And we must even be wary of *why* we say no. 'We're insecure about change. Sex has become a comfortable habit for many of us. But comfortable can easily become dull', and sex must not be 'dull' at any costs, even if we must now not lie back and think of England but go and tog up in rubber.

In this brave new age of sex, the greatest sin is sexual boredom. And there is more than a hint of 'old' ideas about women's sexual roles and the process of their continued construction. The ubiquity of articles about sex in *women's* magazines underlines the persistence of the view that good sex, like good housekeeping, is the woman's responsibility. 'Sexual problems arise when one of you feels frustrated or censored in bed' (*New Woman*, September 1994). The answer is to *learn* the correct way to talk about sex. When is important: 'during a romantic dinner, on a weekend morning or afternoon, taking a walk together or having a picnic'. How is even more crucial: 'never say 'never' or 'always'. Avoid judgemental phrases or personal attacks ... instead of saying 'you're too rushed', tell him how pleasurable it is if he goes slowly. During actual love making use the 'caring sandwich':

A caring sandwich gives you a positive way to verbalise exactly what you need whenever something's not working in love-making without criticism or personal attacks. Gloria was trying to tell Rick how uncomfortable it was for her when he grabs her breast during love-making.

Instead of saying 'ouch!', 'Watch out!' or 'Don't be so rough!' as she had in the past, she said softly 'Sweetheart I love you' (the supporting statement), 'and I need you to be gentle with my breasts' (the 'no'), 'because I really am enjoying the rest of what you are doing' (the supportive statement). This caring sandwich was the first time Gloria could express a dislike to Rick without his getting defensive or sulking.
(*Woman*, September 1994)

Speaking about sex is so difficult it must be done in the right way (in case he sulks), in the right place (when you are both relaxed) and following an ordained pattern. The self-monitoring involved in these exercises is truly breathtaking in its depth and breadth. 'Work as Partners Choreographing a Dance' it exhorts as its final instruction, to ensure synchronous pleasure, the right buttons touched, but avoiding, at all costs, 'threatening his delicate ego'.

This article is followed immediately by another, 'X-Stasy – Legitimate sex aid or degrading pornography? Women are split about the value of erotic videos' (*Woman*, September 1994). It's not enough, it argues, for women to have sex because they are in love or because they want a family: 'There's more to feeling and consciousness, and not to be aware of them leaves one feeling vulnerable and not very confident'. This sets the stage for an 'ignorance anxiety'. 'How does sex work? What are my desires? How does my body respond? What are my boundaries? Should I do this just because everybody thinks I should? What really turns me on?' (ibid.). The heavy implication that lies in both the question and the solution is that the reader cannot trust herself, nor does she possess the capacities to overcome these induced doubts. Such strategies are familiar in other commercial spheres – selling insurance, health foods and child-care products, for example – in which anxieties can be easily mobilized and commodified. So,

Erotica can be very useful at showing people's behaviours, styles, and tonalities which they are not familiar or comfortable with . . . People are simply not aware of the tremendous diversity in style – not position, *style*. And, other than reading erotica you can't get that too much any other place except watching people have sex.
(*Woman*, September 1994)

This is unequivocally language of the contemporary marketplace, where lifestyle is all. Erotica is the equivalent of a fashion show, or a travelogue, devoid of any affective content, its role being to communicate breadth of choice. The endless advice, guidance, warnings and enthusiastic encouragements for new and different sex consciously seek to entice us out from behind the disenabling screens of embarrassment, boredom or just downright ignorance, and to fearlessly make statements, through our willingness to experiment, about our sexual individuality. 'Sex as lifestyle' presents sex as a consumer product. Additionally, the sex as lifestyle discourses seek to create a desire for these commodities in endless variations of 'choices', through which one expresses the self. The omnipresence of sex in the highly competitive and advertising revenue-dependent monthly magazines are testimony to the economic viability of such a project. Yet manipulation of consumption *the patterns of consumption depend on the 'showing of the wares'*

patterns depends not just on the 'showing of the wares', but, crucially, of engendering anxiety about the effectiveness and success of the sexual self we choose to be.

There is no question but that sex will be 'had' in these discourses of lifestyle sex. Desire (and heterosexual desire, at that) is assumed. So we are caught in a pincer movement: on the one hand, a moral imperative to have sex, since this is the central dynamic of a 'relationship'; on the other, if we 'have' it, then we are honour bound to avoid sliding down into the abyss of boredom. This is a lifetime project, and one for which we cannot be pre-pared too soon. 'Sex by numbers . . . Get set to multiply your orgasms', 'Find his G-spot by the second date' (*More!*, November 1994). This twice-monthly journal read by young women aged fifteen to nineteen years has a regular feature entitled 'Position of the fortnight'. An illustration of the copulating couple is accompanied by detailed instructions as to its achievement, and a 'sizzle' rating from 1 to 5.

The emphasis in this 'sex as leisure' is not only on how to speak about it, how often, where and in what positions, but is implicitly on coital sex as the summit of sexual experience. While the difference between male and female propensities for the pleasures of coital sex are acknowledged, their resolution in mutual and simultaneous coital orgasm is a matter of careful planning, education and execution.

> . . . the most blissful act in the known universe practically guarantees the man a flight to heaven, while women are put on standby and must sometimes take other means of transport. If someone could come up with a new position, then maybe this orgasmic inequality would dis-appear. Well, they have. A Manhattan psychotherapist has devised an innovative method of intercourse – a variation of the missionary po-sition – that not only increases the chances of orgasm in women but also tends to bring on that ecstasy of ecstasies, the mutual orgasm.
>
> (*Cosmopolitan*, August 1992)

In the promotion of lifestyle sex, anxieties about inadequacy and boredom are partially clothed in guidelines to attain orgasmic bliss. Hidden within both are assumptions about the primacy of heterosexual coital sex and the masculinist bias this rests on, despite the consistently reiterated theme of erotic equality.

The high-profile promotion of individual freedom does not just mask a commercial agenda, but more effectively dissembles an agenda that silently but no less effectively promotes and maintains key hegemonic ideas. Good housekeeping has been replaced by 'good sex-making' – the how-to-do-it manuals now instruct, direct and cajole the uses of female sexuality where once they instructed and directed in the use of the cooker, sewing machine or duster. Concerns about hygiene and culinary proficiency have been replaced by concerns about orgasmic efficiency and the management of erotic pleas-ures. While appearing to represent the final severance of connections be-tween domesticity and womanhood, the destruction of the 'Berlin Wall' that separates the spheres, there are significant sectors left standing. For the para-meters of sexual and erotic success are derived from those of heterosexual

coitus. This signals the extent to which women continue to occupy a differential position in 'the sexualisation of modern societies' (Evans 1993: 240).

> Just as male homosexuals could not be effectively commodified or
> politically incorporated as long as they remained illegal, passive non-
> objectifying subjects . . . so too actively consuming public women need
> to be reconstituted in commensurate sexually active forms, and this
> indeed is what they have become.
>
> (Evans 1993: 266)

The widely trumpeted sexual freedom has, in fact, been turned on its
head. The key to this, the clitoris, has been commodified through the promotion of women's multi-orgasmic capacity. Possession of these capacities
becomes the imperative to use them:

> A commodity is, in the first place, an object outside us, a thing that by
> its properties satisfies human need of some sort or another. The nature
> of such wants, whether, for instance they spring from the stomach or
> from fancy, makes no difference.
>
> (Marx, in McLellan 1977: 421)

But there is a price to be paid for the legitimation of sexual pleasures,
a tariff which loosens none of the regulatory fetters. Sexual desire, and the
means to assuage it now appears to us, as Marx would put it, in fantastic
form. The constitution of individual sexual desires, derived from our imagination and our capacity for sensual pleasure, is expropriated in a sexual
marketplace of commodified pleasures. The 'real sensual qualities' are obscured
by objectified mechanistic manipulation, in which the real sensuality is not
just assumed but occluded.

Sex as lifestyle is not, literally, selling sex, exchanging sex for money.
This at least is more straightforward. In such a case, there is 'a physical
relationship between physical objects' (ibid., p. 434). In the marketing of
lifestyle sex, what is being exchanged has no material form. It is not packaged,
nor is there a visible exchange of money for sexual pleasure. Moreover,
lifestyle sex is of doubtful worth in the enhancement of human satisfaction
or governance of our sexual selves. Yet it is clearly one which has almost
guaranteed appeal. For this particular commodity appears in a highly
commercialized competition for advertising revenue, without which such
ventures could not survive. Marketing strategies cannot 'get it wrong'. There
is too much at stake. This is a strictly commercial outlet for talking about
sex, on the face of it far removed from the clinical texts and laboratories of
the sexologists – Alex Comfort's 'anxiety-makers'. Nor does it, despite appearances to the contrary, offer the same promise as erotica. These are not
texts to encourage exploration of sensuality. There is an imperative quality
to lifestyle sex, which seeks to fix a sexual agenda through mobilization of
anxieties about physical performance.

In this respect, there are parallels with the masturbation anxieties engendered and promoted in the eighteenth and nineteenth centuries. In the
context of the dissolution of reproduction from sexuality, where the latter is
promoted as *the* principal marker of the individualized self, a new rationale

for normative frameworks has emerged. The anxiety now is not about the essential dangers associated with allowing free rein to our sexual drives, and the threat to physical health which this represents. In late modernity, lifestyle sex contains rather than enables choice. The new 'anxiety-makers' monitor attempts at sexual self-realization through 'choice', through the reiteration of 'old' messages from experts who hold the key to sexual fulfilment.

## Conclusion

The 'liberalization of heterosexuality' is a complex idea because it is both a truth and a non-truth. Considered chronologically, there has been a considerable loosening of sexual mores that can be related to a particular historical epoch or particular decades. Previous chapters have charted the valorization of sex since the turn of the century. Viewed 'from above', there has been a shift from sex-as-danger to sex-as-pleasure. From the inter-war years of the twentieth century, a reluctance to promote sex in any form publicly has apparently been exchanged for its enthusiastic promotion. Taking a variety of indices of social change – extra-marital sex, divorce, onset of sexual activity, availability and use of contraception, censorship patterns of literary and visual material, legal statutes – the twentieth century may be seen by future historians of Western culture as the century that liberalized heterosexuality. Yet a cursory contrast between this and the last century would reveal some striking similarities. In both we might accurately speak of a preoccupation with sex and a compulsion to speak about it. The equally striking difference is that at the end of the twentieth century, we are enveloped in a post-liberation environment in which the 'specialness' of sex – the anxieties, ambivalences, fears and preoccupations reflected in the overt regulation of sexuality we associate with the bourgeois model – appears to have been dissolved.

Such a characterization would be as misleading as the 'repressive thesis' of the previous century. It has been argued that liberalization cannot be understood either as a linear or evolutionary process, sweeping away all 'old' ideas in its wake. The valorization – attaching a positive rather than a negative value to sex and sexuality – has, on the contrary, been halting and highly contingent on particular circumstances and participants. This chapter has criticized the contention that there has been a liberalizing of heterosexuality from the fetters of past regulatory frameworks, which equated sex with duty rather than pleasure, with prudery rather than celebration, with stratified gender inequalities. The complexity lies in the fact that one cannot deny that these 'old' ideas are, if not wholly dissolved, at least marginalized and unfashionable. But just as historians challenged the notion of the repressive hypothesis, which applied to bourgeois sexual ideology, in their critical examination of both its form and content, applying a similar evaluation to the twentieth-century 'liberalization hypothesis' reveals similar intricacies. Proposing the notion of liberalization presumes the question 'from what?' If from the past, then the bird's-eye view reveals an affirmative answer. We are no longer Victorians.

This chapter has examined the processes by which heterosexuality was 'uncoupled', in which sex was legitimately disconnected from the pillars of monogamy and conjugality, while retaining the stabilizing connections with patriarchal sexual relations. It has also explored the promotion of lifestyle sex, as heterosexuality became a vital component in the dynamics of flexible accumulation. This incorporation depended for its viability on the overt promotion of sexual freedom as the mark of the liberated individual consumer, and was arguably one of the major influences in our largely uncritical acceptance of the superficial picture. The notion of liberalization of heterosexuality suggests the release from regulation which stifles individual self-expression. It suggests the attainment of a 'sexual adulthood' in which the paternalistic 'anxiety-makers' are rendered redundant. And it suggests that the high-profile 'specialness' of sex associated with modernity has, in late modernity, been levelled to the status of just another lifestyle choice. Looked at another way, these shifts are illustrative of the elasticity of the heterosexual imperative, a capacity for adaptation that parallels and, it has been argued, is indirectly related to the processes by which strategies for capitalist accumulation have manoeuvred to retain their primary driving force.

# 8  Subverting heterosexuality

We are often reminded of the countless procedures which Christianity once employed to make us detest the body; but let us ponder all the ruses that were employed for centuries to make us love sex, to make the knowledge of it desirable and everything said about it precious . . . We need to consider the possibility that one day, perhaps, in a different economy of bodies and pleasures, people will no longer understand how the ruses of sexuality, and the power that sustains its organisation, were able to subject us to that austere monarchy of sex, so that we became dedicated to the endless task of forcing its secret, or extracting the truest of confessions from a shadow.

(Foucault 1979: 159)

In the previous discussions, heterosexuality has been the central focus. It has been discussed in terms of individual sexual practices, defined as normal/ abnormal, healthy/unhealthy, pleasurable/dangerous, liberating/repressive. It has also been considered in relation to social institutions and social practices – marriage and reproduction – the changing structural demands of capital and the cultural changes associated with late modernity. In all these sets of relations, two features have been prominent: first, what constitutes heterosexuality is what constitutes 'acceptable sex' and, second (and relatedly), while what constitutes 'acceptable sex' has modified and shifted in the period of discussion, heterosexuality remains the dominant paradigm for erotic expression, and the one against which other 'sexualities' are defined and define themselves. This last is important. Where once heterosexuality was uncompromisingly promoted as a sexual choice validated by nature, in the late twentieth century such strategies are considered to be at least outmoded and ill-informed, at most reactionary. Yet at the same time there remains, in the constant reiteration and reformation of the parameters of 'acceptable sex', a clear prioritization of heterosexuality over other possible choices. In more subtle ways, the primacy of heterosexuality is reinforced by equating it not with the dictates of nature, but with those of the reasoned, free-thinking, consciously selecting, sexual self. This is one strand of continuity. The second is less clearly visible but is related to the underlying logic of the promotion of heterosexuality discussed in earlier chapters.

It has already been argued that the parameters of heterosexuality, both in terms of definition and of acceptability, have been shaped by and reflect the dominant features of modernity. Ordered, contained, aim-directed and rationalized, the dividing line between acceptable and unacceptable sex was marked, in some form or another, by a transgression of these. Yet a regulation of sexual expression which promotes heterosexuality over others has a longer history, and thus cannot be ascribed to the process of modernity alone. The continuity in the prioritization of heterosexuality over time suggests the recognition of a disruptive possibility. Left to our own sexual devices, we might be tempted to explore the full gamut of our sensual and sexual possibilities with catastrophic results for the central pillars of social regulation. To let the imagination run rife for a moment, the logic and formation of coupleships would be redundant. Children could be conceived without coitus, not as a last-ditch resort by so-called 'childless couples' constructed as lacking a vital component of their lives, but as an aspect of extended 'lifestyle choice'. Sexual pleasures would be horizontally rather than vertically ordered, disengaged from the categories of hetero/homoerotic images and identities, and gender categories would be dissolved. The responsive flexibility of constructions and reconstructions of heterosexuality are tacit acknowledgement of these disruptive potentialities.

For the subversion of heterosexuality entails the dissolution of more than just how we express sexual desire. There is a further element which Foucault alluded to in his discussion of the deployment of sexuality. He stated that 'we must not imagine a world of discourse divided between accepted discourse and excluded discourse, or between a dominant discourse and a dominated one' (Foucault 1979: 100). The discourse of heterosexuality is not, therefore, a fixed entity, nor is its position or the conditions under which it is constituted inviolable. 'We must make allowance', Foucault continues,

> for the complex and unstable process whereby discourse can be both an instrument and an effect of power, but also a hindrance, a stumbling block, *a point of resistance and a starting point for an opposing strategy* [my emphasis]. Discourse transmits and produces power; it reinforces it, but also undermines and exposes it, renders it fragile and makes it possible to thwart it.
>
> (Foucault 1979: 101)

This chapter explores this notion in the light of the challenges to the heterosexual paradigm that have emerged in the second half of the twentieth century. I begin by reviewing the related yet distinct challenges to the primacy posed by the political deployment of gay and lesbian sexuality. A comprehensive review that would do justice to the complexity of the strategies and their success will not be attempted in the space available. Instead, the deployment of sexual signifiers of 'masculinity' and 'femininity', the relationship between the coital imperative and male domination, the almost aggressive promotion of heterosexual pleasure detached from the confines of monogamy, and the earlier pre-eminence of bourgeois sexual asceticism will provide the focus for an evaluation of the effectiveness of this dimension of the subversion of heterosexuality. I then return to the work of Giddens and the reflexive self and give a brief commentary on the subversive potential of this notion. The concluding sections of the chapter explore the implications of the more recent and rapidly expanding literature of queer, and of the work of Butler and others that seeks to disentangle the 'soldered together' connections between sexual desire and gender identity. These recent developments will be critically examined, focusing particularly on the degree to which they remain dependent, for their subversive meaning, on the continuing centrality and viability of 'heterosexuality'.

## 8.1   The context

Foucault's notion of the subversive potential in discourses of sexuality seems particularly relevant to the developments in, and challenges to, sexual ideology in this period. For immediately following a decade in which apparently a series of long-standing anxieties and repressive structures relating to sexual behaviour had been dissolved, there emerged movements of sexual identity which confronted and directly challenged the normality, even desirability, of heterosexuality for men or women. The appearance of groups that were committed to positively affirming alternative sexual preferences, not in abstract form but through their own 'coming out', might suggest a more tolerant and more flexible interpretation of what constituted 'sexuality'.

To some extent, this might be tenable in the context of, for example, the 'liberalization' of homosexuality in the Sexual Offences Act of 1956. The limitations of this liberalization, discussed in the previous chapter, suggest that this would be a simplistic assumption. One can more easily imagine movements of affirmation developing in the face of overt repression of expressions of sexuality than in a climate which, apparently, *was* more liberal and undoubtedly was engaged in the positive promotion of heterosexuality as an individual personal choice disengaged from traditional constraints. Yet looked at another way, and with Foucault in mind, this aggressive promotion *in the context of* the dissolution of negative attitudes to sex, provided the very climate in which such movements could flourish and from which they could draw their subversive impetus.

To begin, the discourse of heterosexuality offered the ready-made identity of 'the other' to those who were categorized as 'homosexuals'. Moreover, the classificatory project of modernist sexuality which read off types of people and individual characteristics, both physical and psychological, from their sexual preferences, unwittingly created a basis for the emergence of a politically aware sexual activist. Finally, the interrelatedness of the discourses of hetero and dissident sexuality are reflected in the differences evident in the male and female 'resistance movements', both in their trajectories and their preoccupations. Both campaigned for the immediate extension of full citizenship rights, irrespective of sexual preference, and claimed their right to the public expression of these. Yet there were differences in the gay and lesbian challenges that illustrated the extent as well as the depth of the heterosexual hegemony. For in shaping its own parameters and dimensions, the dominant discourse significantly contributed to those of its 'opposing strategies'.

## 8.2   Subversive women

One of the features of the liberalizing decades of the mid-twentieth century was the detachment of women from the disenabling contexts of traditional gender roles and sexual expectations these entailed. The twentieth century was one in which the bourgeois orthodoxy about sexually anaesthetic women was replaced by an affirmation of both the existence and particularity of women's sexuality. A space opened up for the positive promotion of women's sexual autonomy, one which offered more than one arena for its expression. As a number of feminist commentators of the period have pointed out, from its inception this freedom for women was a questionable one both in its scope and aetiology. In experiencing and experimenting with their sensual 'equality', women were simultaneously experiencing the tensions that derived from a conditional freedom in the context of a still intact system of gender domination.

There were a number of ways in which this tension manifested itself. First, there was, in this promotion of sexual equality, an assumption that women *would*, unproblematically, desire men. The rejection of fictions of the past – the sexually quiescent woman – and acceptance of a degree of sexual equality was bought at the price of second ordering erotic alternatives to heterosexual coitus. If we are to understand the liberalization of heterosexuality as a point along a continuum of sexual regulation rather than a fundamental challenge to the prevailing sexual culture, this is not surprising. Sexual alternatives would not only continue to be marginalized but, particularly in the case of those which excluded men, would be silenced.

In this context, there is a critical difference between the two processes. Marginalization of a choice logically requires acknowledgment of its existence, even if it is to deny it. Silencing, on the other hand, is obliteration. If, in the context of past repressions, women were excused the taking of refuge in 'passionate friendships', in the climate of liberalization such palliatives were considered to be redundant. The hegemonic influence was evident in a second sense. Not only was the object of women's desire assumed, but so was the manner in which women would express and experience this desire – it would mirror that of men. In effect, then, women would become, sexually, 'honourary males'. The primacy of the orgasm and of penile penetration were 'sold' to women as the pinnacle of sexual pleasure without, until the work of Shere Hite and Nancy Friday, ever questioning the universality of these male-defined assumptions.

The Foucauldian notion that discourse 'transmits and produces power ... but also undermines and exposes it, renders it fragile and makes it possible to thwart it' (Foucault 1979: 101), is reflected in the rapidity with which these assumptions and fallacies were exposed – and by whom. For women's involvement, even centrality, in this liberalization process illuminated the connections between the primacy of heterosexuality and the mechanics of patriarchal domination. The newly formed second-wave feminist thinking that emerged in parallel though not necessarily in accordance or close partnership with the radical politics of the 1960s and 1970s, mounted a counter-challenge to the assumptions of 'honourary malehood' both in relation to object of desire and to experience of pleasure. This was the challenge encapsulated in the notion of 'compulsory heterosexuality' (Rich 1983). While initially deployed as the basis for the challenge to assumed heterosexuality, the argument challenged assumptions about the representativeness of the so-called heterosexual experience itself. As Bea Campbell (1982: 33) has said:

> The first thing that can be said is that feminism more fully politicised sexuality than the advocates of the Permissive Era ever did, both by establishing women as the subjects of feminist politics, and by proposing the politics of personal life. Women's liberation was initially concerned to make heterosexuality problematic.

But the subversion of the discourse of heterosexuality was, necessarily, a staged process. The potential for a radical problematization of heterosexuality was curtailed, first, by the conflation of heterosexuality with the active and conscious oppression of women by men and, second, the development of separatist political strategies that emphasized the role of self-education for women. It is easy in retrospect to be critical of the distortion of the challenges to heterosexuality into an internal division in the women's movement. While such distortions did occur (for coverage of these, see Segal 1987, 1993), they did so not just because of misguided individual thinking. They must also be understood in the context of the urgency and anger about the more overtly physically coercive practices that were implicitly condoned in the uncritical acceptance of the 'naturalness' of heterosexuality. 'It is hardly surprising that feminist determination to understand and eliminate rape and violence against women (and soon children as well) came to take precedent over other matters in debates around sexuality in the second half of the 1970s' (Segal 1993: 56).

The juxtaposition of the need to challenge heterosexuality and the contexts in which this challenge was mounted deflected the radical rethinking of sexual pleasure itself. In a climate characterized by, as MacKinnon 'the daily eroticisation of women's subordination' (MacKinnon 1979: 221) engaging in a struggle in this particular arena was low on the list of priorities. A feminist erotica to replace the mystified sexual bliss of heterosexual coitus was lacking in the subversive strategy. Instead, male sexuality was problematized as a 'continuum of violence' against women (Brownmiller 1975; Dworkin 1981; Griffin 1981). Speaking of sexual pleasures for women in this climate – specifically *physical* pleasures for pleasure not as a political act – was difficult. This had the paradoxical effect of occluding the possibilities offered in this challenge to heterosexuality of open explorations of 'polymorphous perversities'. Exploration of this territory was accorded a lower status than less specifically erotic directions suggested in the notion of 'women-identified women'. Adrienne Rich exposed important alternatives of seceding from male-dominated sexual and social partnerships and replacing it with the notion of a 'lesbian continuum . . . to include a range – through each woman's life and throughout history – of woman identified experience; not simply the fact that a woman has had or consciously desired genital sexual experience with another woman' (Rich 1983: 156).

Of the many insights offered by Rich's essay, a critical one is the emphasis she places on the issue of 'choice' in women's expressions of sexual desire. The assumption that heterosexual women have chosen, or have been free to choose, this outlet for their desires ignores the powerful coercive elements of Western sexual ideology, which have romanticized and normalized the heterosexual forms of desire while pathologizing or silencing alternatives. The notion of compulsory heterosexuality exposed and confronted the duplicity of the sexual revolution. Yet it did so in ways which, initially at least, did not hold issues of the sexual or the erotic at its centre.

The feminist challenge identified the connections between the taken-for-granted 'pleasures' of coitus and the superstructure of expertise and promoted freedoms erected upon them. The lack of emphasis on the bodily pleasures awaiting those who stepped beyond the boundaries of heterosexual coitus was both the strength of the challenge and its eventual weakness. The strength lay in the necessary deconstruction of the erotic fictions of the coital imperative, exemplified not only in the relentless search for mutual (vaginal) orgasm (nature's proof that *this way* was the best), but in the wider and less often addressed persistent elevation of the sexual experience as *the* human experience which transcends all others.

Yet at the same time, the strategies promoted by the radical feminist alternatives – of which the woman-identified woman was the least didactic – curtailed rather than expanded the possibilities of a feminist erotic. As Gayle Rubin (1984: 67–8) has said, the promotion of 'women-identified women':

> Made heterosexual feminists into second-class citizens and created a decade of problems for heterosexual women in the radical women's movement. In retrospect, I also think it abused lesbians. By conflating lesbianism (which I think of as a sexual and erotic experience) with feminism – a political philosophy – the ability to justify lesbianism on grounds other than feminism dropped out of the discourse . . . In defining both heterosexuality and lesbianism in terms of one's relation to patriarchy, the erotic experience dropped out. Definitions of sexual orientation became completely unsexual.

The challenge from feminist scholarship subverted the notion of heterosexuality as a 'natural order', and replaced it with a conception of an *institution* of heterosexuality by illuminating the sexual power relations it supported and the gender system from which it derived. It illuminated also the processes by which women's sexual bodies had been expropriated and reconstructed in a discourse of sexual 'freedoms', which subverting women exposed as a mystification of the real and persisting sexual social relations of a familiar duo – patriarchal heterosexism.

But in this first stage at least, the challenges remained within the confines of the fixed categories of modernist binaries. For example, the relationship between heterosexuality and gender domination was assumed as fixed, as if by 'nature'. Heterosexuality, liberated or not, was a primary script of male domination. Denial of one entailed emancipation from the other. And while there was a form of essentialism written into the primacy of heterosexual sex, becoming a 'woman-centred woman' sexually embodied a corresponding (and for Mary Daly, a naturally ordained) freedom of expression of women's 'essence'. This was by definition non-exploitative, empathetic and orientated to nature, characteristics not a million miles away from the classificatory parameters of the oppressive gender relations they sought to escape (Daly 1979, 1984). Criticisms of universalism in this challenge to heterosexuality have already been expressed (Campbell, Rubin, Segal, for example) in relation to the dimensions of class and ethnicity. But the silencing of the dimension of a women-centred erotica deflected an effective challenge to what constitutes the category of 'heterosexuality', the connections between this category and gender and, ultimately, to the category of gender itself.

For in the discourse of modernity, still contained within the fixities of a binary model, challenges to the orthodoxy retained the framework within which the orthodoxy itself acquired meaning. Yet the lack of fixity which characterizes the discourses of late modernity arguably had its origins in this first subversive offensive, which empowered women with the knowledge of their capacity to reclaim what had been expropriated, and to regain sexual dominion over their bodies.

The staged characteristics of this subversion are illustrative of the ways in which women were doubly disadvantaged in the binary of patriarchy and heterosexuality. Subverting heterosexuality for women entailed more than a challenge to assumptions about their erotic preference. An effective challenge was not possible without understanding the links between the network of expectations and norms associated with the still fixed categories of masculine and feminine that were mapped on to both expressions of sexuality and gender. The primacy of heterosexuality and the super- and subordinate juxtapositions of 'the masculine' and 'the feminine' rendered the subversion of its hegemony more complicated that just a statement of sexual preferences. The particularity of women's subversive potential can be further illuminated if we examine the strategies and impact of 'subversive men'.

## 8.3 Subversive men

Arguments that inflate the scope and depth of the freedoms in this era and the decades that followed parallel those which misrepresent the economic and consumer freedoms delivered by the post-collectivist 1980s. These, not coincidentally, also framed their characterizations in the fictional context of the deregulated autonomous individual. Those who enjoyed the fruits of the dissolution of traditional mores were heterosexual males and women who continued to inhabit the newly decorated but determinedly traditional sexual roles of patriarchy. The characterizations of the permissive era and of many of the sexual freedoms consequent on it are more accurately understood as fictions of the heterosexual hegemony.

But to leave an analysis in the negative would similarly be incomplete and inaccurate. While the decades in question only delivered a partial and conditional escape from the constraints of traditional heterosexuality, at the same time there was an opening up of spaces from within which alternatives to the orthodoxy could announce their presence and state their emancipation

from the 'margins'. If the permissive era did not liberate sex, the post-war afflu-
ence offered a context for movements that challenged orthodoxies – whether
sexual or otherwise – to flourish. In political movements that confronted the
complacency of bourgeois capitalism and its satellite social formations – the
family and heterosexuality being central in this regard – sexuality became
recognized as a principal site of oppression and therefore of resistance. We
have already seen that the degree to which this role was actually revolutionary in relation to heterosexuality was problematic and contested. What is
less contestable is that the twinning of bourgeois rule and the institution of
heterosexuality illuminated sexuality as a site of repression specifically of gay
men and lesbian women. The perception of this connection and its revolutionary significance, along with the wider political climate in which were
flourishing other challenges to the dominant order, provided an impetus for
the movement of sexual minorities in from the 'margins'. It also stimulated
the conscious rejection of their previously silenced and marginalized position
as 'non-heterosexuals' in the bourgeois hegemony. Those who arguably did
this most publicly and successfully were gay men.

At one level, subverting heterosexuality for men may seem an odd
choice as a political action. If, as has been argued, heterosexuality shores up
and supports a system of domination which differentially advantages men,
sexually and socially, what advantages are offered by attempting its subversion? But in contemplating 'heterosexuality' we are dealing with a complex
entity. At a macro level, it can be both a description of sexual preference and
a social institution. The bonds between the two are cemented by sets of ideas
and expectations about identity and behaviour, about nature and artifice,
about (still) normal and perverse. The assumption that heterosexuality *automatically* advantages men is grounded in an essentialist idea that reads sexual
preference off from gender category. In the making of heterosexuality through
the discourses of the science of sex, this assumption was underpinned by the
marginalization of homoeroticism, and the equation of the homoerotic with
the effeminate. Safely labelled, men who desired men presented minimal
threat to the primacy of heterosexuality and the twinning of sexual preference with gender typology. Subversive men thus had to confront a social
institution, which while differentially advantaging men as 'the masculine',
operated a system of stigmatization which regulated their sexual choice in
more subtle ways.

In terms of potential for subversion, the more confident and visible
sexual affirmation of post-Gay Liberation Front sexual activism, whether
overtly political or not, represented a specific challenge to the hegemony. As
David Evans (1993: 137) points out: 'Much of the symbolic force of homosexuality rests with its extreme representation of all non-procreative and
thus institutionally unconstrained sexualities'.

The challenge posed by gay men's sexuality had specific qualities. First,
they were *men* and therefore did not occupy the same defining space in the
hegemony as women, in which gay women were, arguably, doubly disadvantaged. However, this sharing of biological sex with the sexual 'ruling class'
introduced a tension in the subversion between the reproduction of, and resistance to, the dominant (heterosexual) culture. The shaping of the category

of 'the homosexual' in the wake of classificatory sexology consigned the man who desired men to the margins as a stigmatized figure, recognisable by his departure from accepted indicators of masculinity reflected in dress and behaviour. Marshall argues that this shaping of a figure was internalized by gay men, who saw themselves as 'sexual others':

> For those who believed themselves to be homosexual, these ideas were to have a strong impact. It was not unusual, for example, for homosexual men to distinguish quite clearly between 'homosexuals' and 'men'. Indeed it was sometimes their proud boast that their most frequent encounters were with 'men' rather than with 'homosexuals'.
> (Marshall 1981: 146)

The subversive effectiveness of sexual affirmation lay in the active rejection of the stigmatized role of 'the homosexual' and of its association, if not with effeminacy and weakness, certainly with negatively valued *difference*. This distinctiveness sealed the otherwise disruptive male behaviour off from the masculinist heterosexual hegemony. The 'new homosexual', as Altman (1978: 4–6) puts it, was distinguished by an image which bore little resemblance to earlier characterizations. In the aftermath of the Gay Liberation Movement of the early 1970s, the stigmatized image was confronted as an instrument of sexual oppression by a more aggressively assertive, more overtly masculinized image: 'A celebration of masculinity that allow[ed] them to distance themselves from the stigmatized homosexual' (Blachford 1981: 193).

Blachford (1981: 188–92) argues that in both dress and behaviour, the gay subculture was now characterized by overtly masculinist features: misognynist language, the sanctioning of promiscuous sexual behaviour divorced from emotional involvement or long-term commitment, and a 'studied virility' of appearance. He evaluates the subversive potential of their development in relation to the debate instigated by Hall *et al.* (1968) – the necessarily derivative relationship between the dominant culture and its satellite subcultures. The adoption of overtly masculine dress styles, the preponderance of casual and objectified sexual encounters, and the celebration of the sculptured male body is evidence of the 'reproduction of male dominance' (Blachford 1981: 188). In defending these strategies, Blachford argues that the derogatory language that echoes the misogyny of heterosexual masculinity could equally be read as parody and subversion, and that the promiscuous and objectified sexual relations that are also deemed 'masculinist' in the derivative view are overestimated and come nearer to orthodox stereotypes of gay male behaviour (ibid., p. 209ff.). The terms in which the two concepts 'promiscuous' and 'objectified' are deployed in relation to erotic behaviour are themselves reflective of the dominant culture. The negative connotations placed on casual sex are the counterpart of the valorization of stable monogamy, while the boundaries against which 'promiscuous sex' is defined are those of the behaviour of the 'average heterosexual male' (ibid., p. 190). Blachford *et al.* conclude that the overall picture supports the interpretation of the 'masculinization' of gay men largely as a coping mechanism deployed in the context of the dominant culture rather than outright subversion.

A rather different interpretation of this phenomenon is presented by David Evans (1993). He unpacks the subjective meanings attached to 'masculinization' while retaining some derivative links with the dominant culture in what it means to 'be a man' sexually. On the one hand, he states that 'Gay male sexuality is masculine sexuality in all but sex object choice. It too is organised by "male sexual needs" ideology, objectifying as to fact and fantasy' (ibid., p. 96). He suggests that the masculinization defined in relation to objectification was a phenomenon of the 'earlier illegal homosexual world' and that the masculinity in the post-legislation subculture 'was in part constructed out of the need to fabricate the conditions within which gay sexuality had been learned but no longer prevailed . . . a familiar sexual distance and anonymity' (ibid., p. 99). Looking beyond the apparent appearance of 'the masculine' to the subjective meanings attached to it, Evans concludes that despite the adoption, even parodic overstatement, of masculine codes of appearance:

> Gay men are still not to be confused with the real thing. 'New' styles of homosexual manliness are not conventionally masculine, but 'masculine' to a quite studied and specifically homosexual purpose. The term 'masculinization' is thus misleading in a way that 'eroticization' and 'virilization' are not.
>
> (Evans 1993: 100)

This distinction is important, for the notions of 'virilization' and 'eroticization' in relation to dress and behaviour introduce subjective elements in which lie, arguably, the core of the subversive potential. In addition to rejecting masculinity as in some way an *essential* component of heterosexual malehood, it sexualizes signifiers of 'the masculine' in the context of a style of choice. Rewriting the terms under which masculinity is a sexualized choice – an 'eroticization' of dominant codes – provided a context in which formerly marginalized erotic choice could challenge this position.

The centrepiece of the heterosexual orthodoxy is the unchallenged and assumed connection between the masculine and the heterosexual male. In relation to heterosexuality at least, the primary indicators are not so much the cut of the trousers or the presence or not of facial hair, to choose two such indicators. In much of what has been already argued, there has been a persistent theme of the role of the masculinist position in the definition of the parameters of heterosexuality. The ascendant position of the male has been indicated in the ways in which *all* sexuality has been defined either positively or negatively with reference to male sexuality: sexual 'passivity' against male 'activity'; promiscuity against male norms; the female orgasm against the male 'blueprint'; the categories of 'the lesbian' and 'the homosexual'; and the characteristics of behaviour, appearance or sexualized signifiers imputed to them. The creation and maintenance of the masculine as the reference point crafted a sexual 'centre stage' in ideology as well as practice. Its counterpart was a periphery of concentric circles that corresponded to the degrees of 'difference' from the male and, therefore, the moral as well as scientific norm.

The differential emphasis on, and attention to, gay male rather than female homosexuality is testimony to the revolutionary potential male defection from the orthodoxy offered. Men who desired men challenged the long-standing promotion of *male* sexuality as the template for *all* sexuality. The adoption of overt and celebratory homoeroticism as a principal platform of resistance challenged the centre-point of the rationalized sexual expressions of the hegemony. 'Against a society which employs sexuality itself as means to a useful end, the perversions uphold sexuality as an end in itself: they place themselves outside the dominion of the performance principle and challenge its very foundation' (Marcuse 1974: 46).

If rational sex was one of the cornerstones of the male-centred script of the heterosexual hegemony, gay sexuality was arguably the very epitome of 'irrational' sex. It shared with lesbian sex the irreversible dislocation from reproductive outcome; in this sense, both were without legitimate 'aim'. But gay *men* transgressed further. In their overt promotion of the 'pleasure principle' sexually, they fractured the linchpins attaching the discourses of patriarchal sex and modernist sex – the essential male rationality which modified and contained the more disreputable chaotic tendencies of emotion-driven women. The anxiety with which the 'promiscuity' of gay sex was viewed and its consequences were well expressed by Roger Scruton (1986), who, as Evans points out, 'opposed homosexuality specifically because it encourages a new promiscuity':

> [the homosexual] knows with too great a certainty, too great a familiarity what his partner feels, and has no need for tiresome stratagems of courtesy, courtship and shame. The gateway to desire, which hides its course in mystery, and diverts it to the path of love, has been burst open, and a short path to pleasure revealed.
>
> (Scruton, quoted in Evans 1993: 137)

The appearance of the overtly masculine man whose erotic expression called into question all the stalwarts of heterosexuality disrupted the certainties of the male position within the orthodoxy and, arguably, rattled the cage of the orthodoxy itself.

## 8.4 Fracturing the binary

> The 'biological justification' for heterosexuality as 'normal', it might be proposed, has fallen apart. What used to be called perversions are merely ways in which sexuality can legitimately be expressed and self-identity be defined.
>
> (Giddens 1992: 179)

Late modernity, Giddens suggests, has released sexuality from the confines of a single hegemony and replaced it with 'sexual pluralism'. The significant shift which disrupted these features was not the (direct) consequence of the 'permissive' era, but of a movement in which sexuality as a fixity has been supplanted by 'sexual identity' defined and structured by individual choice, where sexual choice becomes one of many elements in 'lifestyle' choice.

Historically, this shift has occurred in a very short space of time as well as having potentially quite revolutionary consequences. The ways of thinking about sex which gave us a regulatory science of sex, with rigid distinctions between the normal and abnormal, have produced in their wake a series of empirical accounts of 'what people do' sexually – which differ from the work of the first sexologists in two senses. First, they consciously eschew normative pre-judgements in the form of classification. Second, they have not only been made available to (increasingly since Kinsey, whose volumes were published at a prohibitively high price and were subject to restricted sales), but directed towards, popular lay consumption. These studies quite explicitly confronted the previously unchallenged givens. Respondents who volunteered information 'confessed' to non-monogamy, non-committed short-term sexual encounters, even a fluidity in sexual choice. They also revealed the emotional and erotic aridity of those sexual relationships which, superficially at least, adhered to the norms. The significance of these for the notion of 'institutional reflexivity' is that they have become 'part of the frames of action which individuals or groups adopt' (Giddens 1992: 29). It is also through the process of reflexivity that the distinctions between the 'normal us' and the 'perverse them' are blurred if not dissolved. 'Sexual diversity, although still regarded by many hostile groups as perversion, has moved out of Freud's case-history notebooks into the everyday social world' (ibid., p. 33). It remains open to question whether this dissolution of old categories is, in the end, more than semantic.

In the late twentieth century, there is much evidence to support the claim that the notion of perversion has been replaced by diversity, that our expressions of sexual desire rank alongside other expressions of self-identity, that sexual pluralism has replaced sexual monism. Yet some caution is necessary. As Weeks (1986: 81) points out, 'the admitted *fact* of diversity need not lead to a *norm* of diversity'. A discourse of sexual pluralism, in which homoerotic choice appears equally privileged, is not necessarily disrupting or challenging the dynamics that have together constituted sexual modernity. The bringing in from the cold of sexual choice suggested by the decline of perversity and the rise of diversity does not necessarily pose a challenge to all elements of the hegemonic centre. It may even be that the high profile of sexual diversity in contemporary popular culture is another strategy of the hegemony to preserve its primacy (Hamer and Budge 1994). Moreover, 'sexual pluralism' that prioritizes assimilation will inevitably tend towards the conservative. Consideration of the conditions of assimilation, and the ideas that accompany it, raises questions regarding the viability of a radical sexual diversity. Such scepticism echoes the more passionately argued debates surrounding multiculturalism.

There is a danger in assuming that changes in appearances, even in experiences, are evidence for changes in fundamental structuring ideas. The claim that the undoubted shifts in both conceptualizing and experiencing 'sexuality' have successfully dislodged the heterosexual hegemony requires a closer examination. Such reservations are central to more recent work in gay and lesbian scholarship, which have addressed, for example, the 'performative' nature of heterosexuality and the necessity to separate gender identity from sexual desire.

The recent literature of queer, which self-consciously transcends vertically ordered sexual categories, holds as its central logic the dissolution of the binary – an either/or of sexual identity or desire. This is the basis of the queer challenge to the hegemony of heterosexuality. The derogatory term 'queer' has been reclaimed not to indicate another sexual category, as 'the other' to gay and lesbian, but to identify a process by which sexual identities and expressions of desire can be released from such frameworks. Queer does not operate as a label for a new and fixed 'sexual subject', but provides an ontological category within which to confront the binary focus of modernist discourses. ' "Queer" . . . displaces bourgeois notions of the Self as unique, abiding, and continuous . . . substituting instead a concept of self which is performative, improvisational, discontinuous, and processual, constituted by repetitive and stylised acts' (Mayer 1994: 2–3).

Queer thus constitutes a 'radical change to the entire concept of an identity based on sexual orientation or sexual desire' (ibid.). It also implies a challenge to the connections between gender identity and sexual desire. The centrality and the scope of the performative renders meaningless the typing of individuals by their sexual identity and objects of sexual desire cannot be read off from presentation of self. The basing of queer 'sexuality' on a 'series of improvised performances' represents a challenge to the reference points of the bipolar model, which for Mayer is quintessentially bourgeois in origin:

> As a refusal of sexually defined identity, this must include the denial of the difference upon which such identities have been founded. And it is precisely in the space of this refusal, in the deconstruction of the homo/hetero binary, that the threat and challenge to bourgeois ideology is queerly executed.
>
> (Mayer 1994: 3)

There are two aspects to the queer challenge that raise questions over both the hermeneutic as well as erotic primacy of heterosexuality. First, the mechanisms of social construction of 'heterosexuality' are challenged. Second, the ascribed connections between gender identity and sexual desires are severed. In both there are possibilities for a radical challenge that might render the distinctiveness and fixity of the category 'heterosexuality' meaningless. Yet, as will be developed further, the potential for disruption is vulnerable to more conservative influences.

Recent work by gay and lesbian theorists has emphasized the fictionality of the parameters of heterosexuality; in particular, the binary which maintains homosexuality as the other, and the dislocation of sexual desire from gender identity. One of the most powerful support mechanisms of heterosexuality is the existence and nature of the connections between biological sex, gender and sexual desire. The strengths of these associations are illustrated by their almost fully assumptive status. Thus in the majority of individuals, one's biological sex – indicated by possession of appropriate genitalia

– is the signpost to both gendered characteristics and heterosexual desire. The ubiquity of this connection and the extent to which, at a conscious level, it remains unchallenged, is suggested by the disparity between our 'world view' of the universality of heterosexual choice, of the distinct division between homo- and heterosexuality, and the empirical evidence of what people do. (In Kinsey's reports of same-sex sexual behaviour, more than 50 per cent of males and nearly 30 per cent females acknowledge such experience.) The claim of the heterosexual hegemony is that the expression of sexual desire is directed by gender identity, which in turn is 'directed' by our biological sex. Though the now axiomatic challenges to biological determinism have rejected the notion of biological directives, the heterosexual hegemony thus implies the dominion of biology while in constructionist terms it is being denied. In this sense, the constructionist critique, which confined itself to the construction of *heterosexuality*, unwittingly fed and maintained the binary.

Judith Butler (1990, 1991, 1993) provides new insights into the layers of assumption under which heterosexuality has lain undisturbed. For Butler, no gender is a 'true' gender, from which other (performative) replicas are derived. Nor is gender the playing out of an acquired sexual identity. Butler argues that heterosexuality itself is 'naturalized' as the original. The binary model of sexual identity (the 'either/or' of hetero/homosexuality) is inherently unstable, not to mention tautologous, since each requires the other as a reference point. Homosexuality is 'not' heterosexuality; heterosexuality is that which is 'not' homosexuality. For Butler, 'there is no "proper" gender, a gender proper to one sex or the other, which is some way that sex's cultural property' (Butler 1991: 21). There are, rather, 'illusions of continuity', by which heterosexuality naturalizes itself, between sex, gender and desire. This illusion depends on the presumption, in compulsory heterosexuality (which operates, I would argue, largely at a subliminal level), that 'there is first a sex which is expressed through a gender and then through a sexuality' (ibid.).

Butler inverts this model. She argues that a 'regime of sexuality [the heterosexual hegemony] mandates as compulsory performance of sex' (ibid., p. 29). This performance is 'gender'-performing masculinity or femininity. Moreover, performance makes intelligible the binary system of sex and gender. The scripts of gender produce the categories they purport to be directed by – that is, sex and gender. Therefore, a drag performance is not the parody of the original, but, as Butler now famously puts it, 'an imitation of an imitation, a copy for which there is no original' (ibid., p. 22).

Crucially, in relation to the deployment of the notion of heterosexual 'performance', there is little room for artistic licence. Gender performance is 'compulsory in the sense that acting out of lines with gender norms brings with it ostracism, punishment and violence, not to mention the transgressive pleasures produced by these very prohibitions' (ibid., p. 24). And there is an urgency to this performance, which is reflected in the accompanying social sanctions. For in order to construct a 'seamless heterosexual identity', heterosexuality demands a *continuous* performance of gender. The ubiquity and potency of the scripts of gender are testimony to the inherent instability of the connection between sex, gender and desire in the heterosexual hegemony. 'If heterosexuality is compelled to *repeat itself* in order to establish the illusion of its own uniformity and identity, then this is an identity permanently at risk' (ibid., p. 29).

For Butler, sex, gender and desire, the linked chain which constitutes heterosexuality, is necessarily both compulsory and fragile. The fragility of the equation is developed in *Gender Trouble* (1990), in which Butler, in a radical interpretation of Freud's 'Oedipal struggle', gives an account of this fragility in her focus on the original denial of same-sex desire. This is not accomplished through prohibition (which would acknowledge its possibility, even probability), but through obliteration. Butler argues that homosexuality, not heterosexual incest, was the original taboo, a conclusion which, she implies, is the logical consequence of Freud's Oedipal struggle in the acquisition of heterosexual identity:

> The young boy and the young girl who enter into the Oedipal Drama with incestuous heterosexual aims have already been subject to prohibitions which dispose them in distinct sexual directions. Hence the dispositions that Freud assumes to be primary or constitutive *facts* of sexual life are *effects* [my emphasis] of a law which, internalised, produces and regulates discrete gender identity and heterosexuality.
>
> (Butler 1990: 64)

For Butler, the gender identification entailed in the Oedipal struggle is one which is both directed and enforced by the repression and denial of the 'real' promise of the original polymorphous sexuality – that of the primacy of same-sex desire. The disposition which governs the Oedipal resolution is not the cause of this process but the effect of the laws which prohibit same-sex desire. The incest taboo is more inclusive than that of homosexuality, she argues, but its effects are, experientially, more traumatic. The heterosexual incest taboo prohibits the *object* of desire but not the desire itself. The taboo against homosexuality on the other hand results in a more profound loss – not only of the object but of the desire itself: 'In other words, the object is not only lost, but the desire fully denied, so that "I never lost that person and I never loved that person, indeed never felt that kind of love at all"' (ibid., p. 69).

In effect, Butler reverses the argument and much of the subsequent interpretation of Freud's account of the acquisition of sexuality. In laying emphasis on the removal of all desire other than heterosexual desire, she explicates the silencing of other *possible* alternatives and the shaping of a sexual and sensual subjectivity. The performance of gender entails a process by which parts of the body are eroticized, created and acknowledged as sites of pleasure. Thus within the constitution of heterosexuality, expectations are mapped onto the body in ways which relate gender performance to acquisition of sexuality. A 'feminine' woman experiences pleasure from the penetrated vagina, the masculine man from penile penetration. This illuminates the dilemma of 'transsexualism', the belief that successful inhabitance of a gender identity is impossible without the appropriately eroticized body parts. The transsexual's acquisition or removal of body parts to express his or her identity more adequately is thus not a subversive act, but one which reflects the extent to which the connection between sex, gender and desire have been 'naturalized'.

This analysis of Butler illuminates not only the performativeness of gender, but provides cogent grounds for questioning the stability and permanency of the regime of heterosexuality, which earlier social constructionist accounts suggest. Additionally, and centrally for this discussion, it directs attention towards appropriate gender performance rather than erotic sex, thus illuminating further the characteristics of bourgeois sexuality already discussed. The object choice of sexual desire is the Achilles heel in the fragile edifice of heterosexuality, a fault line which, like the edifice itself, is camouflaged by unchallenged assumptions. Thus, the question 'how do I know I am heterosexual' in relation to sexual desires is rarely asked. That it is not suggests the very fragility to which Butler refers.

## 8.4 The 'other' as the 'same'

A further insight into the fictionality which is heterosexuality, on which its effective subversion depends, is provided by Jonathan Dollimore's (1991) deconstruction of 'the perverse'. For Dollimore, homophobia is not derived from a perception of difference but of 'sameness', the recognition of which threatens the precariousness of gender and sexual desire. The 'sameness' constitutes a 'perverse dynamic', which 'discloses not an underlying unity in the name of which social division can be transcended, but a radical interconnection which has been and remains the unstable ground for both repression and liberation' (ibid., p. 229).

For Dollimore, the interdependence of the binary (i.e. homo/heterosexuality) is not that which 'presupposes the other for its meaning'. In the perverse dynamic, encapsulated in the radical formulation of 'the sameness within', there is no 'either/or'. Dollimore's point is that at one level we are aware of our polyerotic potentials, and his argument implies that this knowledge is both individually and collectively disturbing and threatening. Provision of a safe world of heterosexual norms cannot quite obliterate the uncomfortable presence of doubt. Labels do not ever fully conquer subjectivity. Dollimore argues that the binaries by which heterosexuality is defined – normal/perverse, same/different – are defensive strategies against the recognition of the polyeroticism that transcends boundaries. The 'differences' represented by the binary homo/heterosexual are not representative of two pre-existing exclusive categories, but of a conscious effort to reorder the sameness into difference.

The impetuses for this reordering were, first, the existential anxiety engendered by the recognition of 'the sameness within' and, second, the socially disruptive potential of the chaotic sensuality which the sameness suggests. Thus, in the classificatory endeavour of sexology, sexual deviancy became the carrier for anxieties about disorderly and irrational human potentialities, thereby creating both the problem and the solution. As Altman (1983: 72) comments:

... the original purpose of the categorisation of homosexuals as people apart was to project the homosexuality in everyone onto a defined minority as a way of externalising forbidden desire and reassuring the majority that homosexuality is something which happens to other people.

There is a paradoxical consequence of this process. In creating the category of the fictional other (the disorderly, troublesome, irrational, sensuality-without-predictable-focus), the hegemony has created an object of desire. The enduring fascination, whether horrified or delighted, of 'other sexualities' given licence in the tradition of drag queens as well as more recent commodifications of difference (cross-gender nightclubs, straight audiences at the Sydney Gay and Lesbian Mardi Gras), may be evidence of a recognition of the fascination of the forbidden. It may also represent the wistful gaze of the constrained denizens of straight sexual culture on sensual possibilities beyond their experience.

Mark Simpson (1994) has argued that gay sexuality is disquieting because it presents a persona of sex that is silenced in the more rational depleasured scripts of straight (male) sex:

The idea of homosexuality is one of naked 'sex'; sex for pleasure; sex for, in and of itself; sex unmediated and privatised by the family and reproduction, as an undifferentiated and public Eros: homosexuality is, thus, by its very nature 'obscene'.

(Simpson 1994: 144)

Gay sensibility has also intruded on – and is even beginning to eclipse, Simpson argues – traditional male definitions of 'masculine' and, through this disposition, another realignment of erotic codes. In the past decade, or thereabouts, he suggests that there has been a commodification of the male body in advertising and popular art in ways which suggest 'a repaganization of society where the male body rather than the female body is coming to be regarded as representing "sex"'' (ibid., p. 13). In a chapter entitled 'Narcissus goes shopping', Simpson illustrates the remarkable commercial effectiveness of promoting male cosmetics and clothing (most notably jeans). Homoerotically idealized images of the male body are diluted in their 'queerness' by the use of settings or sequences replete with heterosexual signifiers. Nevertheless, the queer potential is there; the preparation and exposure of the partly clothed young male body invites the gaze of the sexual fantasizer first and directs his or her sexual preference second.

This dallying with sexual voyeurism is a game that appears to be played (and subverted) with more ease if the object of desire is a man and not a woman. The making of a woman's body as a site of sexual voyeurism would not have the same queer potential. Yet women have become the object of a form of queering sexual voyeurism that is the same yet different. 'In recent years, references to lesbianism have been making their way into mainstream culture in some surprising ways ... Indeed, given the coverage in the popular media of late, it seems that everyone is now 'one of us' – or aspires to be' (Hamer and Budge 1994: 1).

First in movies, then music, in historical dramas and soap operas, and finally fashion and advertising, 'the love affair with lesbianism' (ibid.) has been flourishing. The issue is not so much that lesbians are being positively valued, even courted, but what in this new high profile is being said about women's sex with women. A sceptical point to begin with, women having sex with other women is an enduring heterosexual fantasy. However, notwithstanding this, the popular inclusion and recognition of lesbianism by Madonna and k.d. laing internationally, and Britain's conventionally attractive soap opera lesbians, are phenomena of less than a decade's standing. One precipitating element has been suggested to be the impact of AIDS on the rewriting of the possibilities of sexual diversity. It may also be that in the late 1990s, women are increasingly detaching themselves from the old certainties of love and marriage. Erotic choice becomes another of their consumer freedoms, in which they might choose a more palatable alternative to the erotic and emotional clumsiness of heterosexual males.

But it is an erotic choice which lacks one element of the dissonance of heterosexual relationships – the ingrained sets of expectations mounted in the still powerful framework of gendered power relations. The emergence of lesbianism on to the 'centre stage' has been nurtured within the language of style and fashion, an element that immediately induces scepticism over the subversive potential. Sue O'Sullivan (1994) alerts us to some of the grounds for these doubts. She argues, like Hamer and Budge, that AIDS 'forced open the door' of sexual diversity in popular magazines in the late 1980s: '"We are everywhere!", the rallying cry of the 1970s gay and lesbian activist, becomes a bizarre and poignant reality within the context of AIDS in the 1980s and 1990s for both gay men and lesbians, when they are *seen* to be everywhere' (ibid., pp. 83–4).

A romance with an 'acceptable lesbian', O'Sullivan argues, is inversely related to the continued vilification of the hairy, butch, *feminist* lesbian – what she calls the 'caricature lesbian whipping girl'. It is the persistent presence of this whipping girl in accounts of this 'change', O'Sullivan argues, that points to one deeply ambivalent feature in this apparent extension of sexual diversity. Much of the erotic meaning conveyed by 'mainstream lesbianism' depends on the maintenance of the stigmatized 'other' – the unreconstructed butch: 'Even the term "lipstick lesbian" indirectly signals that there is another lesbian who overtly shuns makeup in the name of a political rejection of male dominated notions of femininity' (ibid., p. 84).

Another tension in the valorization is shared with the high-profile intrusion, even takeover, of the queerly eroticized male image in advertising – it sells. This raises the immediate response, 'Why, and why now?' O'Sullivan suggests that the current promotion of lesbianism may be an element in the mustering of the still viable defence strategies against feminism as a political force – the expropriation and defusing of a radical sexuality and its incorporation into the mainstream through imbuing it with heterosexual eroticism. Feminism once had a monopoly on lesbianism, its approval and promotion a central plank of its political platform. The popularization of lesbian chic by mainstream sexual culture seeks to appropriate radical sex and make it 'style', while simultaneously defusing its potential and rewriting it as commodity. The close relationship between these 'subversive sexualities' and the commercial world raise immediate questions over the long- or even short-term subversive potentials. There is an uneasy sense, in often aggressively marketed sexual diversity, that by entering this world one is playing the game of the orthodoxy.

The pervasiveness of notions of style and choice in the promotion of sexual diversity arguably have little to do with radical rewriting of sexual desires. For in the deliberately and ambiguously queered adulation of the male body and the notion of lesbian chic, a coy silence is maintained about their impact in the bedroom. Style and image allude to the possibilities of pick-and-mix sexuality, but do not promote it. In an evaluation of subversive potential, recognition does not mean acceptance, less still the dissolution of sexual boundaries required for a pure rendering of the challenge of queer. In the 'gender-bending' climate of the 1990s, the underlying script of assimilation prevails – an assimilation which operates on the terms of mainstream sexual culture.

## Conclusion

The notion of permissiveness in the context of the second half of the twentieth century depends for its meaning on the elevation of the notion of individual choice. It suggests the decline of the rule of the experts who characterized the previous epochs of more restrictive sexual norms, and the replacement of these by informed, 'morally mature' citizens who require little formal regulation. Of course, 'permissiveness' also carries with it a more pejorative meaning, particularly in the hands of the Moral Right. But even in this negative view, permissiveness entails a broad-based relaxation of strictures and traditional norms.

The movements of sexual resistance that emerged in parallel with the liberalization of heterosexuality constituted a challenge to the orthodoxy itself. Yet however transgressive the behaviour of either gay men or lesbian women, their position as 'the other' was not substantially challenged.

While it is predicated on and offers the potential for a dissolution of the binary, the appearance of queer sexual politics does not indicate an unproblematic weakening of the heterosexual hegemony. In the short term at least, the promotion of fashionable play with gendered distinctions dilutes the possibility of severing rather than suspending the connections between gender and sexual desire. This weakening of radicalism operates through the rapid commodification of sexual diversity, itself a notion, like pluralism, which is equally amenable to conservative as 'liberal' deployment. Even in its apparent queering, the popular promotion of sexual diversity retains some significant distinctions. Openly homoerotic images are de-queered by inclusion of images that testify to the 'in the last instance' heterosexuality of the male subject. The recent celebration of lesbian chic is that of the more acceptable 'lipstick lesbian', a strategy which devalues and marginalizes 'the other'.

Even the notion of gender as performative is not unproblematic. To acknowledge that discontinuous sexualities mean freedom of choice ignores the constraining elements of structure. To continue the theatrical metaphor, performances are also dependent on script-writers, availability of finance, even a supportive audience. These elements leave the performance vulnerable to reactionary influences and retain its status as a 'Fringe' to the mainstream circuit. Yet it would be premature to dismiss the possibilities. Viewing subversion as a process rather than an achievement, the genie cannot now return to the bottle. A longer historical perspective may recognize that the fragility of the heterosexual hegemony, and the binary which is its supporting structure, depends as much on enabling human agency as it does on constraining structure.

# Final thoughts *and* questions

A much respected tutor in my undergraduate years once advised me – in relation to the writing of conclusions to essays – to emphasize the points you feel are the most interesting. In following her advice, it seemed to me then, as it does now, that conclusions should, in addition to providing a summary, pose as many questions as they answer. Thinking sociologically about something as commonplace and complex as 'sex and sexuality' provides a wide canvas of possibilities of approach and interpretation.

This book has been informed by the view that thinking sociologically requires asking questions of the past as well as the present. The framework for asking such questions has been the isolation of key ideas that are apparent in contemporary Western conceptualizations of sex and sexuality. My intention was not to convey a sense of grand narrative, nor any direct linearity in their genesis or persistence. My concern was to explore the tensions evident in ways of thinking about sex and sexuality, which are striking both in their contradictory nature and their predominance in Western sexual orthodoxies: between characterizations of repression and liberation, between sexual dangers and pleasures, and between shame and celebration. Despite their contrariness, these pairs of ideas appeared to predominate in the establishment and maintenance of heterosexuality as the defining framework for expressions of sexual desire. The question that originally informed this project was: 'How is it, in the sophisticated environment of the late twentieth century that ideas about sex and sexuality can retain these contradictions and tensions and where did these ideas come from?'

One starting point was the influence of Christianity in conferring on sexual desire negative and fearful connotations. These in particular emphasized the connections between animality and sexual desire, a source of the notion of uncontrollability, which was later to appear in secular theories about sexual 'drives'. A significant facet of this early expression of the fearfulness of sex was its gender specificity – the association of women's sexuality with bodily and spiritual danger. The most familiar of Old Testament extracts vividly characterizes this element in the story of The Fall from Grace in the Garden of Eden. This association, now far removed from its biblical base, is nevertheless a key theme in the subsequent shaping of Western sexual ideology. The antithesis of this fearful and chaotic presence was what might be termed the secular construction of modernist sexuality – the imposition of classified and ordered categories arranged around notions of the normal and the perverse, the mainstream and the marginal. The impact of modernity, or the civilizing process, was that it shaped and directed moral sensibility while restricting the possibilities of wider expressions of sexual desire. What was and was not constructed as acceptable modes of expression reflected, as the work of Elias and Freud indicated, the need for the construction and maintenance of a new social order. Crucial also in both the construction and the understanding of recognizably modern sexual orthodoxies was the influence of Western asceticism and the hegemony of rationality as the ordering framework for social action. These ideas – which were, not coincidentally, the linchpins of bourgeois ideology – are evident in and contribute to the science of sex, the blueprint for modern sexuality.

Retracing these processes and developments raised further issues. First, it illuminated complexities inherent in the dynamics of repression and liberation, which, notwithstanding Foucault's exegesis on these processes, remains central to the concept of modernization. In an uncritical interpretation, there is a sense of progressive enlightenment of sexual mores which belies the complexity of the meanings as well as the complex structuring of ideas, values and knowledge, associated with both 'repression' and 'liberation'. Second, it allowed a more detailed examination of the role of the 'civilizing process' in the management of feelings and desires commensurate with the emphasis on rationalization of all areas of human life. Rationalization of sexual desires was a supremely modernist endeavour. It was no longer appropriate for veils to be drawn over the disturbing aspects of sexual desire. What was demanded was its detailed examination and classification. Too easily interpreted as evidence of 'modernization', the dynamic through which sex became the object of study is exemplary of the moulding and delivery of an epistemology where the untidy and troublesome human passions and desires were ideologically catalogued as 'normal' and 'pathological' under the heading of 'sexuality'.

The review of the immediate antecedents of contemporary sexual ideologies allowed also a re-evaluation of the characterization of the twentieth century as the century of sexual liberalization. Relaxation of the more stringent constraints placed on expressions of sexual desire, which, in one view, defines the twentieth century thus, were conditional on the successful classification and reordering of sexual pleasures into manageable contexts. Central to this endeavour was the motif of 'planning', a structuring of action that was intended to ensure a predictable outcome. The almost religious faith in the efficacy of this strategy went beyond its immediate instrumental advantages. The attraction lay also in older human preoccupations, which concerned, as has been suggested in an earlier argument, the mastery of the more fearful aspects of the forces of nature, which have been equated, over time, with 'the irrational'. The pre-eminence of rational action in the ordering of human existence in the context of modernity, or of the civilizing process, offered an ideological context in which long-standing anxieties about the 'disorderliness' of sex could at last be overcome.

There was nothing magical in this process. The application of rational considerations in the production of orderly sex depended on the presence of a body of expert knowledge, and of experts who would educate and direct human sexuality along paths shaped by informed choice towards a desired outcome – the production of children or of a stable and permanent marriage.

In the wake of the successful strategies of the science of sex, fears about sex once associated with unseen forces of 'animal passion' were exchanged, in the work of the twentieth-century exponents, for anxieties about a failure to perform the scripts of sexual management successfully. This rational secular discourse, whose legitimacy lay in the infallibility of science rather than a deity, performed a similar social role: to direct and internalize what were, in effect, moral precepts legitimized by the objectivity of science. Once internalized, this medico-moral sexual ideology was able to withstand the inroads of the 'liberation' that followed.

The third major theme to be addressed in this book was the shaping and promotion of heterosexual coitus as the centre-point of expressions of sexual desire in the context of modernity. This primacy was strengthened rather than weakened by the movement to positively promote sexual pleasure, which characterized much of the twentieth century. Interpreting this development as modernization and liberalization fails to adequately interpret the significance of the exclusions inherent in its conditionality. The discussion which examined planned sex and conjugal pleasures illustrated some of the terms under which certain modes of expression were validated and disqualified.

The overall pessimism in this account of the constructions of a terrain of sex and sexuality in the context of modernity is mediated by the apparent dissolutions of fixities and the demotion of grand narratives of gender and its integral associations with sexual desire. The promise of flexibility associated with late modernity and the production of self is that the bonds forged between gender, sexual identity and sexual desire will be loosened if not severed. A partial realization of this promise is suggested by the representation of 'indeterminate' gender in club culture, in advertising imagery and most recently as an indicator of its 'proletarianization' on afternoon chat shows. Yet while a judgement about the representativeness and depth of this 'widening of the margins' must to some extent await history, there are some reasons for scepticism. If, as has been argued, these soldered together connections have a specific material basis, then their severance would require a parallel dissolution of the conditions that produced them. In the absence of this, playing at sexual or erotic diversity will remain at the margins, while flexibility of choice continues to be 'delivered' by the present elevation of modes of consumption over modes of production. Behind the façade of erotic democracy remain long-standing anxieties about some implications of this process which remain problematic. Such pockets of resistance are evident in the reluctance to confer equal status on homoerotic choices and the sexuality of the young. In the persistence of these anxieties there are present, though often not openly articulated, ideas about the old inherent 'uncontrollability' of sexual desire. These suggest that a full erotic democracy is not, even in the late twentieth century, considered unproblematic. This reluctance after almost a full century of promotion of the positive advantages of sex seems at one level inexplicable.

But while the *hegemony* of heterosexuality has rightly been a constant theme in this discussion, the manoeuvres that have underpinned this ascendency are testimony also to its fragility. It is this characteristic which contains within it the possibility of the dismantling of the primacy, and as such, sets the scene for a history of sexuality in the twenty-first century. At the end of the twentieth century, the fault lines in heterosexuality are increasingly being exposed. But the seismic shocks necessary for its disruption are not, as yet, measurable on the Richter Scale.

# References

A Physician in the Country (1767) *A short treatise on onanism: or, the detestable vice of self-pollution*. London: Fletcher and Co.

Addy, J. (1988) *Sin and Society in the 17th Century*. London: Routledge.

Altman, D. (1983) *The Homosexualisation of America*. Boston, MA: Beacon Press.

Aries, P. (1979) *Centuries of Childhood*. London: Peregrine.

Barret-Ducrocq, F. (1991) *Love in the Time of Victoria: Sexuality and Desire among Working Class Men and Women in Nineteenth Century London*. Harmondsworth: Penguin.

Bauman, Z. (1987) *Legislators and Interpreters*. London: Polity Press.

Bauman, Z. (1989a) *Modernity and the Holocaust*. Cambridge: Polity Press.

Bauman, Z. (1989b) *Legislators and Interpreters: On Modernity, Post-modernity and Intellectuals*. Cambridge: Polity Press.

Bauman, Z. (1990) *Thinking Sociologically*. Oxford: Basil Blackwell.

Beale, L. (1887) *Morality and the Moral Question: Chiefly from the Medical Side*. London: Publisher not cited.

Birkett, W. (1939) *Report of the Interdepartmental Committee on Abortion*. London: HMSO.

Blachford, G. (1981) 'Male dominance and the gay world', in K. Plummer (ed.) *The Making of the Modern Homosexual*. London: Hutchinson.

Bland, L. (1985) ' "Cleansing the portals of life": The venereal disease campaign in the early twentieth century', in M. Langan and B. Schwarz (eds) *Crises in the British State 1880–1930*. London: Hutchinson.

Bloch, I. (1908) *The Sexual Life of Our Time and its Relation to Modern Culture*. London: Rebman.

Bloch, M. (1967) *The Historian's Craft*. Manchester: Manchester University Press.

Box, M. (1967) *The Trial of Marie Stopes*. London: Femina Books.

Brake, M. (ed.) (1982) *Human Sexual Relations*. Harmondsworth: Penguin.

Breche, E. (1970) *The Sex Researchers*. London: Andre Deutsch.

Brownmiller, S. (1975) *Against Our Will: Men, Women and Rape*. Harmondsworth: Penguin.

Butler, J. (1990) *Gender Trouble: Feminism and the Subversion of Identity*. London: Routledge.

Butler, J. (1991) 'Imitation and gender subordination', in D. Fuss (ed.) *Inside/out Lesbian Theories, Gay Theories*. London: Routledge.

Butler, J. (1993) *Bodies that Matter: On the Discursive Limits of 'Sex'*. London: Routledge.

Campbell, B. (1982) 'A feminist sexual politics: Now you see it, now you don't', in M. Evans (ed.) *The Woman Question: Readings on the Subordination of Women*. Oxford: Fontana.

Chesser, E. (1949) *Sexual Behaviour: Normal and Abnormal*. London: Hutchinson.
Comfort, A. (1950) *Sexual Behaviour in Society*. London: Gerald Duckworth.
Comfort, A. (1968) *The Anxiety Makers*. London: Pantheon.
Coveney, L. *et al.* (1984) *The Sexuality Papers: Male Sexuality and the Social Control of Women*. London: Hutchinson.
Daly, M. (1979) *Gyn\Ecology*. London: Women's Press.
Daly, M. (1984) *Pure Lust*. London: Women's Press.
Davies, C. (1980) 'Moralists, causalists, sex, law and morality', in W. H. G. Armytage, R. Chester and J. Peel (eds) *Changing Attitudes to Sexual Behaviour*. London: Academic Press.
Davin, A. (1978) 'Imperialism and Motherhood', *History Workshop*, 5, 9–66.
De Beauvoir, S. (1972) *The Second Sex*. Harmondsworth: Penguin.
Degler, C. N. (1974) 'What ought to be and what was: Women's sexuality in the nineteenth century', *American Historical Review*, 79(5), 1467–90.
De Mause, L. (1976) *The History of Childhood*. London: Souvenir Press.
DHSS (1974) *Health Service Circular (IS) 32*, May. London: DHSS.
Dickens, C. (1861) *David Copperfield* (undated edition). London: Odhams Press.
Dollimore, J. (1991) *Sexual Dissidence: Augustine to Wilde, Freud to Foucault*. Oxford: Clarendon Press.
Doughan, D. (1981) *Birth Control: The Equal Knowledge Campaign 1922–31*. London: LLRS Publications.
Dworkin, A. (1981) *Pornography: Men Possessing Women*. London: Women's Press.
Ehrenreich, B. and English, D. (1979) *For Her Own Good: 150 Years of Experts' Advice to Women*. London: Pluto Press.
Elderton, E. (1914) *Report on the English Birth Rate. Part One: North of the Humber*. London: Dulau and Co.
Elias, N. (1982) *The Civilising Process, Vol. 1: A History of Manners*. Oxford: Basil Blackwell.
Ellis, H. (1899) *Studies in the Psychology of Sex*, Vol. 2. Philadelphia: FA Davis Company.
Evans, D. (1993) *Sexual Citizenship: The Materialist Construction of Sexualities*. London: Routledge.
Eyles, L. (1933) *Commonsense About Sex*. London: Victor Gollancz.
Faderman, L. (1981) *Surpassing the Love of Men: Romantic Friendship and Love between Women from the Renaissance to the Present Day*. New York: William Morrow.
Fletcher, J. and Walker, K. (1955) *Sex and Society*. Harmondsworth: Penguin.
Foucault, M. (1977) *Discipline and Punish: The Birth of the Prison*. Harmondsworth: Penguin.
Foucault, M. (1979) *The History of Sexuality, Vol. 1: An Introduction*. Harmondsworth: Penguin.
Foucault, M. (1985) *The Use of Pleasure: The History of Sexuality*, Vol. 2. Harmondsworth: Penguin.
Foucault, M. (1990) *The Care of the Self: The History of Sexuality*, Vol. 3. Harmondsworth: Penguin.
Freud, S. (1961) *The Standard Edition of the Complete Psychological Works of Sigmund Freud* (trans. J. Strachey), Vol. XXI (1927–1931): *The Future of an Illusion, Civilisation and its Discontents and Other Works*. London: Hogarth Press.
Freud, S. (1986) *On Sexuality: Three Essays on the Theory of Sexuality and Other Works*. Harmondsworth: Penguin.
Friday, N. (1976) *My Secret Garden: Women's Sexual Fantasies*. London: Quartet.
Friday, N. (1980) *Men in Love: Men's Sexual Fantasies*. New York: Arrow.
Friedan, B. (1965) *The Feminine Mystique*. Harmondsworth: Penguin.
Gathorne-Hardy, J. (1973) *The Rise and Fall of the English Nanny*. London: Book Club Associates.
Gavron, H. (1966) *The Captive Wife*. Harmondsworth: Pelican.

Gay, P. (1986) *The Bourgeois Experience; Victoria to Freud, Vol. 1: Education of the Senses.* Oxford: Oxford University Press.

Gay, P. (1986) *The Bourgeois Experience, Vol. 2: The Tender Passion.* Oxford: Oxford University Press.

Gerth, H. H. and Mills, C. W. (eds) (1970) *From Max Weber: Essays in Sociology.* London: Routledge and Kegan Paul.

Giddens, A. (ed.) (1972) *Emile Durkheim: Selected Writings.* Cambridge: Cambridge University Press.

Giddens, A. (1991) *Modernity and Self-Identity: Self and Society in the Late Modern Age.* Cambridge: Polity Press.

Giddens, A. (1992) *The Transformation of Intimacy: Sexuality, Love and Eroticism in Modern Societies.* Cambridge: Polity Press.

Gilman, S. (1989) *Sexuality: An Illustrated History. Representing the Sexual in Medicine and Art.* New York: Wiley.

Gittens, D. (1982) *Fair Sex: Family Size and Structure 1900–1939.* London: Hutchinson.

Grahame, H. (1989) *Out of the Backstreets.* London: PAS.

Gramsci, A. (1971) *Selections from the Prison Notebooks of Antonio Gramsci* (trans. and eds, Q. Hoare and G. Nowell Smith). London: Lawrence and Wishart.

Grant, L. (1993) *Sexing the Millenium.* London: Harper Collins.

Greer, G. (1970) *The Female Eunuch.* London: MacGibbon and Kee.

Griffin, S. (1981) *Pornography and Silence: Culture's Revenge Against Nature.* London: Women's Press.

Griffith, E. (1948) *Sex and Citizenship.* London: Methuen.

Gurley Brown, H. (1962) *Sex and the Single Girl.* New York: Geis.

Hall, L. A. (1991) *Hidden Anxieties: Male Sexuality 1900–1950.* Cambridge: Polity Press.

Hall, L. A. (1992) 'Forbidden by God, despised by men: Masturbation, medical warnings, moral panic and manhood in Great Britain 1850–1950', *Journal of the History of Sexuality*, 2(3), 365–87.

Hall, R. (ed.) (1978) *Dear Dr Stopes: Sex in the 1920s.* London: Andre Deutsch.

Hall, S. *et al.* (1968) *Policing the Crisis: Mugging, the State, and Law and Order.* London: Macmillan.

Hamer, D. and Budge, B. (eds) (1994) *The Good, the Bad and the Gorgeous: Popular Culture's Romance with Lesbianism.* London: Pandora.

Hardy, T. (1891/1965) *Tess of the D'Urbervilles.* New York: W. W. Norton.

Harrison, B. (1967) 'Underneath the Victorians', *Victorian Studies*, 10, 239–62.

Harvey, D. (1989) *The Condition of Postmodernity: An Enquiry into the Conditions of Cultural Change.* Oxford: Basil Blackwell.

Hawkes, G. (1991) 'Raucous guests at the feast: Young women and sex in family planning', unpublished PhD thesis, Manchester University.

Hawkes, G. (1995) 'Responsibility and irresponsibility: Young women in family planning', *Sociology*, 29(2), 257–73.

Heath, S. (1982) *The Sexual Fix.* London: Macmillan.

Henderson, Sir H. D. MBE (1949) *Report on the Royal Commission on Population.* London: HMSO.

Hite, S. (1976) *The Hite Report.* London: Pandora.

Hutton, I. E. (1926/1953) *The Hygiene of Marriage.* London: Heinemann Medical.

Jackson, M. (1994) *The Real Facts of Life: Feminism and the Politics of Sexuality c.1850–1940.* London: Taylor and Francis.

Jackson, S. (1982) *Childhood and Sexuality.* Oxford: Basil Blackwell.

Jordanova, L. (1987) 'Children in history: Concepts of nature and society', in G. Scarre (ed.) *Children, Parents and Politics.* Cambridge: Cambridge University Press.

Keating, P. (1972) *Into Unknown England 1866–1913: Selections from the Social Explorers.* London: Fontana.

Kinsey, A., Pomeroy, W. and Martin, C. (1948) *Sexual Behaviour in the Human Male*. London: W. B. Saunders.

Kinsey, A. *et al.* (1953) *Sexual Behaviour in the Human Female*. London: W. B. Saunders.

Krafft-Ebing, R. V. (1899) *Psychopathia Sexualis: With Especial Reference to Antipathetic Sexual Instincts. A Medico-Forensic Study*. London: Rebman.

Kumar, K. (1978) *Prophecy and Progress: The Sociology of Industrial and Post-Industrial Society*. Harmondsworth: Penguin.

Lacquer, T. (1990) *Making Sex: Body and Gender from the Greeks to Freud*. Cambridge, MA: Harvard University Press.

Leathard, A. (1980) *The Fight to Save Family Planning*. London: Macmillan.

LeGates, M. (1976) 'The cult of womanhood in 18th century thought', *Eighteenth Century Studies*, X, 21–40.

Lewis, J. (1980) *The Politics of Motherhood*. London: Croom Helm.

Lewis, J. (1984) *Women in England 1870–1950*. London: Wheatsheaf.

Lowith, K. (1982) *Max Weber and Karl Marx*. London: Routledge.

MacDonald, R. (1967) 'The frightful consequences of onanism: Notes on the history of a delusion, *Journal of the History of Ideas*, XXVIII, 423–31.

MacKinnon, C. (1979) *Sexual Harassment of Working Women: A Case of Sexual Discrimination*. New Haven, CT: Yale University Press.

Marchant, J. (1916) *The Declining Birth Rate: Its Cause and Effects*. London: Chapman and Hall.

Marcus, S. (1966) *The Other Victorians: A Study of Sexuality and Pornography in Mid-Nineteenth Century England*. London: Book Club Associates.

Marcuse, H. (1974) *Eros and Civilisation*. Boston, MA: Beacon Press.

Marshall, J. (1981) 'Pansies, perverts and macho men: Changing conceptions of male homosexuality', in K. Plummer (ed.) *The Making of the Modern Homosexual*. London: Hutchinson.

Mason, M. (1994) *The Making of Victorian Sexuality*. Oxford: Oxford University Press.

Masters, W. and Johnson, V. (1966) *Human Sexual Response*. Boston, MA: Little Brown.

Masters, W. and Johnson, V. (1970) *Human Sexual Inadequacy*. London: J. & A. Churchill.

Masters, W. and Johnson, V. (1986) *On Sex and Human Loving*. London: Macmillan.

Mayer, M. (ed.) (1994) *The Politics and Poetics of Camp*. London: Routledge.

McLaren, A. (1978) *Birth Control in Nineteenth Century England*. London: Croom Helm.

McLellan, D. (1977) *Karl Marx: Selected Writings*. Oxford: Oxford University Press.

Mearns, A. (1883/1970) *The Bitter Cry of Outcast London*. Leicester: Leicester University Press.

Mitchell, J. (1971) *Women's Estate*. Harmondsworth: Pelican.

Mort, F. (1987) *Dangerous Sexualities: Medico-Moral Politics in England since 1830*. London: Routledge and Kegan Paul.

Nead, L. (1988) *Myths of Sexuality: Representations of Women in Victorian Britain*. Oxford: Basil Blackwell.

Nietzsche, F. (1990) *Human, All Too Human: A Book for Free Spirits*. Cambridge: Cambridge University Press.

Onlywoman Press (ed.) (1981) *Love Your Enemy? The Debate Between Heterosexual Feminism and Political Lesbianism*. London: Onlywoman Press.

O'Sullivan, S. (1994) 'Girls who kiss girls and who cares?', in D. Hamer and B. Budge (eds) *The Good, the Bad and the Gorgeous: Popular Culture's Romance with Lesbianism*. London: Pandora.

Pearsall, R. (1969) *The Worm in the Bud: The World of Victorian Sexuality*. London: Weidenfeld and Nicholson.

Peel, J. (1963) 'The manufacture and retail of contraceptives in England', *Population Studies*, XVII, 113–26.

Peel, J. (1964) 'Contraception and the medical profession', *Population Studies*, XVIII(2), 133–47.

Peterson, M. J. (1986) 'Dr Acton's enemy: Medicine, sex and society in Victorian England', *Victorian Studies*, 29, 567–90.

Plummer, K. (ed.) (1981) *The Making of the Modern Homosexual*. London: Hutchinson.

Porter, R. (1982) 'Mixed feelings: The Enlightenment and sexuality in eighteenth century Britain', in P. G. Bouce (ed.) *Sexuality in Eighteenth Century Britain*. Manchester: Manchester University Press.

Porter, R. (1984) 'Spreading carnal knowledge or selling dirt cheap? Nicholas Venette's *Tableau de l'Amour Conjugal* in eighteenth century England, *Journal of European Studies*, xiv, 233–55.

Porter, R. (1989) *Health for Sale: Quackery in England 1660–1850*. Manchester: Manchester University Press.

Porter, R. and Hall, L. (1995) *The Facts of Life: The Creation of Sexual Knowledge in Britain 1650–1950*. New Haven, CT: Yale University Press.

Ranke-Heinemann, U. (1991) *Eunuchs for the Kingdom of Heaven: Women, Sexuality, and the Catholic Church*. Harmondsworth: Penguin.

Reiger, K. (1985) *The Disenchantment of the Home: Modernising the Australian family 1880–1940*. Melbourne: Oxford University Press.

Rich, A. (1983) 'Compulsory heterosexuality and lesbian existence', in E. Abel and E. K. Abel (eds) *The Signs Reader: Women, Gender and Scholarship*. Chicago, IL: University of Chicago Press.

Robinson, P. (1972) *The Sexual Radicals: Reich, Roheim, Marcus*. London: Paladin.

Robinson, P. (1976) *The Modernisation of Sex: Havelock Ellis, Alfred Kinsey, William Masters and Virginia Johnson*. New York: Harper and Row.

Rowbotham, S. (1977) *A New World for Women: Stella Browne, Socialist Feminist*. London: Pluto Press.

Rubin, G. *et al.* (1987) 'Talking sex: A conversation on sexuality and feminism', in Feminist Review (ed.) *Sexuality: A Reader*. London: Virago.

Salisbury, J. (ed.) (1991) 'Bestiality in the Middle Ages', in *Sex in the Middle Ages*. New York: Garland.

Sayer, D. (1991) *Capitalism and Modernity: An Excursus on Marx and Weber*. London: Routledge.

Schofield, M. (1965) *The Sexual Behaviour of Young People*. Harmondsworth: Penguin.

Scruton, R. (1986) *Sexual Desire: A Philosophical Investigation*. London: Weidenfeld and Nicholson.

Segal, L. (1987) *Is the Future Female? Troubled Thoughts on Contemporary Feminism*. London: Virago.

Segal, L. (1993) *Straight Sex: The Politics of Pleasure*. London: Virago.

Simpson, M. (1994) *Male Impersonators: Men Performing Masculinity*. London: Cassell.

Sims, G. (1889/1984) *How the Poor Live*. London: Garland.

Smith, F. B. (1977) 'Sexuality in Britain 1800–1900: Some suggested revisions', in M. Vicinus (ed.) *A Widening Sphere*. Bloomington, IN: Indiana University Press.

Snitow, A., Stansell, C. and Thompson, S. (1983) *Powers of Desire: The Politics of Sexuality*. New York: Monthly Review Press.

Stanley, L. (1984) *The Diaries of Hannah Cullwick*. London: Virago.

Stone, L. (1977) *The Family, Sex and Marriage in England 1500–1800*. London: Weidenfeld and Nicholson.

Stopes, M. (1918a) *Married Love: A New Contribution to the Solution of Sex Difficulties*. London: Putnam.

Stopes, M. (1918b) *Wise Parenthood: The Treatise on Birth Control for Married Women*. London: Putnam.

Strachey, L. (1948) *Eminent Victorians*. London: Chatto and Windus.

Stycos, J. M. (1977) 'The desexing of contraception', *Family Planning Perspectives*, 9(6), 286–92.

Szasz, T. (1980) *Sex by Prescription*. New York: Anchor Press.

Taylor, B. (1984) *Eve and the New Jerusalem: Socialism and Feminism in the Nineteenth Century*. London: Virago.

Taylor, C. (1911/1972) *Principles of Scientific Management*. Westport, CT: Greenwood Press.

Thomas, K. (1959) 'The double standard', *Journal of the History of Ideas*, XX, 195–216.

Thomas, K. (1983) *Man and the Natural World: Changing Attitudes in England 1500–1800*. Harmondsworth: Penguin.

Thompson, E. P. (1967) 'Time, work-discipline and industrial capitalism', *Past and Present*, 38, 56–97.

Thompson, R. (1979) *Unfit for Modest Ears: A Study of Pornographic, Obscene and Bawdy Works Written or Published in England in the Second Half of the Seventeenth Century*. London: Macmillan.

Trall, R. T. (1903) *Sexual Physiology and Hygiene: An Explication, practical, scientific, moral and popular of some of the fundamental problems of sociology*. London: Simpkin, Marshall and Co.

Trilling, L. (1964) *The Liberal Imagination: Essays on Literature and Society*. London: Mercury.

Trumbach, R. (1989) 'Gender and the homosexual role in modern western culture', in D. Altman *et al.* (eds) *Which Homosexuality?* London: GMP Publishers.

Trumbach, R. (1991) 'The birth of the Queen: Sodomy and the emergence of gender equality', in *Hidden from History: Reclaiming the Gay and Lesbian Past*. Harmondsworth: Penguin.

van de Velde, T. (1934) *Sex Hostility in Marriage: Its Origin, Prevention and Treatment*. London: Chapman and Hall.

Venette, N. (1750/1984) *Conjugal love; or The Pleasures of the Marriage Bed consider'd*. Facsimile Edition. New York: Garland.

Vicinus, M. (1989) 'They wonder to which sex I belong: The historical roots of the modern lesbian identity', in *Which Homosexuality?* London: GMP Publishers.

Walkowitz, J. (1982) 'Male vice and female virtue: Feminism and the politics of prostitution in nineteenth century Britain', *History Workshop*, 13, 79–91.

Weber, M. (1974) *The Protestant Ethic and the Spirit of Capitalism*. London: Allen and Unwin.

Weeks, J. (1985) *Sexuality and its Discontents*. London: Routledge.

Weeks, J. (1986) *Sexuality*. London: Tavistock.

Weeks, J. (1989) *Sex, Politics and Society: The Regulation of Sexuality since 1800*. Second Edition. London: Longman.

Weeks, J. (1990) *Coming Out: Homosexual Politics in Britain from the Nineteenth Century to the Present*. Revised Edition. London: Quartet Books.

Wellmer, A. (1985) 'Reason, Utopia and the dialectic of the Enlightenment', in R. Bernstein (ed.) *Habermas and Modernity*. London: Polity Press.

Westheimer, R. (1994) Contributor to 'How to have hot sex again', in *She*. London: National Magazine Company Ltd.

White, C. (1970) *Women's Magazines 1693–1968*. London: Michael Joseph.

Wolff, C. (1986) *Magnus Hirschfeld: Portrait of a Pioneer in Sexology*. London: Quartet.

Wolff, K. F. (1950) *The Sociology of Georg Simmel*. London: Collier Macmillan.

Wood, C. and Suitters, B. (1970) *The Fight for Acceptance: The History of Contraception*. Aylesbury: Medical and Technical Publications.

Wright, H. (1935) *The Sex Factor in Marriage*. London: William and Norgate Ltd.

Wright, H. (1947) *Sexual Fulfilment in Married Women*. London: William and Norgate Ltd.

# Index